THE VON AUFSESS OCCUPATION DIARY

The von Aufsess Occupation Diary

Baron von Aufsess

Edited and Translated
by
KATHLEEN J. NOWLAN

Phillimore

1985

Published by
PHILLIMORE & CO.LTD.
Shopwyke Hall, Chichester, Sussex

ISBN 0 85033 543 4

Printed and bound in Great Britain by
BILLINGS BOOK PLAN
Worcester, England

Contents

Preface

The following pages cover the last stage in the German occupation of the British Channel Islands, from the time the islands were cut off from the mainland of France in the summer of 1944, to the end of the war in May 1945.

It is a purely personal chronicle of the times, written rather for the relief of confiding to paper thoughts, which could not be expressed aloud, than with the interests of the future historian mind.

As Head of the Civil Affairs branch of Military Administration, however – a post in which I acted for the greater part of the occupation as liaison officer between the German Military Command on the one hand and the island authorities on the other, often I suspect to the satisfaction of neither – I probably had a closer insight into the workings of both sides than anyone else in the islands. So, my observations on events should at last, perhaps, be made public.

The diarist, I am well aware, is apt to offend more people by his candour than he pleases by his veracity. My diary faces the extra hazard of being the first voice from 'the other side of the hill', and its first publication, moreover, is in the English language.

The date on the calendar persuades me to set aside my misgivings. Forty years have elapsed since the events described took place and most of the leading protagonists on both sides are now dead. In retrospect, much of my censure of them seems unduly harsh, but it was written under the stress of circumstance and at least was impartially bestowed upon both sides alike. The reader must exercise the forebearance which the diarist would do if he were writing today.

The situation in the last ten months of the war was probably without precedent in the annals of military history and international law. These small islands, so foolishly transformed by Hitler into 'island fortresses', planned to withstand the heaviest attack, and, similarly heavily garrisoned, were marooned in the backwaters of war; bypassed by the Allies' advance and left isolated from the continent and all sources of supply. On them, cut off and cooped up together, lived 35,000 German soldiers and 60,000 islanders.

Food and fuel reserves for the troops and the civilian population were sufficient for only a limited period, which could be prolonged only by the small gains from intensified agriculture and ever more frequent reductions in rations. This created tensions and gave rise to special problems, inherent in the situation as between occupiers and occupied, of a magnitude which could not have been forseen and which seemed impossible to overcome. Yet, they *were* overcome, by agreement between the occupying forces and the island governments. In these small islands agreement between nations was actually put into practice. And the States of Jersey and Guernsey remained the same before, during and after enemy occupation, a fact surely in itself unique.

HANS MAX VON AUFSESS

Aufsess, June 1984.

Chapter One

July – August 1944

30.7.44. The advance of the Allied battle front on Granville touches me deeply. In these last three years, Granville had become of special significance as the place where I first set foot on the Continent again, when going on leave, a sort of anteroom to home. The many happy little acquaintanceships I had struck up there, in the way one does in France, with the little fisherwoman, the girl in the newspaper kiosk, the diminutive *commis* in the cafe, the woman who sold butter under the counter, had made me feel more at home there than in any other foreign town. And on the return journey, the inevitable long wait for transport back to the islands meant one was on extended leave, could feel free, wander at will, with no responsibilities beyond enquiring when the next ship was sailing.

Most of the food parcels I sent home originated from this friendly little harbour town. How riling it is that the Americans will soon be there. How are we ever to get home again when one port after another falls to the enemy and is so badly damaged that, even if the fortunes of war should turn in our favour, it will be impossible to land at for many months to come?

Yesterday a few of us got together and were talking about our prospects for next Christmas here, without coal, without light, without bread, without news, etc. The conversation took a macabre turn. War is the forcing-ground of cynicism and extremes. Such items of news as get through to us serve only to confirm this. For instance, the army service corps which evacuated the pigs before the girls operating communications. Or our French buyers[1] who, as conscientious objectors, fled from rather than to the advancing Allied forces. Or the bomb, dropped by a plane, which missed the harbour but hit a mine just outside, causing a double explosion and a waterspout of imposing dimensions.

11.8.44. I reproach myself for having made so few entries. In justification, it has still been possible to correspond with home, and as I have taken full advantage of these last opportunities, there has been no time to devote to the diary.

Yesterday St Malo fell. We are finally cut off. The day was extremely clear and we could distinctly see the clouds of smoke rising above the shattered city out there across the sea. Reflected that all the pride and splendour of this ancient seaport was literally going up in smoke. Our situation is extraordinary; we and the Jersey people are alike prisoners of the islands. As the map shows, these small islands now lie in insignificant isolation at the centre of a British-dominated area. The dogs of war have passed us by. We joke about the forgetfulness of the British at leaving us behind.

The Bailiff[2] came to see me. In my absence some measure had again been commanded without any consideration of whether, if the island governments refused to comply, we could or would wish to force them to do so. Result: we withdraw an order already issued, and must now either abandon the project or try as best we may to carry it through ourselves. The Bailiff, cold and vulpine-visaged, departed as justified victor of the day. He is our sworn opponent, not so much because he hates us – he is too wily an old lawyer for that – as because he understandably chafes against the restriction to his authority and feels wounded in his self-esteem. It is easily foreseeable that in the future he will twist everything against us to his own glorification.

A new table-companion, a military lawyer from Saxony, has been assigned to our mess. He is a genial little man, who quickly found his way around and is adept in small practical matters. He had the washrooms fitted up with new screws and hooks in no time at all. Every mess member suddenly acquired a napkin-ring and had his sugar-tin neatly labelled with his name. The little Saxon has put up a new aerial and changed all the bulbs in the mess, to his and our benefit. He is a great exponent of 'a place for everything and everything in its place', and other similar such useful tags and precepts find appropriate expression in his everyday life, with his boots ingeniously hung up outside his door at night and every shirt and nightshirt with its special hanger (brought with him) in the bathroom. On one occasion when he was being ragged as a typical Saxon, etc., he embarked on a suitable defence based on his storehouse of axioms, but the application became so involved that I lost the thread of the argument.

12.8.44. In the morning with Colonel Heine of A2, siege commander of the Jersey island fortress, in his stuffy bunker. 1,400 naval men from St Malo have come to grace our table and share our short commons. They would have done better to have gone to the assistance of the hard-pressed army. But one must not be insularly egoistic. They could have been dead or taken prisoners but can now enjoy life roistering round the streets in gangs.

There are also American prisoners-of-war here. One would like to know more about them. With what convictions did they come over to fight in Europe? At the moment they seem interested only in arrogantly demanding more and better cigarettes and sweetstuffs – commodities which we have long since ceased to enjoy. One man's face has been badly burned by a flamethrower, and he has shots in both shoulders. But the enemy receive the same meticulous nursing as our own wounded from St Malo.

Six propaganda people from the navy arrived at the same time, and soon made themselves known to the fortress commander. They want to open an office here to function as a big news distributing centre. I can hardly imagine, in our present hopelessly isolated situation, anything more superfluous.

Delicate problem of allocating the last supplies of gas between the public soup kitchen and the local newspaper. Sonderführer Hohl[3] (*nomina sunt omina**) spouts propaganda and holds up any objective decision. I sense behind this the conflict which the attempt on Hitler's life has set up in people's minds. Reason and a sense of proportion have become suspect as reactionary. Rational argument no longer applies. The shadow of the gallows hangs over us all, especially the nobility.

On the beach complete amity still reigns between the German soldiers and the local girls. With a few exceptions the girl will surrender to her partner readily enough, provided this can be effected in proper privacy. The Englishwoman is astoundingly simple, effortless and swift in her lovemaking. While the Frenchwoman involves herself totally in the game, which she likes to be conducted along intellectual lines, for the Englishwoman it is a surprisingly straightforward physical matter. This direct and uncomplicated fashion of making love is not to be underrated; in its openness and honesty it precludes all that is wanton or furtive. If the Frenchwoman, after prolonged kissing, would murmur some word of love or quote a romantic couplet, the Englishwoman would surely only laugh at such tactics.

13.8.44. A long conference at Colonel Heine's. He is a gentlemanly old fellow, modest and with a great concern for the proper conduct of affairs, but at the same time a typical military bonehead, narrow, inhibited and over-cautious. Just the stiff set of his head above his high collar conveys an impression of rigidity. Still, this very lack of drive and flexibility means that he will undertake nothing without lengthy consideration and is thus, from the viewpoint of Military Administration, far preferable to a more forceful commanding officer, who might rush into precipitate action.

Lt.-Colonel Lindner is a good-natured giant from east of the Elbe, with a huge round head and tiny eyes. He does literally nothing and is entirely dependent on his staff. To compensate for his lack of

*'Hohl' means 'hollow' in German.

knowledge he repeats in stentorian tones such points of the discussion as he has grasped. But he is full of goodwill and personally likeable.

14.8.44. This evening invited to the General's. We pulled the little Saxon's leg about his practical way of dealing with the small problems of life, with astonishing results. He promptly emptied out the contents of his trouser pockets, knife, keys, cigarette-lighter, etc., and happily demonstrated how he suspended these objects in his pockets so they could not get lost or damage the lining. Then, having really got into his stride, he went on to expound the method he had devised to drain manure off his garden! In his enthusiasm, he started to stutter, and we were hard put to it to repress our laughter.

The first long-term report on the besieged fortresses has been drawn up. We can hold out until the end of December; after that famine is inevitable. The figures give a clear picture of the supplies necessary to support life and the productive capacity of the terrain.

Afternoon on the beach. The wooden skeleton of a ship, half burned-out, has been cast up on the shore. A great attraction to the children, who are playing all around it. Graphic confirmation of an idea which has often crossed my mind, that war is a game for children, a malicious lad's prank. Certainly pleasure in destruction and in what has been destroyed is common to soldiers and to small boys alike.

Visit the military lawyer, Dr. Harmsen. A clear legal brain, but dry as dust and with a rather sardonic cast to his emaciated features. I see eye-to-eye with him on the judgement reached, but not on the length of the sentence. It requires a level head and human warmth of feeling in the impersonal balancing of the offence against weeks or months in prison, to ensure that the sentence is nevertheless humane. We have a mutual respect for each other, although each doubtless sees in the other faults of character which the possessor probably regards as his special virtues.

I am writing in the evening at the window of my office. There is a wide view over the sea. The trees are a luminous green-gold in the setting sun. From St Malo there is a continuous muffled rumbling of gunfire. Sometimes the whole house shakes. No doubt it is the final phase of the battle for the coastal fortifications. After that, the war will pass far beyond us – until it returns for the final reckoning.

I am just listening to the *Schatzkästlein*[4] programme on the radio. How typically German, deadly earnest, sentimental and pompously instructive it sounds here on English soil.

15.8.44. This morning Heider (the Platzkommandant) demanded that the beaches should be closed, as a reprisal against the civilian population for the escape of a prisoner from the local gaol. At first I was furious at the absurdity of this request. Then annoyed with myself for this hasty reaction. After all, if a lot of escapees were being kept hidden in the island, we should have to take some steps about it. But in our present hopeless situation it seems foolish to drop the velvet glove which has hitherto served us so well. Where is the happy medium between undue severity and undue leniency? I have nobody to advise me and can only rely on what I feel to be right. But I realise there is no ideal solution.

In the afternoon at the cinema: Luise Ulrich in Ibsen's *Nora*. She holds one spellbound. The happiness of married life floods back to mind. To some extent the daily routine dulls the pain of parting, but the pain can never be totally stilled, nor will it be, when one is a prisoner-of-war or for however long the parting may be. Watching events inactively here brings melancholy realisation of how the noose of captivity is tightening around us and that there will be no escaping it. To think of the family in time of defeat with the thousand miseries that will bring, is past bearing.

We discuss the delicate question of reprisals against the civilian population for sheltering escaped prisoners. I am the only one in favour of restraint. We should not, on account of a couple of unimportant escapees, drop the velvet glove which we have used with success in the past. We exhaust our strength prematurely on trifles.

In the morning the medical corps brought the horses down onto the beach again. I first rode Toni, an elegant little horse which at the gallop bounds along like a hare. Then came Froni, the white mare, wild, intractable and never tiring. I rode her bareback in my bathing trunks and managed to keep her, if with difficulty, under complete control. A marvellous feeling, with a mettlesome horse beneath one and miles of beach ahead. We varied the procedure by riding into the sea. Froni swam out to deep water and balancing above her, I gave her free rein. There was an occasional very high wave, bringing her muzzle under water, so that only her pink distended nostrils showed, poking up like the snout of a hippopotamus. Then she quickly drew a deep breath and surfaced again, snorting and baring her teeth, evidently disapproving of this salty taste. I sometimes take small boys up on a horse and give them a ride, which they vastly enjoy, but Froni is too untamed to take such liberties with.

It seems that Froni and I were quite a sensation on the beach. B. told me afterwards that people were asking 'Who is it?' but most knew well enough that it was 'the Baron'. I have become thus known everywhere and am never, like my colleagues, addressed by my military title.

The lovely afternoon, with its deep blue of sea and sky, was followed by an equally beautiful evening. I went out to my second bungalow, a little house which I had lent to a young English couple. Played the

violin again after a long break. Took my friend the dog Tim some
succulent rabbit bones. Returned at last, tired out and suntanned, to
the west window of my office. The last rays of the setting sun were of
unusual splendour, staining the clouds a deep crimson. This evening
there is no sound of battle, so it would seem that the last resistance in
St Malo is wiped out.

It was a very disturbed night. A convoy to Guernsey must have been
engaged in action at sea. All the military hospitals here are already full
with the wounded from St Malo. Planes flew over us so low that I held
my breath, expecting that at any moment that they would fire into the
gables of the house. But this time, exceptionally, they were German
planes. They had been bombing the American communication lines.

A book by Churchill on his great contemporaries has come into my
hands. I first read the chapter on Hitler, written in 1935. I should have
expected a more personal appraisal of the man, but the writer merely
relates him to the background of events and draws his conclusions from
that. I am inclined to think that Hitler will not be of much attraction to
the biographer, certainly to nothing like the same extent as Napoleon
or Bismarck. His life is lacking in human interest. He has no complexity
of character or breadth of appeal; on the contrary, he is crude,
unintellectual, and bigoted in disposition, forged by a singleminded
drive for power into a narrow, stereotyped figure. The times which
produced him may well be of greater interest. These called for dynamic
personalities to help steer the ship of state off the rocks. But if, this
purpose achieved, the dangerous power thus unleashed is allowed to
forge ahead unchecked, and without adapting to changing circumstances, all will end in total shipwreck. Hitler is incapable of changing
course. He is straitjacketed by his own narrow aims and ambitions. He
has, starting with Stalingrad, already sacrificed army after army and
division after division. We too, in our fatal situation here on these
isolated islands, are equally victims of his mule-headedness, intransigence and inability to make up his mind until it is too late. What the
young Alexander, conqueror of half the world, could permit himself, is
not to be aped by this little upstart, World War I corporal and
house-painter, whatever his personal magnetism.

Swam far out to sea from the bathing pool to my bungalow, against a
light east wind which tossed the little waves in my face. Pleasing
reliance on one's physical strength in this alien element. Along the
beach, children were building sandcastles in face of the incoming tide,
which eventually stormed and swamped them. Most exciting moment
is when the outer bastions of the sand walls still hold, and the child
stands on a little dry island surrounded by the sea.

Heaviest bombardment of all in St Malo. The island trembles as if in
an earthquake. The seabed transmits every quiver like a tautened

drumskin. Amazing what a protracted resistance they are putting up over there in that hell of St Malo.

Today the second front has started with an invasion in the south of France. This no longer makes the impression one feels it should. The pattern of withdrawal and retreat has become a commonplace.

Conference with police over minor problems shows that the island is peaceable, and justifies my conviction that any over-nervous provocation of the population on account of trifles is entirely out of place. Discussion with the Bailiff on lighting restrictions, exchange of local horses for army horses in better condition, etc.

16.8.44. Sonderführer Woelken is the typical intellectual. He is very well-read and knowledgeable on a host of subjects, has opinions galore but no judgement. It is as if his brain was a mechanical adjunct, supported by but not part of his body; intellect and feelings are unconnected. He has a high but not interestingly-shaped forehead, the bulge above the bridge of the nose and bespectacled eyes denoting a critically observant rather than a creative or philosophical mind. His cheeks are plump and childlike, indicating emotional immaturity. He is well-built but slack and unco-ordinated in movement. His ruling passion is collecting books. Books mean more to him than any living creature, more than women, dogs or nature. He delights to read paragraphs aloud to his girlfriend – who plays up to his vanity – naturally only from English books, as in his spineless way he has become the complete Anglophile and despises everything German. As we have often taken him to task about this, he has developed a curious sort of double-think dialectic, designed to let us know that at heart he loves what is German too. He has not stuck to a profession; has often changed jobs: after a year as a lecturer in Scotland, was last a bookseller in Munich. He is altogether too brainy and ingenious. Still, it cannot be denied that he has some excellent attributes. His mental agility enables him to distance himself from his subject, to set it on a pedestal as it were, and view it from all angles. He speaks excellent English and has the enviable ability to translate only half-expressed ideas immediately and in entirety of concept. So he is a useful instrument rather than a good co-operator and a work of reference rather than an adviser.

Sonderführer Bleuel is a completely different type. With his close-set bespectacled eyes, forbidding expression and protruding upper lip, he appears the typical school teacher. He is in fact a secondary school master and has that pedagogic manner which at first tends to put people off. But on closer acquaintance with him and his work, it soon becomes evident that his virtues outnumber his failings. His pedantic persistence is just what is needed in the overall work of administration. Where accounts need to be checked, muddled statistics have to be sorted out, and all sorts of small tangles are involved, his tenacity of purpose makes him just the man for the job. For an assignment requiring the light touch and some exercise of charm and humour, he would not be the man to choose. But he is a very obliging fellow and much attached to me, as I am one of the few people to recognise his merits, and I have established a friendly relationship with him on our frequent bathing expeditions. On these occasions he is more relaxed and human and a certain versatility of mind, acquired on his teaching stints abroad, shows him in a more favourable light. It has been well worthwhile to cultivate him and discover behind the stiff facade of the school master the approachable human being.

He is a dedicated sunbather and can make the proud claim to be the brownest man on the island. He has become so deeply tanned that even the pronounced *embonpoint* of the hearty trencherman is not particularly noticeable. He has an odd attitude towards girls, tends to snap his fingers at them and give them a long follow-up look reminiscent of southern climes.

18.8.44. Am reading a very fluently-written book about the medical profession, *Many are Called*, which gives a vivid picture of the world of doctors and hospitals. The characters are acutely observed and well delineated. Tension is maintained to the end as the leading character qualified as a doctor by cheating at his examinations.

In the afternoon shown over a tobacco plantation by a cranky, querulous old man who used to be a tobacco planter in India. He is a curious mixture of races, half Chinese, half English. Also a *mixtum compositum* of character. Obviously the complete egoist, yet affecting a desire to be helpful. One suspects he is motivated not so much by charitable concern, for us or anybody else, as by a spirit of opposition to the States and for that matter to mankind in general. I have seldom seen a suit so patched as his, yet he wore it with a certain panache. A very odd type.

There will soon be a new moon. At this spring tide the sea retreats almost over the horizon. The place we have been bathing from suddenly seems very far from land. The rocks and seaweed appear sombre, dark brown and alien. There is a tinge of variation in the seaweed, from yellow – the complementary colour to blue – to reddish-brown, produced by such of the sun's rays as penetrate to this comparatively shallow depth, but the colours of the living world are lacking. On the dark seabed here, one can imagine some alien planet, similarly dun-coloured and unblessed by the light of the sun, in comparison with which our world would be a veritable paradise.

19.8.44. Yesterday afternoon caught an apple thief in my garden and administered summary justice in feudal style. I was reminded of 'the best joke of the year' which I saw in an American magazine. A cat-burglar broke into a skyscraper apartment which happened to be occupied by a boxer and was met by a knockout blow which catapulted him down to the street below from the 20th floor. Significant that Americans should consider this 'the best joke of the year'?

In the evening by the sea, where the majestic breakers crashed along the shore and the golden evening light was warm on our bodies. Bleuel and I have become so well-known on this stretch of beach that we mingle with the local residents, playing with the children and offering cigarettes to the adults. As a lark, we grabbed a young girl, ran with her into the sea and ducked her under a couple of breakers. A young fellow we know showed us some American occupation money, and an American helmet, made of some incredibly tough synthetic material, light as a feather.

The fall of St Malo was officially announced yesterday. Colonel von Aulock was taken prisoner. The front is now some hundreds of miles away from us: we are deep in Anglo-American territory. The General[5] rang up and asked me for news. Our extraordinary situation causes him great anxiety. He has still not been able to obtain any ruling on his return to the island from Army Headquarters, which is milling around somewhere in the depths of France.

Inspected the threshing. Thank God it is a splendid harvest. With careful planning, we should be able to spin things out until the end of January next year.

20.8.44. Strident propaganda has now reached the ranks of the poets and invaded the halls of fame. I have just put down with deep repugnance a book on the poet Josef Weinheber, glorifying in extravagant terms as a typical representative of his race and age a man who seems to me totally unsuited to the role. The forty or so illustrations showing the poet in his village, at his desk, at breakfast, in the garden etc., the unnaturally set expression on his face, presumably intended to convey poetic inspiration, merely evoke laughter. A photograph showing him shaking hands with the local Party leader is captioned 'Politics and Art shake hands'. Perhaps the artist had in mind the portrayal of the Muses as goddesses, but overlooked the fact that here were no classic beauties but merely a couple of potbellied members of the petty bourgeoisie. This does no credit to the men themselves and presents politics and art in involuntary caricature.

It was a rainy day. In the afternoon went riding with Satan, but we were both affected by the low state of the barometer and were heavy and sluggish. Took a gallop through the wet stubble but without our usual verve.

In the evening the sky cleared, and as there was a new moon and the spring tide was at the flood, I went out to our bungalow again to bathe. The narrow strip of sand between the surf and the seawall was covered with millions of sand-hoppers, which come out at this time of day and had been driven into the small space by the rising tide. The seagulls were having a wonderful feast. A whole flock of nimble, graceful tern was also present; unlike the native herring-gull, they keep together in swarms and make only an occasional appearance.

Swam far out to sea in the red-gold path of the sun, with nothing in sight but the far horizon where the sea and sky merged. In the absolute calm the long lines of breakers fell in superb momentum along the shore. There was a continuous mighty rise and fall of the sea, dousing the beach with rollicking foam as the great waves broke. Coming ashore, one saw the familiar faces of the local residents, who, leaning on the wall above, were also enjoying the beautiful evening.

The gunfire this evening was an attack on a convoy to Guernsey.

21.8.44. The pessimists of this war are unfortunately proving to be right. Pokorny is one of them. In fact, his debilitated appearance and forward stoop give him something of the air of a bird of ill-omen. I have often mentally compared him with the suffering figure of St Sebastian in the engravings and wood-cuts of the Middle Ages. Then too, there is his religious fanaticism, which also lends his fine features a strained and suffering look. I like Pokorny immensely, he is sensitive and clever. He is over-swift and dogmatic in jumping to questionable conclusions, but he is fair and kindly, even malleable, in character. He is conscientious too, and is never caught out by an emergency, however much his health suffers as a result. He has a heart condition, in fact, and needs looking after. If anything goes wrong in his section, he is upset to a degree which would affect other people only in their private affairs. He needs independence, but at the same time a firm guiding hand, and having found this gives his full loyalty.

Yesterday evening we were gathered, as so often, around a map of France discussing the desperate state of our military dispositions, with our islands now almost three hundred kilometres inside a British-controlled area. In his usual precipitate fashion, which it must be admitted has often enough led him into error or given offence to other people, Pokorny, without a shadow of doubt in his tone, advanced the view that as we were now *de facto* prisoners of the British, they would have no hesitation in providing us with the necessities of life, as they were bound *de jure* to do for all prisoners of war. Can there be some grain of sense in this? At any rate it has given me an idea. I have been weighing this up all night. Perhaps some solution to our problems could be hammered out along these lines, although there is more to it than this suggestion so hastily thrown out.

We would have to be guided by three considerations: first our honour as soldiers, second, commonsense, and thirdly, humanitarian motives. It is now pretty obvious that the British do not intend to take the islands by force, but to spare them and let them fall into their hands like ripe fruit at the end of the war. If Germany is defeated this year, the safety of the islands is assured. But if the end is further delayed, the British must either take possession of the islands or do something about supporting the civilian population, unless the islanders are to starve, which one may safely assume would be the last thing the British government would wish.

An attack on German forces in their rear, which for all practical purposes are already cancelled out of the war, would involve an outlay in men and materials better employed in expediting final victory. The spirit of the defenders of St Malo has set a dangerous example, which could be emulated here, which the British would surely not wish. And what would become of these beautiful islands and their inhabitants then?

If the British are wise, they will continue to refrain from any premature demand for the surrender of the islands, through which they might be forced into an attack upon, and the senseless destruction of, territory which to all intents and purposes is already theirs.

If the end of the war is to be further delayed, the next urgent task will be to arrange for Red Cross ships to bring supplies for the islanders, and they might well at the same time bring supplies for the German garrison. As long as the Germans are masters in the islands, it would hardly be expedient to let them starve.

If, therefore, it seems likely that there will be a delay in the cessation of hostilities beyond the calculated time limit for existing supplies to run out at the end of January 1945, the enemy must be given requisite advance notice and called upon, under the threat of impending famine for the civilian population, either to take the islands by force or to send them supplies. As we are cut off and so far from our Headquarters, negotiations could best be effected by an envoy sent under a flag of truce to one of the neighbouring harbours.

The note must be formulated in the first place to satisfy the military code of honour, but must then leave the way open for some sensible agreement, taking into account the needs of the indigenous population and the unique character of the situation. The text could be roughly as follows:

> From 31st January 1945 supplies for the civilian population can no longer be
> guaranteed. There is no question of a voluntary surrender of the islands before

Germany is defeated. We therefore challenge you to battle. If you will not accept
the challenge, ships with supplies for the civilian population must be sent under
the conditions set out below. Otherwise the civilian population will face
starvation.

I shall revise the above paragraphs and write to the General along these
lines, letting him know my chain of reasoning. It will at the same time
be a good exercise in determining one's mental capacity to assess the
situation and plan in advance.

22.8.44. Today I moved from White Lodge to Linden Court. I have
lived in the former house for over three years and spent a happy time
there. Turning out the stuff which had accumulated brought the
wretchedness of defeat poignantly to mind. Photographs of my wife and
children taken on happy leaves at home. The battered suitcase I used to
take on leave was also pulled out from under the bed. What joy it used
to be to open it and spread out all the gifts I had brought back. A
snapshot of the Reitzenstein family fell out of some papers: Anna
Sybilla killed in an accident and Ruppie killed in the war. A guide to the
beautiful city of St Malo, which meanwhile has been razed to the
ground. A happy little souvenir of Paris, now being evacuated by
German troops. Also found a bottle of cognac with part of the contents
remaining. I sat down in the gracious drawing room and discovered for
the first time what a consolation drink can be, exhilarating and
befuddling at the same time.

Major Heider got back to the island today and brought news of our
total withdrawal from France, except for the last distant zone of defence
on which our forces have fallen back. Poor, overcrowded Germany,
which will now really know hunger and have to endure still further
sustained bombardment. One may have to think seriously of making a
life for the family abroad. How will life be possible in a Germany which
has been totally destroyed?

23.8.44. A lengthy conference with the Attorney General[6], Duret
Aubin. Such a very decent chap, clever, modest and conscientious,
every inch a man. His rather low wrinkled forehead and corpulent
figure suggest a man of deep feelings. Without the chilly and inhibiting
presence of the Bailiff, he was clearly rather at a loss how to proceed.
He is a man ruled by his emotions, and all the more likeable for that. In
fact, his visit today turned out to be more a social than an official
occasion. He made a brave start with a well-prepared disquisition on
the possible effects when the gas supply gives out in about ten days'
time. He believed that on this account alone an immediate approach
must be made to the Red Cross. But of course the practical implications
cannot yet be assessed, and we shall have to wait and see how things

turn out. We parted, as usual, with warm-hearted feelings of mutual understanding and regard.

This evening I made the final move to Linden Court. It is a charming place and the food and service a good notch above that provided by the good Helen and former military policeman John.

I have been working this evening on a lecture which I have been asked to give to the Island Commanders tomorrow. The task here assigned me, in its far-reaching implications and responsibility, weighs heavily on me; I feel deeply involved in and moved by this work, and hope that the urgency of my convictions will come through in my speech.

In the night had frightful dreams about my wife being involved in an accident. (On that day, as I afterwards learnt, she had been arrested by the Gestapo.) Then lay in a waking nightmare conjured up by all the horrors of the unknown future.

24.8.44. The lecture is over. It was an unexpected success. It seems the time has come when people would rather listen to reason and moderation than propaganda and exaggeration (the last two of course being synonymous). Above all I found myself borne along by the force of my own feelings, which enabled me to carry conviction to the audience, and to marshal my arguments in such a way as to make them more easily acceptable.

Three of the Commanders have already asked me to repeat the lecture to their officers. I am not at all keen on this. I am no orator. But it may be an opportunity to disseminate a little sweet reason and to point out exactly what our situation here is and what our responsibilities are. It might avert some foolishness and facilititate the work of Military Administration, not to mention lending me some greater authority in decisions which will have to be taken in the future.

In this respect all honour is due to Major Heider who, unlike his predecessor the Colonel, is not jealous of my position and as a result accords me full acknowledgement and credit as Head of the Administrative Groups and Director of Military Administration.

In the evening in absolutely calm weather and a sunset sky of Bengal lights, went swimming again. Sonderführer Bleuel stood his radio on the seawall. It was tuned to a station playing English lovesongs. There was soon a crowd of children and adults gathered round, listening raptly and gratefully. They were mostly friendly neighbours with whom we have long ago concluded a true peace, of a sort which it will take decades to establish between the German and British peoples.

Have been conducting an amusing little game of 'to know or not to know' with Ella. When she dived into the water, I climbed up the ladder and got dressed. This brought speedy results in the shape of Ella

herself. In spite of her former reluctance, as an Englishwoman, to speak
to me in public, she stayed talking longer than usual and we exchanged
our customary badinage. Women cannot bear to be shown that one is
not entirely independent of them.

25.8.44. A big conference on the price of vegetables, how they are being
bought up by the troops, how they are put on the market. A large batch
of long-keeping bread baked with seawater has gone bad. Delivery of
milk-cans from the dairy for water supplies to the garrison of Fort
Césembre near St Malo, where German troops are still holding out.

In the afternoon greatly enjoyed the film *Three Sisters* with Gisela
Uhlen. It is heartwarming to consider that Germany can produce and
distribute around the world such an excellent, genuine and moving
drama. Our country can have no better publicity than its art, to which
such a film as this properly belongs. Art awakens understanding and
with understanding comes liking. It is by art that we must reconquer
the world which we have lost by arms.

29.8.44. Nothing is more depressing than stupidity in the mass. I have
given my lecture again, first to our local paymasters and officers of the
Service Corps and this evening to officers of the M.G. Battalion. Those
not sunk in total apathy and vacancy could be moved to some brief
spark of interest in the situation only as it affected themselves. Their
minds were working only through their empty bellies. How much effort
one expends on a cause already lost. Death suddenly appears as a
welcome release from this society, where one encounters nothing but
opposition and lack of understanding. Thoughts of emigration cross my
mind again. How can one live in the company of such barbarians,
lacking all sense of a higher justice?

In Guernsey an islander has been shot by some soldiers when trying
to prevent them from stealing his potatoes; a first intimation of the
coming battle for food in the beleaguered fortresses. The Intendant, my
opposite number on the military side, has had a nervous breakdown.
Probably only a matter of time before one follows his example. There is
opposition all along the line to moderate behaviour. Severe sugar
rationing. Cuts in electricity. To produce enough wood for heating will
mean virtual deforestation. I have opposed this to the last, as it would
have a drastically adverse effect on the future of the islands' agriculture
and ecology.

Have had a depressing glimpse of the slaughtered horses in the
abattoir. I shall go without meat if it means having horse-flesh. Feel a
responsibility for their death and ready for death myself since I have
seen the gory haunches of those well-loved and gallant beasts hanging
up there.

30.8.44. The worsening weather brings reminders of the changing season. It gets dark quite early now. One is driven to compare the season with our own situation, with darkness increasing and a gloomy fate awaiting us in the months ahead.

After a long break, Ella came to see me again. She has wonderful colouring; her hair near pure gold, her suntanned complexion a rosy brown. She is extraordinarily slender, yet well-built and feminine in contour. She would look enchanting as a dancer.

I took her into the drawing room and stood her beside the two statuettes of Javanese dancers. One is gracefully formed but lacks the expressiveness of the partner piece, which is evidently the work of a master. Every movement of the body conveys a sense of spiritual fulfilment and surrender to the dance. The face is rapt and self-absorbed. The body is fuller and riper. Even the posture of the hands conveys an inward grace which has no connection with the mere prettiness of the first figure. The one might represent youthful beauty, flighty and insouciant, the other complete womanhood, with body, mind and spirit mystically fused in full dedication to love in its fullest sense.

I expounded on this to Ella and pointed out how closely, with her over-slim figure, flightiness, addiction to pleasure and lack of responsibility, she resembled the first figure. This seemed to make some impression on her. Perhaps her curiosity will lead her to that richer depth of human experience which seems unknown to Englishwomen, but which is so much more lasting and rewarding than a limited physical attraction.

The gap between a gay, pert English girl and a Javanese temple dancer with her half-religious, half-erotic dance myths, is wide indeed, but it was precisely this remoteness of circumstance which enabled me to read a little lesson on the difference between the two figures, as I saw it.

At the cinema saw *Mother Love* with Käthe Dorsch. I find I am becoming increasingly affected by such films (my comrades say the same). Perhaps this is because, in our desperate situation and complete severance from home and family, such portrayals, with their speaking illustrations, bring all too vividly to life memories and anxieties best left unstirred. The fate of the deserted mother left with her children is to some extent the fate which most of our wives are now enduring. Just to survive, one strives to draw a veil over these memories in day-to-day activities. But then one reads a book or sees a film and realises that the sorrow it depicts is one's own.

Chapter Two

September – October 1944

1.9.44. Now the lovely month of August is over, no doubt the last of those comparatively free from care. Now every month will become more trying and fraught with worry. Tomorrow the gas comes to an end. The public kitchens and bakeries are beginning to close down. Yesterday the States presented a memorandum, raising a number of complaints of a general nature, all leading up to a protest against our time-limit of 31.1.45. Supplies are insufficient for the civilian population to hold out until then, and the memorandum concludes with a barely-veiled threat to bring the guilty persons to justice after the war, if the civilian population should suffer. The situation, as described, is chiefly concerned with the lack of fuel, and is clearly based on reports from the manager of the gasworks, an embittered man who must have exercised considerable pressure on the States. I think our reply to this document must in general be negative, but that there must be some pretty far-reaching concessions with regard to medicaments, soap and possibly sugar, in order to avert the threatened resignation of the States.

How pleasant to be able to resign when things get too difficult. I wish I could do just that. The burden is heavier for us. I am here as a lawyer in a post in which any mistake may cost me my life. I ask myself if there can in fact be any solution to the problem which would be acceptable to both sides. We wish to hold out as long as possible, the islanders wish to see the earliest possible end to the siege. One can surely find no middle path which would be both just and legal. And with the end of the war, I shall be held finally responsible here. It seems a position in which one is condemned from the start, unless a miracle happens. It is as well to have this clearly in mind. Thus one will not jeopardise personal or national honour in hopeless compromise.

Our daily setbacks are now so great that it is hopeless to believe any longer in a reversal of the military situation. The miseries of the homeland and of one's own family after the war prey on one's mind. If only one could be there to stand by them.

Yesterday Lieutenant Wetzstein came to see me. He is the only man with brains I know here. He attributes our downfall to the failure of intellectual leadership in the German nation. As a former National Socialist, one of the earliest members of the movement, when its aims seemed genuinely national and idealistic, this depresses him greatly.

I would not like to say that the Germans can thus be judged as a whole. What happened was that we called to power a class of the population which was totally unfitted for the task. Every age reflects its governing class. Our present one, the National Socialists, is that of the half-baked, the semi-literate, the small schoolmaster, upstart and adventurer. And nobody is so apt to lose all sense of proportion as the parvenu. It is the poor people as a whole who suffer for this.

3.9.44. The States' memorandum has given me a sleepless night. In it they challenge the possibility of holding out until the date set by us, 31.1.45, and threaten to withdraw their collaboration in spinning out supplies. They also threaten, in veiled terms, an ultimate calling-to-account of the persons concerned, if the lives of the civilian population should be endangered by our date-line.

In my endeavours to scrape through at my task here in a fair and humane fashion, yet without being too soft or compliant from a military point of view, it has often occurred to me that a final decision by force of arms would be the best and most honourable solution, a thousand times preferable to this slow strangulation. Well then, if the States believe they cannot hold out so long, we will willingly pass on their S.O.S.; perhaps our opponents will then take a hand. Yes, we must pass on the responsibility with which the States has saddled us to our British opponents. Then they can either attack us or send supply ships. If they do neither and if the islanders then suffer want, it will no longer be through any fault of ours, and the States will no longer be able to threaten to resign if we order further retrenchments. This seems the only just solution, particularly as the States' memorandum claims that, according to an expert survey, a state of emergency for the civilian population will arise before 31.1.45, owing to the lack of fuel for the public kitchens and bakeries.

In the morning I called my 12 assistants in civil affairs to a conference. Pokorny, in his sensible, levelheaded fashion, was the first to acknowledge the soundness of my suggestion. The intellectual, Woelken, followed with some brilliant digressions from the theme; one or two objections were raised among the rest, but all quickly came to the conclusion that this was the only answer to the problem. Colonel Heine, who happened to call, was also soon convinced. Now I shall prepare a detailed report and send it over to the Commander-in-Chief's Headquarters in Guernsey. I am nervous about reporting by telephone, as misconceptions can so easily arise and there is nothing I dread more than having this plan stifled at birth through lack of understanding.

There is a full moon tonight and, with the approach of the equinox, a great storm has blown up. No doubt there is some connection between these mighty movements of air and water. The high tide and the storm produced fantastic scenes on the beach. I went down there quite early with Bleuel. The water came up nearly to the wall, raging and thundering like the brown swollen waters of a mountain torrent, but extending almost as far as the eye could see. We could advance only by moving sideways. Then an untoward encounter with a breaking wave pulled us head over heels high up on the sandy shore. If one can get past the first breakers, one can swim far out to sea. As I faced these gigantic waves, even before they broke, I was conscious of a very real fear, racing heart and pumping breath. But fear brings courage and I plunged in. One is rocketed to the top of a mighty roller, submerged in spume on its crest and then finds oneself, fighting for breath, coasting down the other side. Often the next great wave follows close on the heels of the first, with another building up beyond, but proving to be not so dangerous, as it collapses before it breaks. There can be no more wild and exhilarating experience, even on the back of a horse. It is a completely physical pleasure. One could yell with joy like a child, and with all the noise around nobody could even hear. I think it is the release from mental effort, the abandonment of the body to the elements, which bear it up, toss it around and subject it to their own laws, which gives the keenest pleasure.

This morning, Sunday, rode Satan out to Mont Orgueil Castle. A couple of touches with the switch restored the old horse to all his former mettle. I rode into the ancient fortress, like the knights of old, over the drawbridge and through the forecourts. I was received by Major K., who insisted on showing me round and giving me full particulars of the old building, and how it had been adapted to meet modern requirements to serve as a pocket of resistance in the present war. Old dilapidated rooms suddenly assumed their possible former roles. The whole fortification reminded me of a child's toy, to which we too have now added some low walls along the rocks and set up rifle ranges. So, throughout history, war remains a wicked boy's game for grown men. Fortunately, our additions have not involved any structural alterations to the venerable pile. But the knights of yesteryear would have been astonished at our complicated methods of waging war – the artillery plane and estimation tables.

I have been reading *Les Confessions de Talleyrand* and have come across a saying I find particularly pleasing. 'One must treat serious things lightly and unimportant matters with great earnestness. This has the advantage of precluding the person of average intelligence from joining in the argument'. I would add that it has the further advantage of relaxing stress, and thus leading to the best solutions being found in the most difficult situations. It is for lack of ability to adjust to Talleyrand's advice that the Frenchman so often appears frivolous, the German humourless and the Slav gloomy and unlikeable.

There is news of an armistice in Finland and Bulgaria. The external signs of defeat are piling up. There are still a few people who believe in miracles. If only the new weapons would arrive, they say, everything would change.

Lieutenant Wetzstein came to tea at Linden Court. He is the only man here of ideas and intellectual standing. The talk inevitably came round again to the depressing future. One can no longer get it out of one's mind. We spoke about likely future developments in Germany and agreed that the war would change our lives as fundamentally as some great natural catastrophe: that there would be an end to individualism and that European culture would be as effectually destroyed as that of the Greeks after Pumae in the Persian Wars. Europe will, of course, like Greece, continue to be regarded as a teacher and cultural yardstick for many years to come, but it will not again attain political importance. We concluded with economics, and agreed that with defeat the currency would be devalued and that only then would the full extent of our impoverishment, brought about by the war, come to light. Capital and credit will be wiped out and only a stringent financial system could save us from inflation.

4.9.44. Repeated my lecture to the naval officers. They paid close attention, which put me on my mettle and helped me to speak with a conviction which I think got over to them. I have noticed that, to hold the attention of an audience for more than an hour, it is necessary to introduce a flattering allusion to the listeners here and there. Humanity in the mass is primitive in character; according to Le Bon, 'reacting by instinct, touchy, credulous, and uncritical'. So one can safely introduce a little flattery. Afterwards there was a lively discussion. I sat between Captain Breithaupt, who has the Iron Cross with oak leaves, and Captain Lentsch. Was delighted by the sound common sense these old salts brought to bear in expressing their views of our situation. It was also a relief to know that, besides their much lauded and undoubted courage, they could take a realistic view of our present hopeless plight. A youthful officer of the flotilla joined our circle. He saluted like a hero on a postcard, grim of visage and with upflung arm. So many people are unaware that they are acting out a self-imagined role!

Every day brings further depressing tidings. It has got to the stage when one can only hope that our defeat may be speedy. These dismal days are followed by restless nights. Late last night I had news that the military bunkers were flooded by the high tides, and found it very difficult to get to sleep again. Brussels has fallen, the Dutch frontier is passed and Metz under siege. There is complete collapse in the West. It seems doubtful if we can set up a new line of defence.

5.9.44. This is a time when the clear-sighted and the ill-advised part ways politically. In the news bulletins our propaganda still dares to refer to the loss of France as an actual advantage. And there are still people who repeat this and talk about the coming 'new weapons' as if, in this desperate situation, they could quickly bring about a complete reversal in the military position, and only some small delay in their issue had caused our retreat. Meanwhile, hundreds of thousands of brave German soldiers are dying and whole armies are being decimated. This exploitation of the people's good faith and credulity will later take its place in the annals of history, as the loss of faith on the home front did after the last war. The next few weeks may well decide whether the war will end this year, or whether, held up at the German frontier, it will continue over the winter.

The Attorney-General came to see me to talk over various problems, with the avowed aim, as he put it, of taking the venom out of them. There is such a strong bond of personal liking and understanding between us, that all questions which might have led to difficulties were quickly cleared up. We joked that, at the next Hague Conference on International Law, we should be able to report two examples from Jersey: the fire brigade has refused its assistance in pumping out the military bunkers, in the one instance wrongly as the lives of the soldiers were at stake, in the second rightly, as the salvage of ammunition was also involved.

After that, Mrs. Riley turned up and with some embarrassment diffidently suggested that, if someone were needed to go to England to put the islanders' needs before the British government, she would be willing to undertake this mission. She wouldn't, I thought, be at all a bad choice as an envoy, and rather jokingly, I went into all the details with her. She was much moved, and told me I must certainly end up as the next German ambassador to Great Britain.

6.9.44. In the morning called on Colonel Heine. In spite of the air conditioners, howling like sirens, the bunker was as stuffy as ever and the Colonel a bit on edge. I handed him a copy of my memorandum, with a personal covering letter.

In the evening Ella came to see me, first at White Lodge and then at Linden Court. She was glowing with health and her own lovely colouring. With her fantastically slim figure, she took up only a third of the big armchair she was sitting in. She is always ready for fun and her merry, bright eyes light on something new to laugh at every minute. We are having a little flirtation, the most superficial and light-hearted, but, in these times of severe mental depression, a welcome relaxation. If I can no longer look after my family at home, at least I have someone here whom I can spoil a little.

7.9.44. Yesterday evening we were invited to Captain Halbritter's. He is a quiet, cultivated, likeable man, although perhaps, behind a composed front, a little self-opinionated and touchy. The discussion soared to great heights, culminating in the question of the existence of God. Pokorny, with his deep religious faith, was able to testify to a belief in a personal God. For me, the answer to the question was summed up in a well-known quotation from Goethe: 'As natural scientists we are pantheists, as artists polytheists, and by ethics monotheists'. I have always interested myself in natural science, as I feel that this brings us nearer to the spirit of the universe.

8.9.44. The Bailiff came to see me about the electricity works. He probably thinks that he can dominate me, but it is his vanity in this respect which gives me a hold over him. I have now had so much experience of conceit, that I believe I know how to deal with it.

The Bailiff already sees himself as the chosen of his people, going over to England and returning like Father Christmas with coal, soap, sugar and eventually peace. This would give him great satisfaction, not on account of the islanders, but on his own account. He casts himself in the role of a saviour, as illustrated in the closing lines of his recent memorandum regarding 'the survivors of his government, who would one day call us to account'. His heavily-lined face takes on an air of sanctimony when he speaks of being the '*voix de mon peuple*'. Yet, such is his adroitness, experience, and ability to adapt, that I really get on very well with him, and even hope in time to establish a more cordial relationship.

Today ships laden with precious wheat set off for Guernsey. Their safe arrival is essential for us to hold out in the islands. There are heavy showers, alternating with a blue sky. The weather has not yet settled down after the seasonal storms.

It is often inexpedient to throw an irrefutable argument in the teeth of one's opponent; better to wait and introduce it diffidently and rather as a side-issue. Then he cannot immediately attack it, but is led round to it gradually, if inexorably. The Bailiff's arguments, when he came to see me this morning, were so flimsy that I just let him talk himself out, until he was defeated by the weakness of his own case.

9.9.44. Such a beautiful morning. A delicate gold-tinted haze over land and sea. One takes a deep and grateful breath. One should be glad at the prospect of another lovely day, but the cares of the night still weigh on the spirit. What can things be like at home now?

It is not in my nature to regard the future with total gloom. But my optimism reaches out to the period after the war, rather than clutching at any vain hopes of postponing our defeat. I know now that we cannot win the war, but I still hope and believe we may win the peace. And after the war, we shall need Talleyrand's vision, but no more visionaries. Of course, if I were standing, rifle in hand, on the banks of the Rhine, I might feel differently than here in this indefensible spot which is already half a prison-house.

10.9.44. Yesterday a big sensation hit the headlines. The German police, having discovered that the Labour Representative of the States' Superior Council (Deputy E. Le Quesne), was in possession of a wireless set, arrested him out of hand, without any previous reference to us. It is now the common topic of conversation and there is no means of suppressing the scandal. This is unfortunately a typical example of the example of the power the police have attained in our National Socialist state. The police force, which should be merely the executive arm of the law, has become a power in its own right. Indeed, our territorial army is headed by a policeman, S.S. Führer Himmler.

If the police had informed me first, I should have clapped Le Quesne on the shoulder, and taken his set into my own custody – thus consolidating our good relations and avoiding losing this valuable and important States official. Police Inspector Bohde, of the Secret Field Police, however, although I had previously found him a peaceable enough chap, was of the opinion that he had the right to arrest anyone in the island, but no-one had the right to arrest him! Well, on this rating, the worthy inspector evidently takes precedence of us all!

There has also been another unpleasant incident. The States' memorandum has been circulated as a pamphlet, by whom it is not yet known. But if this took place with the knowledge of the States, it is a serious breach of confidence and an indiscretion which contravenes all previous usage. I confirmed to the Bailiff that I have passed on his memorandum, at the same time repudiating the veiled threat which it contains as irrelevant and prejudicial to sensible negotiations. 'A threat must be regarded by a soldier as a challenge and can only have an adverse effect'.

I have been dwelling on the idea that the specialised and the general fructify each other and are interdependent. I can only love my native land because I am completely at home, not everywhere, but only in one particular corner of it. I can achieve success only in a subject of which I am completely the master, but to do this need some knowledge in many other fields. No man can comprehend the true nature of love unless he is able to love one woman with all his heart. Yet he could not make a woman happy if he had not the innate versatility to recognise the charms of many others. He loves this one particular woman because she unites in her person those desirable qualities he had observed only singly in other women. We have some deep-seated need of the

matchless, the unique, to counter the world's overwhelming multiplicity and variety. Thus in each of us, our specialised knowledge and our
general knowledge achieve some sort of union, which happily produces
satisfactory progeny.

For the first time paid a visit to the local gaol, which impressed me as
all very clean and neat. I looked at it with the interest one always has for
the seamier side of life, but in this instance with mixed feelings too. The
small cell typifies imprisonment, and are not we all, in a certain sense,
prisoners here? That is certainly what it looks like at the moment. Yet,
in one of these bare cells, on a plank bed, would I not still have freedom
of mind? Yet how heavenly it was afterwards, to have a long gallop with
Froni, and in the afternoon to swim from the wide shining beach.

This afternoon Miss Gricht came to see me. I had walked out on her
so often; now at last the invitation must be honoured. She is pretty, very
pretty, not a doubt of it. But what is more tiresome than a silly, callow
girl who always laughs at the wrong moment, not out of an amusing
naïvete, but from suppressed complexes and a misplaced shyness. She
is the product of a false middle-class upbringing. A girl who normally
never drinks or smokes but who, out of sheer self-consciousness,
suddenly puffs her way through a whole packet of cigarettes and downs
one schnapps after another, fails to notice that in the end one is just
dying to get rid of her. It is too much. After her departure I fell asleep
from sheer boredom, as if I had been pole-axed.

12.9.44. Am again occupying myself with biology. It is more to my taste
than materialism, which interprets life as passive and mechanistic and
is thus not qualified to answer the fundamental questions posed by the
living organism in its universality, vital activity and imminent goal.
This does not mean that natural philosophy, to which I am admittedly
irresistibly drawn, is not reconcilable with material facts; rather it is
richer in ideas, which it seeks to put into philosophical concepts.

13.9.44. I am greatly depressed by Lt.-Colonel Helldorf's failure to
follow the reasoning of my memorandum. He just tries to make light of
the matter and patch up the situation. What his actual motive may be I
don't know, but in view of his customary astuteness, combined also
with his autocratic egoism, I am inclined to think it must be a personal
one. Against the General's wishes, he has taken that girl to Guernsey,
where she is now living with him. In this he has scored a victory over the
General, and shown that it is he, not the General, who is the real
commander. His intention must be to hold out as long as possible to try
to achieve at the end a free withdrawal of German troops from the
island. Only in these circumstances would he be able to take the girl
back with him to Germany. He intends, in the total derangement of his

senile infatuation, to marry this little servant-girl. So do the private concerns of the individual affect the welfare of the many.

14.9.44. I have been battling all night with the vexed question of Helldorf. In imagination I wrote an eloquent letter to the General and would have got up and put it on paper then and there, but the electricity is cut off at night as an economy measure. When one is totally immersed in a problem, there is a pressing need to take some action while one's arguments are still fresh in one's mind. Spontaneity lends them force, even if, as I have generally found, some modification is necessary later. So I am writing my letter to the General from my heart, as a basis for the modified version which will actually be sent.

My dear General,

Lt.-Colonel von Helldorf's attitude with regard to the present situation, as expressed to me on the telephone, causes me the greatest alarm. I feel myself so much responsible for the situation here that I do not hesitate to express to you quite freely all my doubts, suspicions and concern. I can understand that it is not possible to pass on the islanders' demands directly to the enemy, indeed that it would not be proper for us to do so. But in playing down the gravity of the situation which they have brought to our attention and trying to patch it up by giving some minimal assistance from our own resources, we are not dealing with it adequately or helping enough.

Although, if the Jersey government were to resign, I should of course do my best to carry on alone, I think the difficulties which this would cause would be greater than may be assumed. The moment the island government sets itself against us, the islanders will range themselves behind it. Even if it is not particularly popular with the broad masses, the adage 'right or wrong my country' still holds good. The allocation of foodstuffs and the running of the electricity and water works could not be more economically and securely managed than they have been up to now. It would also be very maladroit, after over four years of occupation, to change the mode of government at the eleventh hour. Conditions in Guernsey are different. In the first place the local population still has a gas supply, and in the second the local Statesmen are weaker characters and that island, half the size of this, has not such a politically sound and stable government.

In my opinion, the fact that soap and medicaments for the civilian population will run out on 1st November and coal, salt and sugar on 1st December, must be put before the highest authorities in the Reich, with the urgent plea that they help out by sending supplies of the first by air, and that in regard to the other commodities they inform the British government via the International Red Cross. Whether or not the States' threat in their memorandum is unjustified, the fact remains that the responsibility has now been placed firmly on our shoulders.

Although von Helldorf has always been very tolerant and sympathetic in all questions affecting the civilian population, he seems in this instance to have become a fire-eating Anglophobe and has even quoted the treatment of civilians at Le Havre. At any rate, he has quite failed to grasp the legal standpoint which I have put forward, in arguing that we must clear ourselves of the implied guilt with which we have been saddled, by passing on the responsibility to other authorities. I am aware of, and think highly of, von Helldorf's clarity of judgement and his ability immediately to grasp a clearly presented case, that is in all my dealings with him up to now. In this instance, I cannot help feeling, other considerations play a part. He is always highly reasonable, broadminded and obliging insofar as his own interests are not concerned. And so far one can get on splendidly with him; I would be the first to acknowledge it. But he is equally pitiless: unjust, unscrupulous and capable of any intrigue if his own interests are affected. Dr. Auerbach and I often called him 'the arch-intriguer', and compared him with such Machiavellian figures as Pope Urban, Alexander or one of the Borgias. I hold him quite capable of sacrificing the whole German staff, the troops and his best friends, if they should interrupt his little love affair.

According to what he has written to me, his intention is (a) to hold out as long as possible in order (b) to effect a free withdrawal of German troops from the islands. Both these aims would appear praiseworthy and in the interests of our soldiers, but a free withdrawal of our forces could scarcely be effected – if at all – if the civilian population had already suffered losses through starvation and we had taken no measures to avert this. According to what his girlfriend says, he has promised to marry her and is completely infatuated by her. I now fear that his motives, however reasonable his arguments may appear, are not to be trusted and that his sole aim is to maintain the status quo and to avoid any such risk and challenge as would undoubtedly be involved in passing on the States' S.O.S.

Von Helldorf is certainly in a very influential position. He is regarded by local officials as the final authority. He has himself not neglected to foster this view, as there are numerous instances to show. I have therefore ventured to draw the General's attention to this darker side of his character, of which I am only too well aware, the more so as I am equally well aware of his otherwise unimpeachable judgement and lack of bureaucratic inhibition in carrying through any necessary unbureaucratic measures.

Quite apart from the question of how our fate may turn out here, the fact remains that Germany is already partially occupied by the enemy, and that this process is likely to continue. It is therefore vital that we deal in proper legal fashion with this sole small corner of the British Isles to be occupied by German forces, if only from sheer commonsense. And that means we must take all steps to avert a state of emergency for the civilian population before that state arises. Britain must be fully informed of the state of the affairs by reliable channels. Responsibility will thus be transferred to the opponent. Britain may then attack us, which will be more to our taste than being slowly strangled, or it may send ships with supplies for the populace, whch would admittedly strengthen our powers of resistance. Or it may do neither, in which case at least the States could no longer refuse to co-operate with us in spinning out available supplies, otherwise they would be laying themselves open to the charge of irresponsibility. German Headquarters must therefore be informed, with the urgent recommendation that they pass on the States' memorandum to the British.

15.9.44. Have discussed the draft of my proposed letter to the General with Pokorny. We agreed that, by the light of day, the accusations against von Helldorf seem too monstrous to be credible, without any firm evidence to back them up. Even though I am 100 per cent convinced of their truth and am perhaps the only person who would be able to enlighten the General – better leave it. I am reminded of a saying of Napoleon's that 'all the evil in the world results from one being not good enough or not bad enough'. I feel guilty in perpetuating this human failing by remaining silent.

I have discovered a black-market restaurant in a lovely setting in St Aubin's Bay. They still serve a wonderful meal without any coupons. Of course I shall have to have it closed down, painful as this may be after enjoying such a good meal there in the role of snooper.

Von Helldorf accuses us of unfairness in apportioning the beer between the islands. In fact we have nothing to do with it, we merely manufacture it here. A spirit of mistrust, jealousy, and ill-will is growing up between the German Staffs of the two islands, which ironically reflects local historical precedent. The General no longer phones me. He too is obviously out of humour and I for my part am too proud to ring him up. So, when times are hard, people make them harder. I am now afraid that the States' memorandum will be put to other uses than those which we intended.

I am continually nagged by doubts about whether I shall ever return home. The risk of ultimately being held guilty and called to account hangs over me day and night. The deceptive peace of our present existence in these golden autumn days merely masks a fate that nonetheless advances inexorably upon us.

16.9.44. This afternoon I drove round alone in the neighbourhood to seek some distraction from depression, but I found no ease from my grim thoughts and gloomy imaginings of home and the family. There is no proper autumn here. I sought out the one small corner of woodland, but in spite of the sunshine, the brilliant colours of autumn were lacking. The leaves turn brown, then black and soon fall. It is now eight years since I enjoyed an untroubled autumn with my wife; it is our favourite season. Six years of war and two of training for war intervened. In the evening I found some consolation in reading. The study of biology seems to bring me an understanding of the universal spirit and leads to an extraordinary conviction of immortality, not of the individual, but of the universal spirit which dwells in us all.

All over the island Germans are sedulously engaged in learning English, a sign on the part of those clear-sighted enough to make the best of a bad job, of what they already anticipate. My own day seldom passes without an hour of language study.

I called on Miss White at Samarès Manor and confided to her this unhappy state of affairs in my relations with the General. She was far too tactful to ask for details. But she was so distressed at any kind of breach between her two best friends on the German Staff (in her difficult task of administering the Manor in the absence of its owner) that I ended up by trying to console her. She is a very wise and percipient old English lady, and in fact a much better judge of character than the General. She had long since seen through Helldorf and summed up his intriguing ways.

My room is full of gorgeous full-blooming asters. This is the one extravagance in which I can still indulge.

17.9.44. Began this Sunday with a ride into the golden morning. A thick white dew still lay on the meadows. One must look out for skids, but Froni knows her business even better than Satan, and one can practically leave her to make her own speed on curves. Without her iron shoes she would be in no danger of slipping at all. The poor beasts still cannot accustom themselves to these manifestations of civilisation.

In the afternoon, accompanied by Pokorny, I made a tour of the bakers' ovens, where the civilians can have a warm meal cooked now the gas has given out. We by-passed the queues of waiting people, but there was not a surly look or a cross word from the waiting women and girls. Rather they regarded us in quite friendly fashion, and were inclined to crack jokes with us. This made me feel more at ease, as our visit was out of genuine concern for these people, and not just to estimate how long they could hold out. One lives constantly with this odd contradiction, of being the enemy on British soil, yet of sympathising with the inhabitants and wishing to help them.

The contents of the dishes were very meagre, mostly a few potatoes cooked without fat, and some tomatoes here and there. Fortunately, with this eye-witness knowledge fresh in mind, I was able to stop the publication of an article in our island newspaper for the troops, referring to the islanders' 'good supplies' and the 'interesting contents' of the dishes they took to the bakers' ovens. (This 'skilful' German propaganda!)

Spent the whole afternoon shooting. It was a wonderful relaxation. I stood under the towering oaks and beeches at Rozel Manor, all vigilant for any pigeon which might cross my sights. At the same time, not a movement in the air escaped my notice. Every titmouse, every falling acorn, made its impression on my sharpened senses. The sluggish flight of the crows, the see-saw motion of the magpies, the hovering gulls, could only deceive me for an instant. The flapping wings of pigeons and the fuss of their arrival and departure were unmistakeable. The beech trees are full of beechnuts and these tempt the pigeons. I was able to shoot two, and at dusk bagged a rabbit, which had ventured out to nibble on the lawn, instead of waiting holed up in the dahlia bushes until I had departed. These rabbits are shabby creatures, their hide dirty through living underground, and their front legs curiously malformed. I thought of the hares at home, which would scarcely venture into a well-kept garden, but which are statelier and cleaner beasts.

A noble spaniel lay in the morning sun on the asphalt road, enjoying the warming rays. A picture of mental ease, well-being, peace and breeding. I led the horse round him in a wide circle, so as not to spoil this happy hour in a dog's life.

Have been reading Paracelsus, who says 'The human being is a microcosm, the macrocosm is all the divided parts of a human being'. In fact, the human organism contains all potentialities within itself, its own poisons and its own antidotes. When the microcosm is endangered by illness, man senses that he is a meeting-place of the cosmos. Thus the homeopathist advocates treatment by minute doses of medicine adapted to the organism's own self-defensive processes, just as the wise wife guides her husband by an intuitive understanding of his needs.

18.9.44. The reply to the memorandum has arrived from Guernsey. At first sight, reading it leaves a rather confused impression, as it consists of two documents of almost identical content. The first, obviously written by the General, starts in factual fashion, but ends on a warmer and more human note; von Helldorf's contribution is confined to facts and figures. What is most disappointing is that it is not in itself a reply to the States, but an exposition to us of the C-in-C's (and his adviser's) views on and reactions to the memorandum. These views, with a more or less subjective expression of displeasure, we are asked in conclusion to convey to the Bailiff in 'a suitable form'. (At least they realise that the present form is not suitable.) Of course, in formulating the reply, everything will depend on the exact wording and terms employed. So we shall have to think up some form in which to express views with which we cannot altogether agree. We are again saddled with the responsibility and all the work involved – the difference between expressing annoyance and conveying this in a diplomatic note which will be preserved in the archives of the States is as great as that between the tubes of paint and the finished picture. As usual in all such important matters, I shall lay it aside and put it out of mind for the time being. Then I shall return to it with a better sense of proportion to give it the close attention it deserves.

In the early morning was at the harbour, which is full of warships. In the hazy atmosphere of a misty sunrise it reminded me strongly of Hamburg harbour, which is always swathed in smoke and fog; the oily water glittering in the weak sunlight, the bustle about the tall ships' ladders and the long-necked cranes all around, lending the scene an odd and legendary air. The human figures in the scene, in their bustling activity, seemed like wound-up puppets. There was nobody else to view this picture of the harbour in the early morning sunshine as a whole, nobody to catch, in the clatter of the old ships' machinery, the faded paintwork, the threadbare uniforms, the loading of battered gun-parts, the flavour of a war nearing its end. Nobody sees the full picture, although there is something awe-inspiring about it. One could wish to have been a painter of historical scenes.

It seems to me remarkable how we all, to a greater or lesser degree, keep up our spirits in the face of overwhelming odds. Common sense tells us we could never prevail against them. Yet, if we were called upon to fight, nobody here would count the cost, even if it only meant defending our lives for a few more days before inevitable defeat. This fighting spirit and a deep sense of military honour is inborn. Nobody who has not worn uniform and shared the soldier's creed can understand it. This is why the Bailiff, that well-clad civilian, fails to grasp how sorely his threats offend our honour. He is completely the wily lawyer; if he were a sportsman, even, he would have a better understanding of the case.

19.9.44. Our housemaids are just too superior. They behave like the ladies of the house, expect to be included in parties, refuse to clean shoes, fetch vegetables from the garden or light the stove; the gardener must attend to these chores. One even feels inhibited about lighting a cigarette without offering them one. They are mad on cigarettes; no doubt a good deal of ash falls into the kitchen saucepans. Unfortunately many officers permit them liberties far in excess of their domestic status. Frances was so horrified to find a flea in my bed, one would think she had been offered a personal insult.

20.9.44. Yesterday morning called on Colonel Heine to pick up the Division's reply to the memorandum. At the same time he handed me a legal report composed by a young lawyer who had attended my lecture. This proved to be a logically constructed thesis of suicidal, cannibalistic chauvinism. According to this document, the civilian population, following a brief ultimatum to Great Britain, should be abandoned to starvation straight away. They should be rounded up in camps, where they would be cut off from any further food supplies. The legal justification for this was that the state of emergency, imperilling the troops, had already arrived. It is a shattering document, full of the bias and bluster that make Germans hated all round the world. It lacks all sense of proportion or sound legal concepts, and is informed only by bestiality. I know the writer, a sinister-looking man, completely bald despite his youth. The born hangman and the personification of ruthless fanaticism. What is still worse, the major, his commanding officer, has written a covering note, signifying his agreement with this irresponsible composition, with the illuminating comment that the fate of the Germans now in British hands need no longer be taken into consideration, as it is now a matter of victory or death for all Germans. So effective is propaganda!

I formulated an immediate retort: 'In your young jurist's arguments with regard to the problem of a state of emergency, which is now under discussion by the superior and competent German authorities, the only thing that is lacking is the proposal that the liquidated men, women and children should be utilised as soon as possible, before we all grow too thin, to supplement the meat ration for the troops and for the manufacture of urgently-needed soap!'

But better for me to make no reply, at least not yet. The Colonel has already done that and torn them off a few strips – he was incensed because he was urged to pass on this document to the General by official channels, which probably annoyed him just as much as the contents. He is a great upholder of official channels, and nothing could irritate him more than their misuse.

This shameless document must surely take pride of place as an indication of the state of mind of that class of our contemporaries, brainwashed by propaganda, to which the writer belongs. I would try to preserve it, except for the risk of damage to Germany's reputation if it should fall into enemy hands.

Only this afternoon I encountered a lieutenant who, in know-all tones, proclaimed that the present hold-up of enemy forces on the strongly-fortified German frontier was a sure sign that the tide of battle had now turned in our favour. Touching as such faith may be, I can find no common ground with these clever people who are unable to take a wider view of events. Much as I love my country, and have great hopes for its future, I believe it is just such mental immaturity and lack of moderation which have brought about our downfall. Victory for such a spirit of unreason is too frightful to contemplate. This negative aspect of the German character was brought to power in times of need, unrest and social upheaval, when, perhaps, it had a part to play in achieving a new and juster social order. But it was never qualified to rule. Poor Germany, which produces good ideas, but leaves them to men utterly lacking in ability to carry them out! Nobody is such a worldly innocent as the German in putting a good theory into practice. Yet the cynic might say that nothing is more practical than a good theory.

After this really shattering day, had Ella and John to supper in the evening, and for a few hours escaped the pressures of the times in lighthearted companionship.

21.9.44. Went with Bleuel to the Soldiers' Shop and requisitioned the remainder of the children's underwear, in order to have it taken apart and made up into desperately needed underwear for the troops. A lot of the soldiers have already been thus equipped and are going around with corners of pink, bright green or yellow shirts proudly sticking up from their uniform collars. On sleepless nights my mind is plagued by bright ideas and the means of carrying them out. They are clear, penetrating and logical but, I know, to be distrusted in the brighter light of day. It is rather like viewing the countryside through a telescope; one recognises distant objects anew, but fails to relate them to the countryside as a whole.

22.9.44. A night and day of concentrated mental effort behind me. I felt obliged to refute the validity of the legal case as presented in such inflammatory and pseudo-authoritative terms by the young lawyer and to demolish his arguments one by one. This was not difficult in terms of jurisprudence. He is better trained in rhetoric than in law, but none the less dangerous for that. I brought all my acumen and irony to bear in deflating his claims and reducing them to nonsense. The dangerous ideas propagated in this document demand the sharpest rebuttal, both in themselves and in the attitude of the writer, and this I think I have achieved in the clearest, most carefully considered and definitive terms. Sad that here, so far from home, one must engage in an additional battle of law and ethics, with the fate of thousands in the balance.

This afternoon an enemy vessel approached Guernsey, bearing a white flag with a blue star. A German boat went out to meet it. It seems that the surrender of the islands was demanded. Up to now no state of emergency has been proclaimed. Perhaps the state of siege may continue for a while. Helldorf answered my enquiry on the 'phone with the nonchalance of a grand seigneur slighly incommoded by a buzzing fly. When I asked what the enemy emissary wanted, he replied 'The usual', as if such trifling demands for surrender were an everyday occurrence. As far as I know, this was the first. When I asked what he meant by 'The usual', he answered with great good humour, 'Oh well, surrender, of course'. The old fox certainly has style and as a diplomat outranks the worthy military commanders by a long chalk. Perhaps his craftiness may yet pay off.

Today in warm, overcast weather, waded far out to sea at low tide and enjoyed a swim. Poor Lucienne, who has a great crush on me, followed me into the water but soon gave up. Was overjoyed to leave her behind and kick and splash alone. The way she sticks to me like a leech is so irritating. But I do deplore her silly infatuation and was sorry it led her to venture into the sea and spoil her elegant swim-suit which was really only designed for a promenade on the plage.

Today, after the usual complicated deliberations, the Bailiff and I were able to reach speedy agreement on one less difficult matter, on which we found ourselves in full accord. This led to an exchange of pleasantries and jokes and put us both in high good humour. The jokes we crack here tend to be on the grim side, in keeping with the situation. One thing that is certain is that everything is coming to an end, food stocks, the occupation, our life in comfortable billets, the present system of island rule and our present sparring matches over this as well.

In view of the uncertain future, the smallest decisions become a ticklish political problem. How shall the last 100 shotgun cartridges, the last 1,000 bottles of beer, the last 100 kilograms of chocolate, etc., be allocated? The latest agricultural plan for planting and sowing in the new year has become a weighty matter of state.

23.9.44. Every morning, before I go to the office, I spend some time with a good book. The early morning sunshine floods into my room, making a dancing golden pattern through the lattice work of leaves. The well-kept garden is still full of roses, dahlias, petunias and asters, and two elegant clumps of Prince of Wales' Feathers, tall blooming pampasgrass, stand silvergilt on the small lawn. I look forward happily to what this sunny day may bring, on the beach or under the old trees on the wait for pigeons or driving round the countryside. As long as one still has all this, one must still also have some measure of content, in spite of longings for homeland and loved ones. I can only hope that they still have as much good fortune at home.

Colonel Heine has passed on my sharp refutation of the young cadet's legal thesis to his commanding officer, Major Gebhardt, who so short-sightedly and enthusiastically sponsored it. I am greatly relieved about this. It seems to me essential, in these times of delicate political decisions, to clamp down on such dangerous radical manifestations and stifle them at birth. Today I took the colonel a couple of pigeons I had shot at Rozel Manor as a small token of genuine gratitude. This decent and honourable old man, with his heavy burden of responsibility, deserves such recognition, but is unlikely to get it from anyone else, I fear.

24.9.44. Have viewed the grounds of Mrs. Resch's house, in which a large wall has collapsed. She is asking for a ton of cement to repair it. The wall served no useful purpose and was erected merely at the whim of a rich man. Old habits die hard and do not keep pace with the changing times. There are still many rich people in the island but very few tons of cement.

Mrs. Resch is a pretty, well-dressed woman of undoubted charm. Her husband was a German Australian. He seems to have been genuinely devoted to her. He died at the beginning of the occupation. Now, as a comparatively young woman, late 30s perhaps, she is left to bring up the rather shy child of this union with a much older man and to cope with the burden of riches. She is bound to be a target for exploitation by adventurers. In chatting about her future plans I tried to convey to her some of the difficulties of her situation and I think she was properly impressed. Today, over a glass of vermouth, she showed us some snapshots of Australia and of her childhood.

In the morning, Sunday, went swimming in a stormy sea. In the afternoon the naval M.O. Hartmann and his girl-friend Karin came to tea. She is Flemish, but a nursing sister in the German Red Cross. Hartmann is an attractively informal character. At one time he wanted to be an artist or a singer. Now, as a doctor, his sober Swabian virtues of efficiency and uprightness are offset by a Bohemian tendency to drink and loose living. But one can't help liking him, as he is clever enough to strike a balance between these opposing elements of his nature, to work hard, play hard, and enjoy each day as it comes. And he is very good company.

Sister Karin is also a character in her own right. How she came to the island in the first place is a mystery, bizarre and extravagant, and undoubtedly depending on contacts in the right place and much string-pulling. The war must have come as a godsend to her, as she simply loves men, the more numerous the better. In particular she is devoted heart and soul to the navy and addresses everyone from admiral to able seaman with the familiar 'Du'. She embroidered a heart on the admiral's bullet-ridden shirt when mending it. She is stupid but pretty, sensual and vivacious and inspired by a passion for good works which nothing can dampen. She bakes the best cakes, occupies herself with a thousand trashy enthusiams and leads a whirlwind life shuttling between all her men. She has no time for women; they might bake better cakes or be more attractive than she is. Needless to say she is an ardent National Socialist and believes in victory and in herself as if they were one and indivisible. She has extraordinarily melting, carnal eyes under an exceptionally low brow. In talk she fervently supports the Party line and only gets upset if the talk passes beyond the bounds of her small circle or touches on the virtues or cooking of some other woman. Then she is like a clucking hen in defence of her domain, the harbour sick quarters where, as sole nursing sister, she has hitherto ruled the roost and, to do her justice, put in a lot of hard work. She can probably make a lot of men happy, but would be death to the individual.

I slipped away from the tea-table before they left, to join Pokorny in listening to the Sunday evening programme of classical music. We heard a romantic piano concerto by Schumann, in A minor, opus 54.

The commander of the ship of truce did not demand surrender but wished to make personal contact and to set up means of communication by direct telephone cable and also to acquaint the island military commanders with the military situation. It was thus only a preliminary feeler.

25.9.44. I have only written at such length in my diary since it became impossible to write letters to my wife. This interim period must not be lost to us. What I would formerly have written to her is now confided to the pages of this diary. Only the loving greetings and the warmth and lightheartedness and understanding which made letter-writing so much more easy and joyous are lacking. But if I do not survive perhaps this diary may do, and eventually come into her hands and show her how I lived out the last lonely months of my life without her.

I have also found another means of giving expression to my feelings: in a prodigality of flowers. I pick and purchase the finest blooms and put them in vases around my office. I had never done this before; my personal tastes are frugal. This is in dedication to all the beauty, charm and grace which are now missing. It is in homage to my wife and in constant evocation of her dear presence to my side.

Sonderführer Wegner came for the evening. Not a special friend of mine, as he is very much the materialist, devoted to the good things rather than to the higher things of life, with the corresponding weaknesses of character. In short, he is an out-and-out sybarite, but a genial fellow, doubtless well-read, good-hearted and humane of outlook, also a good musician and agreeable conversationalist. We spent a pleasant evening over the old port which I customarily offer guests and he clearly welcomed the opportunity to speak his mind freely, which is seldom possible at the rather stiff military gatherings.

This morning the military court heard the case against the States' labour representative, Le Quesne, for possessing a wireless set. The sentence was seven months' imprisonment. I appeared as a witness to testify for the previous good behaviour of the accused.

In the afternoon had a long discussion with the Attorney-General, Duret Aubin, about the present situation and various resultant problems. This was conducted most amicably. He acknowledged that the decision against a final report on the allocation of manpower was justified. In connection with Le Quesne's sentence we got to talking about judicial acumen, with which so few are blessed, but which is one of man's most important endowments. He told me the story of the English bishop who wished his nephew only one blessing in life; that was good judgement, from which all other blessings would stem.

Helldorf rang up to say that the States' appeal for help had been sent on by ship to the International Red Cross in Geneva. What a weight off my mind! So there was a wise man at the top after all and the responsibility for the imminent state of emergency for the civilian population has been shifted to other shoulders.

In the afternoon we had invited Sisters Ruth and Karin to tea. Karin (not the nurse of the same name previously referred to) has Hungarian blood. Round-cheeked, low-browed and rather plump, she appears the

typical country cousin. But she has great vivacity and is so imbued with
the spirit of music that when she dances her stocky figure no longer
seems incongruous in the stiff Red Cross uniform, but embodies
liveliness and grace. Ruth comes from Saxony. She has a quick wit and
nimble tongue and delights in an exchange of philospohical axioms, of
which she has a ready store. A pert, jolly and very pretty girl. She was in
high spirits and we mimed a sophisticated couple dancing together. She
got the right facial expressions but in movement maintained the reserve
proper to a well-brought-up German girl.

We talked about home and our families and how surprised they
would be to see us enjoying ourselves here, with tea, drinks and music.
But we all owned to a heavy daily load of care and anxiety for the future
and agreed we felt entitled to this little break.

Ella, who is growing more closely attached to me, came to see me in
the evening. I told her a French love story in English, which is good for
my English. We fooled lightheartedly and imagined how we would act
in the same situation as the characters in the story. I jokingly told her
she would later have to try a French boyfriend and an Italian boyfriend
and of course an American. Never, she replied in honest indignation,
never a dirty Frenchman or an oily Italian and she could not stand
Americans as they spoke such atrocious English.

I was reminded that the States' financial adviser had spoken of these
people in much the same terms when recalling his business experience
with them; of the Frenchman, he said, you must be particularly wary, as
he always had some trick up his sleeve to try to do you down.

I am just reading what looks like a dreadfully trashy book, *La Pantoufle
de Sapho*. It is a Montmartre edition, with a suitably titillating
frontispiece, and is by no less a writer than Masoch, who gave his name
to masochism. It was recommended to me by the secondhand
bookseller Burger, and to my pleasant surprise I have found that it
contains some enchanting love stories of high literary merit. It is by no
means concerned solely with the perverse, but rather depicts the
pleasures of love-making in the most delicate terms and varied
manifestations. *La Feuille Blanche* is a classic example of the good short
story and I am tempted to try a translation into German.

Burger is quite a character. He is the complete pacifist, soft-hearted
and kindly, a shambling awkward bear of a man. His face has retained
its youthfulness, with its candid gaze and broad smile. At the same time
he is sensitive, withdrawn and, despite his 40 years, quite unworldly,
especially where women are concerned. He once remarked that the idea
of possessing a woman was utterly repugnant to him. He has always
lived at home with his mother and sister and devoted his obviously
considerable talents to building up his business. This is literally built
up around him, as his office, which is the anteroom to the store, is piled

ceiling high with books and pictures. To have created an undertaking of such scope, he must of course have some judgement and business acumen, yet he will practically give his books away to anyone who takes his fancy. Presumably the business must support such quixotism. I enjoy a chat with him but have to be on my guard to ensure that he does not sell me some volume, which he sees I like, at a completely unrealistic price.

27.9.44. The General and Helldorf arrived here by ship from Guernsey this afternoon. This led me to call on Miss White at Samarès Manor in the evening . She is the most upright old lady and my best friend in the island. She greeted me in her broken German as an 'unfaithful monster' because I had not been to see her for over a week. There is a bond of absolute trust between us, rather as if we were mother and son and I discuss all my problems with her in full reliance on her discretion. In the First World War she made a unique collection of recorded instances of chivalrous behaviour between the opposing British and German forces; proof enough that her heart is on both sides. This evening we hatched a little plot. This was concerned with how best to gain the goodwill of the General, who is Miss White's other great friend on the German staff. His warmth of human feeling on the one hand and his rather limited military outlook on the other, combine to make him susceptible to the nearest influence, at the moment that of Helldorf. This influence must be counteracted. That wily diplomat had, as a first step, already paid his call at Samarès Manor, no doubt with a similar object in view to my own. But he got no encouragement from Miss White, who saw through him long ago. Now she will use her good offices with the General, and represent to him in what high regard I am held by everyone here. I would find this despicable if only my own interests were concerned. But the General's trust and support is essential to me in carrying out my duty here, as I see it, for the good of all, and to ensure that confidence I must call on every conceivable support, even from 'the other side'. In fact I am trying to consolidate a base from which to advance my commonsense policy. Miss White and I agreed on parting that our little plot was amply justified, on both sides, if commonsense were to prevail to the benefit of us all.

I cycled home in a brisk wind, much fortified and refreshed. I have a formidable task here, in trying to steer a just course between the claims of our own soldiers and their military honour and the welfare of the local inhabitants. Is it worth it, I wonder; do the latter even know I am trying to help them? But I have to act according to the dictates of my conscience, which this evening led me to a conspiratorial meeting with an old English lady.

On my way back I ruminated too on how, in my role as liaison officer between the military and island authorities, I was so exactly acquainted with all the facts and figures of the situation and with all the personalities involved and in how far I could utilise their various weaknesses and strengths to further my aims. And of how little I could foresee the fate of this mixed community, German and British, thrown together by the chances of war, but who must inevitably soon part company and go their separate ways.

The forthcoming talks with the General and Helldorf will also do little to throw light on this riddle. I have no great expectations in this respect. To ask advice is to admit one's own limitations, to give it is to appear arrogant. One can only really advise when one is involved in carrying out the project and can influence its progress. Bismarck once said that the wisest and best-informed statesman could not, with certainty, foresee the events of the next day. What a consolation!

It sometimes occurs to me that I might well have attained an equally high position in times of peace, but united with my family. What indescribable happiness.

28.9.44. One is haunted by gloomy pictures of the future; bondage and oppression, poverty, perhaps the loss of one's loved ones. A terrible fate is catching up with Germany. One can no longer feel any ease of spirit. One senses that everything that has gone before is only a pale reflection of the sufferings to come. These pages I am writing now may then appear to stem from a happier age, for which the reader may spare a smile but will scarcely be able to comprehend. Events pile up on me and drive me to despair.

Today the arch-intriguer Helldorf continued his round of visits. It was our turn in the morning and we continued the discussions over a cup of tea in the afternoon. The General remained cool and reserved. No doubt influenced by Helldorf, he will not commit himself until the latter has visited and tried out all the local authorities, to ensure that no decision will be taken or even discussed here without Helldorf's knowledge and consent. There is no doubt that his influence over the General has increased, also his personal authority. He drives around in a large and luxurious car, while the General contents himself with a much more modest one. But, apart from the car, everyone knows that it is Helldorf who wields the real power and that he is not a man to cross.

The note concerning urgent supplies for the civilian population has now been sent on to the Red Cross, and we can only wait and see whether they send us ships. I asked Helldorf what his expectations were. Vain and ambitious people always like to be asked their opinion: they take this as a tribute to their superiority and will thus always make some response. He said he thought it would depend upon the way in which the note was worded, whether or not the British sent supplies. With its open loophole, a not unadroit reply.

I am reading a well-written biography of Goya by Manfred Schneider, and supplementing the text by referring to a portfolio of reproductions of Goya's paintings. How startlingly vivid his portraits are. These reproductions add enormously to one's enjoyment and understanding in reading about his life. His range covered the whole of life and experience, from the most delicate and poetic to the most terrifying and soul-stirring. His range of expression is inexhaustible. He is a careful psychologist, yet has an unbridled imagination. A complete artist of the rarest kind. If I could have had the choice, I should have liked to be a great painter, to make all the beauties of the world my own.

29.9.44. My sole communication to my wife in the last three months has been reduced to a numbered message, with pre-set text and nothing personal about it except the address, to be broadcast in a radio programme for forces' families at home. This is surely the last stage before a total break in contact, perhaps before death. In these bleak autumn days there is nothing to dispel melancholy apart from the occasional social meeting. Even a good film only underlines the pleasanter aspects of life which are lacking.

On the third day after his arrival the General has still not called on me, although it seems to me no exaggeration to claim that, in this state of siege, the administration of the island, cultivation of the land, conservation of supplies and maintenance of order among the civilian population, together with a sensible line of policy, are all more important than military exercises and the state of defence, which has long since been settled and cannot now be changed.

I fear he holds it against me that I am sharing quarters with Heider, whom he dislikes. But I cannot help that, as I had to move out of White Lodge. Perhaps he also takes it amiss that I wrote to him that I had been getting on much better with Heider since I moved in with him, that in fact we had become quite good comrades. I feel rather piqued by this undeserved neglect and inclined to demonstrate my independence, as I don't have to put up with this Grand Mogul moodiness. On the other hand, in trying to carry out my task here, I am determined that all personal feeling must be put aside. I must not take him, or myself either, too seriously.

Basically I think I am an unsociable sort of person, inclined to cut myself off from human contact. I notice this at the cinema. I see how the officers make their way to the seats reserved for them with a certain self-consciousness, enjoying playing their own particular role, looking round and exchanging greetings. I am happy if I can slip into a quiet seat, unrecognised by anyone. If it were not for my wife, I should probably have been well on the way to becoming some sort of odd recluse.

30.9.44. I have seldom been so deeply incensed. Helldorf was in conference with me, when suddenly he said he must be off to keep another appointment. I had previously specifically asked that the Head of Military Government should always be called in to any discussion with the Bailiff and that in Guernsey Counsellor Schneeberger, the Head of our branch office (Nebenstelle) should take part in such talks. And where did Helldorf go, without telling me a word about it? Taking Wegner with him, he went straight to the Bailiff and, without my knowledge, talked to him for over an hour. Apart from going behind my back, this amounts to disowning the military government. It is also a political blunder. If we are disunited and do not act in concert, the Bailiff can play us off, one against the other. No doubt I shall hear from the Bailiff in due course what they talked about. And why does Helldorf bypass me like this? No doubt to represent himself, at the cost of others, as the one person primarily interested in the welfare of the civilian population and to avoid playing this false role in my presence.

But this time I will not put up with such treatment. I shall put the matter to the General. He is welcome to have me recalled but cannot demand that I continue to take part in such a farce. Helldorf's action is equivalent to the General calling a meeting of battalion commanders without notifying the regimental commander. What is worse, it will not escape the notice of the sharpwitted island officials. How tragic that in matters affecting our national honour and our own interests we Germans cannot be united. But I shall not confront Helldorf, red-faced and blustering, rather I shall show him the cold shoulder and counter his wily actions by his own wily methods.

1.10.44. The first day of October, a Sunday; harvest festival is over. We face another month of increasing problems. This morning the General asked me to call on him, and then gave me an invitation for this evening. Helldorf sat there looking rather guilty. They had no doubt heard all about my indignation through Wegner. Now they joined forces to explain that Helldorf's visit to the Bailiff was a special mission on behalf of the General, on account of the Bailiff's threats in his memorandum, but I could see that this was a story which Helldorf had concocted with the General after the event.

To celebrate harvest festival we gave a little coffee party to our immediate circle at Linden Court. We had made a cake from samples of flour from the new harvest and as there was sufficient cognac to provide a few glasses for all, the party was soon in a festive mood. John, the military policeman, made his village pub-type quips, in which the would-be humour lies in an inversion of the usual polite phrases. Offered a glass of cognac, he would say 'I'll not only have a glass but another one after this', or would adjure the company to 'tuck in, we've got to let our hosts know they've invited us'. The German enjoys his crude, literal jokes. Such witticisms would be inconceivable in the mouth of a Frenchman.

At night drove out to the electricity works with a cask of beer. They are working like mad there, trying to patch up the three ancient boilers, but without much hope of getting the job done.

Tomorrow will bring the big confrontation with the General and Helldorf.

4.10.44. The last two days have been devoted to long and detailed discussions between the General, Helldorf and me. Now at last we have caught up on information and confidence has been more or less re-established between us. I am now completely in the picture; have been made aware of the dangerous machinations of the naval commander, Admiral Hüffmeier, a dedicated Nazi and an ambitious man of unstable character, and have glimpsed the tortuous workings of bureaucracy up to the highest levels. Any decisions we take can only be tentative and dependent on events. But at least I can visualise more clearly the intricacies of planning which lie ahead. There are so many differing factors, to cover the needs of the forces and of the civilians, under differing circumstances in different places and with varied time-limits, to take into account and try to weld into an overall plan. Helldorf has just the coolly calculating mind for such work. He is undoubtedly a man of stature. It is a pity that calculation plays such a large part in his make-up. He has considerable but not absolute confidence in me.

It is the General who is personally so likeable. He has a warmth of human feeling and an affability which is perhaps all the more appealing in view of his high rank. And behind his age and high honours one glimpses the youthful spirit ready for any joke or escapade. He has a good memory and an instinctive feeling for what is right, not in the coolly calculating way of Helldorf, but spontaneously and impulsively, although on this account he is more open to influence and less able to weigh a problem as a whole.

Two possibilities seem to emerge from the present situation. Ships from a neutral country may bring supplies for the civilian population, in which case we shall be able to fall back on local stocks, which might enable us somehow to hold out until the end of May next year. If these ships are not sent, the most drastic measures will have to be taken. In fact the chief difficulty will be not so much food as the fuel to cook it, coal for the bakers' ovens and to provide meals for the hospitals and the needy. Under these conditions we should be hard put to it to hold out until February/March 1945. The sowing of 4,000 tons of wheat has now been countermanded.

Yesterday we put a semi-official notice in the local paper informing the people that a note had been passed to the Protecting Power.

It has suddenly been announced that we may write a letter home. An aeroplane is expected. What a rush to try to get all the accumulated news on one sheet of paper within the hour.

7.10.44. Helldorf is planning to confiscate all civilian stocks before the Red Cross ships arrive. He issued a feeler about this in his discussion with the Bailiff, whose response was that the States would strongly protest. I should think the Red Cross Commission would be equally disapproving of any such precipitate action before the legal position has been established. It could only have an adverse effect on negotiations. It is obvious that this must ultimately be a political decision. As the only jurist present, it is very difficult for me to bring sufficient legal weight to bear in these discussions. Helldorf is all for ill-considered and high-handed decisions. He treats the General rather like an errant youth whom he must protect from the dangers of solitary drinking and from any private conversation with another person, so that he, Helldorf, will not be called upon to straighten things out afterwards. He plays up his self-imposed role in this respect, intimating that all sorts of follies would have been committed but for his timely intervention. And the General, who cannot be concerned with all the highly complicated factors involved and therefore cannot see the situation as a whole, gladly believes him. However, in view of his undoubted ability, it is perhaps better that he should be actively involved rather than indifferent.

The dangerous question of the possibility of evacuating the civilian population has now come under discussion. I fear this may lead to some hare-brained order from the High Command. Our previous experience of their orders does nothing to mitigate this dread. To take forceful action is always the quick and easy way out of any situation and the military are only too prone to this solution. It is the first possibility which offers itself and saves a lot of thought. But it is lengthy consideration alone which produces the right solution in the long term.

Helldorf juggles with facts and figures and plans with an audacity I cannot match. In comparison with him, I am inhibited by my own responsibility for the figures and by my legal process of reasoning. He has also a rather arbitrary and lordly way of dealing with such matters. When the problems pile up and become too boring, he just abandons them and goes off to have tea with someone or to some other diversion. There's something to be said for this attitude, I suppose.

He has something in common with the Bailiff, in that they would both stick at nothing to attain their own ends. Helldorf is perhaps the figure with the greater panache, rather a latter-day Borgia who, in keeping with the times, deals out poison in words instead of the wine-cup. The Bailiff is more the wily lawyer, with none of Helldorf's polished hauteur; an obstinate negotiator, an always well-dressed but rather tired Mephisto, whose surface good manners tend to give way under stress to direct and hectoring abuse. Perhaps he is the more honest of the two, or has had the most to suffer.

In the evening, after seeing a good film, we invited Lieutenant Wetzstein back to Linden Court to join us round the fire. His whole trim, exceptionally smartly uniformed figure seems to exude vitality and enthusiasm for life. He is so well-groomed and polished from cap badge to boots that he almost makes the impression of a wax figure. I esteem him for his above average intellect, agility in argument and open mind. But he does tend to let his hobby horse (where the Nazi government went wrong) run away with him. So it turned out this evening when, before long, he was holding the floor in monologue, his small red eyes getting smaller and moister and his face redder. I can see we shall have difficulty in getting rid of him at a reasonable hour.

Now another foolish blunder has been made in the case of the States Labour Representative, Le Quesne. After he had served only two weeks of his seven months' sentence, he has been freed and the rest remitted. This does nothing to help his cause or our own. It brings our reputation for impartial justice into disrepute, and leads to the obvious accusation that we have one law for the highly-placed and another for the ordinary citizen. Although I would willingly have helped him in the fist place and hushed the matter up if it had been brought to my notice in time, I cannot agree with this reversal of judgement and it took place without my agreement.

8.10.44. Autumn comes earlier here. The trees are already nearly bare, without having borne the full brilliance of autumn colours. I dream of autumn at home. If someone should be called on to advise the German government in negotiations with the Red Cross, the choice might conceivably fall on me. It would be wonderful suddenly to turn up at home, too wonderful, I fear, for this dream ever to be realised.

I am still cogitating on Lt.-Colonel von Helldorf's motives in breaking off in the middle of our conference and rushing off to the Bailiff. This seems to offer some sort of clue to the whole situation. Probably he was getting bored with petty detail, but intended in any case to make his own arrangements and follow his own course. The brisk and confident way in which he got up and turned his back on us made that clear enough. He has the power and obviously intends to exercise it. So perhaps I do not, after all, bear the full responsibility. Perhaps I have been plaguing myself unnecessarily on this account. It would seem that the best that Military Administration can do, as an indispensable instrument in any action he may be planning, will be to try to put a brake on any wilder scheme and confine the action within reasonable bounds.

This afternoon felt an urgent need to get away from it all and think things out by myself, so set off on my bicycle. But I returned almost immediately, horrified by the senseless destruction of an avenue of magnificent old beech trees.

Have just read Bergengrün's biography of E.T.A. Hoffmann. This makes clearer to me why I have never felt any particular attraction to this poet. He has an eccentric rather than a poetic imagination, and is more at home with people than with nature. One observation struck me: 'The son of an hysterical woman does not inherit her hysteria, but it engenders in him an extraordinarily lively and eccentric imagination'.

9.10.44. Helldorf and the General departed by ship early this morning, after dodging each other in a hunt for alcohol. Each appeared in person to replenish his stocks without the knowledge of the other. Helldorf has left a trail of irritation and scheming behind him. The dancing teacher, Miss Lillicrap, has spread it far and wide that 'Helldi' is looking after everything, has the rescue ships laid on, etc. She is extremely well-informed, down to the latest and still secret details. So, the great man, playing the hero to women, adds the last touch to the picture of our arch plotter.

Spent Sunday evening at Wetzstein's. It was his birthday and he provided an opulent dinner. The troops engage far too much in black-marketeering and the wangling of supplies, especially this enterprising and crafty rogue Wetzstein. There was even a choice of dishes from a menu. I played with his lovely golden spaniel and noticed how it lacked the affectionate demonstrativeness towards its master which usually typifies this faithful breed.

10.10.44. A lovely mild autumn day, with the sun behind a veil of cloud so light and airy that one could not see where the cloud ended and the blue sky began. I drove alone round the whole island to inspect the terrain. At some particularly beautiful spots I pulled up for a while and thought with nostalgia of the countryside at home, now wearing that glorious mantle of autumn foliage which I so much miss here. Standing on some high spot where the cliffs fall away, with the coast of France visible in the hazy distance, the scene is not only one of beauty but of geographical significance. It shows, as on a map, how the island is lost to and cut off from the European continent.

Swarms of finches in transit whirr around at frantic speed seeking their route. Behind them swoop the gulls, dazzling white against the dun coloured earth. The remaining pigeons lead a harried existence, continually potted at by service marksmen on the hunt for food rather than sport.

11.10.44. The days race by. Thefts and robberies increase, by soldiers and civilians alike. Even the States try to cheat and we have to give many a stern word of warning. I have informed the Medical Officer that, unless the agreed quota of milk is delivered within the next week, the special milk supplies for the sick must be halved. And I have put it in friendly fashion to Deputy Le Masurier, the States' representative for Essential Commodities, that I will take over his office myself if there is another issue of foodstuffs without our authorisation. At this of all times, when fresh vegetables are most plentiful, he has just chosen to distribute three tons of tinned ones.

We are sending soldiers to inspect the threshing and to accompany the milk controllers. I am being invited to visit officers of the forces who seemed previously unaware of Military Administration's existence. One has sent me a pigeon and a roast chicken. Such cupboard-love is easy to see through and does not endear them to me.

In the afternoon I went to look at a farm. It is in the last stages of decay. The two sons and the little wrinkled bearded mother, as dirty and neglected as their background, appeared like those ugly and primitive figures which the painter and caricaturist Hoegfeld delights to depict. They showed me their fields and the stables. In one dark stall, dirty but royal, stood an enormous white Normandy horse. He turned his great head towards us and whinnied gently. My disgust at the dilapidated surroundings vanished at the sight of this noble beast. I simply had to make him some offering and finally mustered up a couple of green apples, which he took gratefully and gently from my hand.

In the evening went to the officers' club, to a concert given by an officers' quartet. The chief judge of the military court, Dr. H., played his instrument with great clarity and command. At the *fortissimo* passages I was reminded of the resounding severity of his sentences, so was glad that he was able to render the softer chords with equal mastery.

Sister Maria, middle-aged and certainly in all her life never spoiled or made much of, enjoyed her big moment, sitting in the front row between the two colonels. For her at least the war has brought her, as the leading Red Cross sister and manageress of the officers' club, to a position she could scarcely have enjoyed in peacetime.

Returned home with Woelken. His intelligence is of such a high order that it can scarcely be put to practical use.

12.10.44. Was invited to a meal aboard ship by Captain Lentsch. All very smart and orderly in the best naval tradition, yet with a pleasant feeling of freedom from restraint. We ate in the small officers' mess. Afterwards Captain Lentsch unburdened himself in modest and deprecatory fashion about the navy's needs in the way of vegetables, wood and clothing. The sailors from St Malo had brought nothing with them but what they stood up in. The officer sitting next to me admitted that he had no underpants. All he had got away with was a pair of gym shorts. This affects morale and in the circumstances it is difficult to enforce discipline. The sailors feel like stranded vagabonds. But there are far too many of them for me to help. Civilian resources have been exhausted long since.

In the evening I received the first letter from home since July, a letter from my mother dated 27.9.44. A 'plane carrying mail has at last got through to the island. Two had previously been shot down. As I look at the familiar writing, I wonder what hazards this letter has passed through on its way to me. These pilot postmen and their crews, who risk their lives to bring us news from home, are heroes. From this letter I can form only a partial impression of what is going on. It seems that my family is planning to move from Altaussee in Austria to our family home of Oberaufsess in Bavaria. What a difficult move that will be in these difficult times.

13.10.44. I have to keep a continual watch on all administrative details. My instructions are only partially or half-heartedly carried out, and minor peculation and dishonesty abounds. At night I lie awake for hours to plan fresh measures with which to face the morning. The Medical Officer, ignoring my reminder of the quota agreed with the States, has presented a report which is clearly designed to block any attempt to reduce the milk ration for the sick. Members of my own staff try to exploit our key position to their own advantage. This precludes a smooth and friendly working relationship. I must be vigilant day and night to guard against petty encroachments by friend and foe alike on our regulations for the maintenance of law and order and an equitable distribution of supplies. Nobody seems any longer concerned with such concepts, only with his personal advantage, and unfortunately our leading officers do not set a good example. Honour and decency go by the board, it seems, when it comes to self-preservation. These practices must be combated before the situation gets out of hand.

There are frequent storms and heavy rain. October is cold and autumn has set in early. One's mood matches the weather. Even the lovely countryside no longer affords consolation when, driving out, one meets with the sorry stumps of hacked-down trees, houses left derelict and bereft of combustible contents. Open ground is overhung with traceries of cables, erected against parachutists, and the earth is churned up where still more strong points are hastily being set up round the coasts.

Everywhere, too, one senses a mood of fatigue and depression, a sort of mental claustrophobia at being cooped up in such narrow confines for so long without any change of scene. Everything is stale; we know the island too well and each other too well. We have seen all the films and read all the books.

Yesterday I saw a detective film which was well acted. I was again struck by how the average German, like the policemen, innkeepers and workmen in this film, is always portrayed as a thickset, round-headed individual. It is true I see enough of them around me. This is the German as popularly conceived and widely disliked: a hard-working philistine, loud, self-assertive and lacking in tact and delicacy of perception. He is full of sentiment but coarse-grained, has a soft heart but a rough exterior. The Englishman is said to be cold of heart but mild of manner, and the Frenchman is credited with good manners, social adaptability and a quick wit. The German sings his own praises in local dialect on radio programmes for the masses, as 'a rough diamond but the better for being honest'. The Frenchman might disclaim absolute probity but would certainly claim courtesy. I find the latter the more attractive attributes, perhaps because of the French blood on my mother's side.

The average German is slow-witted but imbued by strong sentiments and an urge for acceptance by his fellows. He is temperamentally disposed to conformity. Hence, at his 'Stammtisch', his acknowledged corner of the local pub, he joins with his cronies in singing sentimental songs and drinking until his wits are fuddled and the singing becomes a meaningless bawl. It was this lack of critical thought, this urge to conform and blindly to render unto Caesar without questioning Caesar's edicts, which enabled the worst elements of the country to set up a one-party state, where the few who still criticised or questioned were soon swept aside, like weeds from the farrow before the monolithic plough. If this historic miscarriage of judgement in the conduct of the affairs of the nation is to be remedied in the future, the reaction must come not from right or from left, or from above or below, but from the average German himself, re-educated by bitter experience to self-thought and self-determination.

14.10.44. One conference follows on the heels of the other. There are 101 matters to decide. The control of milk supplies; recording sugar, apple and root vegetable crops; further measures against increasing thefts; the replanting of the fields left bare by the decision to withhold the seed-wheat for sowing; water and electricity rationing; finding more space for storage; taking over the mills; combating the rot in potatoes, etc., etc. The date to which the garrison can hold out has now been re-estimated as 31 May 1945.

Spent the afternoon at Rozel Manor with Mrs. Riley, who is a worthy representative of the breeding and cultural interests of this ancient family. She has natural wit and good humour and loves good talk and good books. She belongs to a local 'brains trust' and the members meet once a week. She showed me some of the questions set by a clergyman for last week's quiz, including: 'Do you think children need corporal punishment?', 'Could we get along without convention?' and 'Why is 13 generally accounted an unlucky number?'. Why indeed? I have always been fascinated by the significance mankind has attached to particular numbers and by the odd and coincidental way in which some numbers seem to crop up in one's own life.

We exchanged views on the news with good-humoured raillery. Churchill's visit to Stalin, which strikes us as a cap-in-hand affair, Mrs. Riley maintains is proof that in a democratic country a statesman is free to travel as he chooses, while the tyrant dares not venture beyond his own shores. She lent me an English book about Germany, which is quite interesting and deals instructively with the various stages in the evolution of the nation. Thus we try to appease our mutual need for the mental stimulus which is so sadly lacking in the island's isolated position and above all in the absence of newsprint from both sides of the Channel.

15.10.44. October is half over and we are still without a reply from the Red Cross. As far as medicaments are concerned, the state of emergency has already begun. So it's a good thing that the States, and we too, have rather underestimated than overestimated in our official returns, so that supplies will probably last out for another month.

On Sunday afternoon entertained the two flotilla commanders, Breithaupt and Lentsch, who, assisted by Heider's good supply of brandy, became very merry and expansive. The leading naval officers are, as I have already had occasion to note, far easier to get on with and less bound by convention than their army counterparts. Breithaupt does honour to his name.* He is a broad-shouldered giant of a man with a leonine head; his eyes under their beetling brows, very direct and piercing. He is also sagacious, experienced and independent of

---

*In this context, 'Breithaupt' is taken as meaning 'of wide intellect or understanding'.

judgement as befits his age, but still full of youthful drive despite his 50
years. What a pleasure it would be to serve under such a man. Lentsch
is the typical Hamburg merchant seaman. He could well be the captain
of a large, luxurious ocean-going liner.

With the exception of a brief spell during a test alarm, I spent the rest
of Sunday reading a delightful French novel set in Mont St Michel, *Sous
le pied de l'Archange*. The writing is in the best style of French narrative,
too well-disciplined to weary the reader with long or detailed
description, yet bringing the background of the sea, the fisherfolk's
daily round and the beauty of the ancient fortress vividly to life with
masterly ease. I am again tempted, with such an example and following
the same rules of composition, to try my hand at a German novel.

16.10.44. Perhaps inspired by the French novel, I left my office in the
afternoon to drive out and survey the stormy sea. I could already see
from my window that there was a mighty tide, backed by a strong
south-wester. I first went to the little wooden bungalow from which we
had bathed and spent many happy hours in the summer. I stood for a
while on the low sea-wall, a strong wind blowing stinging particles of
sand into my face and eyes. It was about two-thirds to flood. This was
indicated by the line of seaweed left by the last tide. I measured the
height of the breakers with knowledgeable eyes, remembering the
tossing I had taken the last time I has swum through them. The sky was
an April sky, squally gusts of rain alternating with blinding patches of
sunlight. One of the small boys we had played with in the summer had
come running up at the sound of the car and now stood staring at me in
fascination. Youngsters make no difference in nationality. For them a
soldier is the embodiment of war and an object of powerful interest.
And he was probably as much attracted by the car, as the last time I was
there I had given them all a ride in it, whizzing excitedly round the
corners. But now I was seeking solitude, so moved on.

Viewed across the harbour, the raging sea was an impressive sight. A
cloud had momentarily obscured the sun but behind the veils of falling
rain Noirmont Point stood out clearly, limned in fire, and shafts of
sunlight fell on the churning waters.

I indulged myself in the further run out to the west coast. Off-duty
hours must be made the most of when the elements stage such dramatic
spectacles round the shores of a little lost island. At Corbiere new
combinations of sunlight and shadow chased across the turbulent
attacking tide. The white crests of the breakers flung themselves above
the highest rocks and subsided in foaming streams down the clefts of
the granite. There were many fascinating variations in the tide's
advance. Sometimes, I noticed, the incoming sea threw up no dramatic
cascades, but rolled in quiet majesty clear over the rocky barrier. On

the lonely outer cliff path I met a young woman who pushed a pram bristling with the branches of firewood and sprays of broom she had been collecting. Beside her, her small daughter pushed a dolls-pram from which also emerged a ragged crown of brushwood. In their headscarves, tightly knotted against the wind, their faces appeared so small and elfin. There was something touching in their appearance as they rounded the bend of the path and approached me coming up from the sea. Perhaps, besides the practical purpose of their expedition, they had also been drawn by the turmoil of the waters, which provided such contrasting background to their small frail figures. As they drew near, I could see the young woman was not pretty at all, but workworn, poor and unkempt. But the encounter retained its odd magic, here on the edge of the world in a setting not far removed from an Eden before history began. Curiously enough, after passing, we both kept turning round to look back. An impersonal encounter, not a word said, not even a hand waved. Yet some sort of human contact must have been established between us.

I stayed by the sea a bit longer, but at last lost interest, and wandered into a little garden, the last in the island on the Atlantic coast and appropriately named 'West End'. The old house bore a faded sign advertising a heated tearoom. A lingering reminder of the long forgotten tourist trade.

17.10.44. Yesterday I sat by the fire and treated my heavy cold with inebriating quantities of rum. This led to the maddest ideas about what might happen to us in our present position. Internment in Spain, transported there in our small ships; our return, unmolested to Germany, in return for leaving the island unmolested, as in the case of Crete. Holding out until the end, starvation or death or a prisoner-of-war camp. The better one is acquainted with the situation, the less one can foresee its outcome. I surveyed my rather shaky reflection in the big wardrobe mirror and found my whole world equally shaky and uncertain.

Am reading an interesting English book about Germany, *The Dear Monster*, which acquaints the reader not so much with the German as with the Englishman and how he regards Germany. This is, most unjustly, as a martial monster, blindly bent on destruction, a dragon which should be slain in the interests of the human race. But on closer acquaintance, it seems, the German is really too good a chap to suffer such a fate. So the problem remains unresolved and mankind remains under the monster's threat.

After a busy day, dealing with all sorts of vexed questions, drove out to see my old friend Miss White, armed with a flask of cognac. Roy, her Scottie, gave me a rapturous welcome. We first went to feed

Marmaduke, the rather incongruously named duck, in the pool under the bamboos. She is moulting at the moment and was very shy and hid herself among the exotic water plants.

We chatted about the people and the situation here. We see so much eye to eye that our mutual trust and liking could hardly be greater. She is absolutely the only person here – friend or foe alike – who fully appreciates the fairness and integrity with which I try to carry out my duties here, with the help or hindrance of others, also friend or foe alike. We parted with special warmth and agreed we would remain friends whatever time or politics should bring.

My office desk is decked with three bunches of chrysanthemums, even lovelier than the last, rosy-red, gold and creamy yellow. How happy I should be if I could take them home to my wife. I hear on the radio that the railway installations at Salzburg and the town of Linz have been heavily bombed, and on the English news this evening it was announced that the Russians had broadcast a message to the people of Austria, urging them to rise against the government. That looks as if the Russians are going to occupy Austria.

18.10.44. With the worsening of the situation here, I become increasingly preoccupied with the problem of correct behaviour. I am convinced there is always a fair and just, or at least justifiable course of action. And if no such course remains open, there is always suicide as a last resort to preserve personal honour.

Attempts by young islanders to escape to the mainland are on the increase. French bargemen and labourers are also trying to get away. Such attempts are made from the smallest bays, though very few have been successful. Last week a woman was shot when she was caught in the glare of a Very light at night. As a result, the stretches of beach which had been opened to the public have now been closed again. I thus have a possible preview of my own fate if, in the event of the island falling, I go into hiding, as planned, and try to escape to France.

19.10.44. For days the island has been lashed by storms such as only occur in coastal areas. The last autumnal colours have been obliterated, the dahlias laid waste and the deciduous trees robbed of their last leaves. The rain falls in torrents. The house shakes with the force of the wind and one cannot leave a window open any more than one could a cabin window on a ship in a stormy sea. Otherwise wind and rain would sweep through the house as through a ship. The sea reaches heights which I had never before experienced. As the breakers hit the rocks, they explode in cascades that one might expect if a munitions ship had been hit by a bomb, and the watching children shout aloud in joy and exultation. The little bay from which we used to bathe is protected from the full fury of the tide, as it faces east and the strong wet wind reduces the height of the breakers and tames the raging sea.

Not Hitler but Himmler spoke on the radio about the setting up and training of the Volkssturm. There was no longer any reference to victory, only to encompassing the enemy advance. With all one's genuine sorrow for a Germany on the defensive and literally bleeding to death – indeed because of it – this notion of a 'People's Army' composed of greybeards and schoolchildren, marching behind the local party bigwigs, can only arouse derision.

In my office, where the deep leather armchairs are generally occupied by leading officials of the States and the top brass of the local command at some meeting I have laid on, I was today confronted by 10 private soldiers, in peacetime all farmers. They had been picked to supervise the threshing. Each face differed completely from the next, but it was pretty easy to guess what part of the country they came from. One cunning-looking, dark-haired soldier, whom I instinctively picked on, came in fact from Upper Franconia, quite near where I live. Incongruous as they appeared in my luxurious office, I felt much at home with these tillers of the soil, in origin as richly diverse as the rolling acres of the regions from which they were drawn, across the length and breadth of the land. Now these canny farmers, instead of bringing in their own harvests, were to supervise their local counter-parts on the job. They were clearly gratified, in the first place at having been chosen for their own particular skills, in the second, probably for the first time in their lives, at the prospect of not having to do the work themselves, merely to watch others on the job.

What a sense of bankruptcy and disaster prevails. Every day is a dreary repetition of the one before. Everyone steals, everything is lacking. There is no small corner to which one can creep away and escape the prevailing wretchedness. It faces one on waking. Today a branch of a tree in our garden was blown down by the storm. It had scarcely touched the ground before an army of women and children hurled themselves upon it, hacking and tearing at the coveted firewood. Schoolchildren drag home great lumps of timber which they have hunted out somewhere or other, loads beyond the puny strength of such small fry to carry. Well-dressed ladies stoop to pick up every twig in their path. In the evening there is a veritable pilgrimage of people coming back to town from the country, with all sorts of mysterious bundles, on their backs, on rusty old bicycles, in home-made pushcarts or, most often, in ancient perambulators. There is no help for it, even this wretched traffic in misery and need has to be checked. For the most part it consists only of rabbit-food, brushwood, cabbages and apples, but sometimes there are sacks of flour, pounds of butter and large quantities of potatoes which of course have to be confiscated. I often wonder if, in the event of having to smuggle in food from the country for my own family, I shall have learned any worthwhile lessons from my experiences here.

Like the house made of sweetmeats in Hansel and Gretel, our wooden bungalow at Grève d'Azette has been disappearing bit by bit, day by day, as further planks are torn off. Now it has been broken into and the carpet and crockery stolen. It now seems best for us to demolish it entirely and thus gain some firewood for ourselves.

This evening our housemaid, Frances, who claims to be the daughter of an English colonel, brought me some gramophone records of classical music. After Heider, who is sadly insensitive to music, had put them on at the wrong speed, I retired with them to my own room. One is a lovely recording of Chopin's piano music. It was Chopin who first made me fully aware of the enchantment of the piano, just as Beethoven brought me to a full appreciation of the string quartet and Brückner to enjoyment of the symphony orchestra in all its perfection.

In the English book on Germany, the writer accuses the Germans of being overly enthusiastic. Enthusiasm is certainly a German character-istic, but an admirable one. It makes us a nation of musicians and artists. Admittedly and unfortunately, it also makes us a nation vulnerable to political exploitation. We are all too apt to give enthusiastic and honourable support to concepts which we have not properly examined and weighed in the light of more mundane considerations. Enthusiasts are spiritually the equal of the gods, materially they are the scapegoats of their fellow-men. Poor enthusias-tic Germany.

20.10.44. Yesterday I called on a very important man, Oberzahlmeister (Leading Paymaster) Mispel, who runs a piggery for the troops and issues them with rations. From his well-nourished appearance it is obvious that here, as everywhere else, it is the custom to take a personal cut of the proceeds. Looking round the sties of fat sows, it was impossible to repress the notion that the four-footed occupants' double-chins bore a remarkable resemblance to that of their keeper. Mispel is a schoolteacher and it is as well not to invoke the full flood of his pedagogic eloquence with too many questions, otherwise one can never get away.

In the afternoon was invited aboard ship by Captain Breithaupt. As usual, I found the free-and-easy but disciplined background of naval life very pleasant. Breithaupt is a most engaging and impressive personality. He cannot be called a handsome man; taken separately, not one facial feature would conform to such a standard, but his whole countenance is informed by so much intelligence and goodwill that one is irresistibly drawn to him. We talked about what might be the outcome of our extraordinary situation here. The current rumour is that we may be exchanged for British prisoners of war and returned to Germany. This is based on an unconfirmed report that German troops are being allowed to evacuate Crete with the tacit approval of the British Government. This would of course establish a valuable precedent for our own case, although not one which Great Britain could openly acknowledge, as it might imply some secret collaboration with Germany to deny Russia access to the Mediterranean, to which Crete is the key. So such an exchange of prisoners seems to lie within the bounds of possibility. For Germany it would mean the freeing and immediate availability of a strong division of troops, for Great Britain the return of the Channel Islands undamaged and a large-scale return of prisoners of war. Our own ships could not cope with such an operation, so Great Britain would have to supply the supplementary shipping. There are not a few here who would scarcely welcome such a hasty return to war-torn Germany. But I should welcome it. I might even be able to see my family again. We should be able to wind up things here in decent and honourable fashion and I should be freed of these frightful responsibilities which render my life a nightmare.

According to a recent 'phone call from Helldorf, a Red Cross Commission is already on its way to the islands. The subsequent negotiations should be of great interest.

When I consider Breithaupt's powerful and straightforward character, I cannot help feeling somewhat let down by the General in these critical days. He is kindly and charming as ever – could charm a bird off a tree – but lacks Breithaupt's strength of character. He delegates far too much to Helldorf, who, able as he is, denigrates the work of others to increase his own importance and influence, and has thus caused a serious rift in confidence between the General and me. The General is genuinely good of heart and anxious to be just, but too open to influence and apt to dispense justice to the last man who leaves his door. Propinquity is a great thing. Here we have to combat Helldorf's daily exaggerations and denunciations from a distance, and it is essential that our replies leave him no possibility of disproving our arguments.

At the conclusion of my shipboard visit, a modern minesweeper, of racy design but showing signs of the battles it had been engaged in, gave a demonstration run around the ship. Going aboard and debarking, one was piped on and off with full ceremony, as if one were an admiral. On parting with Breithaupt, I felt more than ever convinced that here was a man one could rely on in an emergency. And if an emergency arises, it is to him that I shall turn.

The stupid person is never bothered by his stupidity, as he is unaware of it, in himself or others. If I were called upon to describe the

German frame of mind in the last 20 years, I should head my thesis 'From Psychoanalysis to Fanaticism'. Psychoanalysis was the popular cult of the first 10 years, the last 10 have been characterised by narrowness of vision. Psychoanalysis led to the destruction of values. The psychiatrist reduced everything to complexes arising from habit. Love was just a hormonal compulsion. Even the genius of Goethe could be explained away in analyst's jargon.

Just as liberalism carried to an extreme led to national demoralisation, so National Socialism also proceeded to the extreme, in the opposite direction. Suddenly there was only one state, one party, one policy, one race, one law. In complete opposition to the open-minded society where all ideas are examined impartially in the interests of knowledge and truth, the nation became mentally blinkered, on the pattern of Leibnitz's 'monad', the one-celled soul without windows. This narrowness of vision, hardening into fanaticism, has led the nation to where it is today, well on the way to self-destruction. One can feel only the deepest sorrow for a people which can thus hurl itself from one extreme into another, when the only happy solution lies in the golden mean, the impartial weighing of all factors and the maintenance of all true values.

21.10.44. Poor Satan, that gallant horse, is weary; he can no longer summon up the proper enthusiasm for a good gallop, nor, I daresay, the strength. The few horses still remaining, after so many have been slaughtered for food, now stand hungry and tired on hard concrete, where they formerly bedded comfortably on straw. They are dying off in advance of us.

22.10.44. At last the weather has become milder. On Sunday morning, I drove out to some favourite spots on the east coast. The sun, shining obliquely through the clouds, cast a circle of gold on the sea. There was not a stir in the air, except for the swarms of birds assembling and scattering. I left the car at the top and scrambled through the wet fields, between laurel hedges and past a group of wind-blown oaks, to halfway down the hill, enjoying the physical exercise and the climb. The sea was smooth and unruffled, yet full of murmurous sound, as the incoming tide splashed gently round the rocks. A real Sunday morning outing and I am grateful still to experience such tranquil hours.

In the afternoon Heider and I went pigeon shooting at Rozel Manor, in the sole remaining piece of unspoiled woodland in the island. I concealed myself in the gold-brown ferns and kept a close eye on a beech tree richly laden with nuts. The poor birds have been so harried and decimated that they have become extraordinarily wary, but I was able to bring one down.

What unforgettable moments I have experienced when shooting pigeons here. When I stood among the hydrangea bushes and gazed spellbound at a storm-tossed cypress, or, hidden among the gorse, saw a palm tree etched against a blazing sunset sky, I often reflected that fate had dealt kindly with me in allowing me to become so thoroughly acquainted with this foreign land, with all its variety of land and seascape and climate. So many pictures of this rich and lovely place are stored in my memory as indestructibly as the snapshots in my little book on the islands.

Since I have taken to reading English books, I am struck by the number of publications on political themes and by how surprisingly alike they are in form and content. An historical survey of recent events is diversified by anecdotes of the writer's own experiences in the political field. They have such titles as *Since Then*, *Searchlight on Europe*, *Talks between European Statesmen*, etc. From this one must deduce a considerable interest in politics and a politically well-informed public, which, as any discussion with an Englishman confirms, is indeed the case.

Helldorf rang me up to say that we may expect the arrival of the Red Cross Commission within the next few weeks. I am on tenterhooks at the news, and all the rumours about a possible exchange of prisoners of war fades into insignificance.

In the evening a second lot of mail arrived. There was another letter from my mother, although of an earlier date than her previous one. From this I learn with deep sorrow that my cousin Hugo has fallen. Among all my relatives and friends, he was the one man who combined in his person the most attractive German qualities of candour, cordiality and widely-based erudition. He was of the rare type who meets everywhere with instant respect and affection. I had often thought of him as a model for the German gentleman. Perhaps he represented not only what is best in Germany but best in Europe. At any rate, his unfailing courtesy, his good humour, his moderate opinions, based solely on his own good judgement, made him for me, as for so many others, a valued friend and arbiter of all that is best in life. He belonged to the class and type of person who should have been ruling Germany. That it is not, is why we are now sliding into perdition.

23.10.44. A day of prolonged and trying negotiations. The Attorney-General came to me, positively shaking with anxiety and indignation, to protest against the requisition of butter. The recently appointed expert in this field, Ten Harmsen, had gone about the business in a clumsy and tactless way. He is altogether too hot-tempered and irascible in his dealings with the islanders. This had resulted in a complete misunderstanding, while I was assuming that all was proceeding smoothly.

This commandeering of supplies shortly before the arrival of the Red Cross Commission is proving very difficult to implement, and does in fact amount to the severest measures we have yet undertaken against the civilian population.

The States of Guernsey have addressed a very sharp note to the General, accusing him of requisitioning a disproportionate amount of local produce in support of the troops and failing to maintain the civilian population in accordance with the rules laid down by the Hague Convention. I can hardly help feeling some malicious glee. When I forwarded the memorandum from the States of Jersey, Helldorf informed me that in Guernsey they managed things better and were not subjected to such tiresome communications, as he arranged everything in personal discussion with the Bailiff. The Guernsey note seems to go far beyond the moderately-worded Jersey memorandum.

The takeover of the mills by German millers resulted in the immediate resignation of the local staff, who objected to being bossed about in military style. I had already carefully vetted the German supervisors in most leading concerns and weeded out the unsuitable types. There is nothing the Britisher is more touchy about than mistrust and supervision. The highly sensitive electricity works are run entirely by local men. They do a splendid job, largely because we have left it to them.

Dear old Lindner, the Silesian squire, is a decent and amiable fellow, but at conferences I find it hard to accord him the deference and attention due to his rank. Lindner and Helldorf are diametric opposites, although superficially they have much in common. The first thing that strikes one is that they would both be in their true metier in a Berlin Guards' regiment. Both are Lieutenant-Colonels, both are cavalrymen, neither has the Iron Cross, Ist Class (an unforgivable shortcoming in military circles). Both are true representatives of the North German Junker class. Both hold the office of Quarter-Master-General, responsible for supplying the troops in their respective islands. And both are one-eyed! There the resemblance ends. Lindner is the soul of honour; direct, uncompromising and upright, if apt to shout and bluster when he comes up against opposition. In contrast to the elegant Helldorf, he appears a shambling, rather uncouth figure, but one's heart warms to him as an always reliable comrade. I have already said enough about Helldorf not to need to point the contrast. Helldorf is probably the most elegant and imposing military officer in the islands. With his monocle, he incorporates the image of the German officer, as caricatured in the communist press. He is also well able to support this image and to impose his superiority on all with whom he comes in contact.

24.10.44. In the early morning drove out with a German supervisor to check the milking. Some of the cows are as thin as skeletons, yet still give milk. They are bred for their milk-yield, not for meat. (Veal is scarcely known here.) The farmers were at first very mistrustful, but my knowledge of the countryside enabled me to establish some contact with them. A German dairyman came up with the bright suggestion of mixing more water with the butter, which would give an immediate 5% increase in production and tide us over the crisis for the time being.

From what I can hear of it, the States of Guernsey's note is lacking in objectivity and composed in highly rhetorical style, unsuited to a *note verbale* from a governing state. One suspects that the originator may be some minor but aspiring advocate on the States Committee. At the same time, Helldorf cannot be absolved of all blame. By now perhaps, his dodges and subterfuges have been seen through and have at least helped towards this explosion of indignation on the part of the representatives of the local population.

I have had a letter from Le Quesne, thanking me for my testimony on his behalf and his resulting early release from prison. At the same time he asked me to exert my influence in securing the release of the other Jerseymen who are still in prison for the same offence, of being found in possession of a wireless set. I am doing my best, as it seems to me a worthy cause. In fact instead of worrying about such paltry 'crimes', we would be better employed in devoting our energies to dealing with the numerous would-be escapees and black-marketeers, with whom the prison is already full to overflowing. So, not without an ulterior motive, I first got the Attorney-General to supply me with the current figures for prisoners and then engaged his good offices in helping me get the men freed. Now I expect, the military judge who sentenced them, Dr. Harmsen, will go rushing to the island military commander to complain. I would certainly prefer not to have to face Heine on this issue; I try to avoid all unnecessary confrontations with him, as, in his stiff, bone-headed, military fashion, he has the knack of pouring cold water on my more altruistic projects. It sometimes occurs to me that some British officer, of similar temperament to my own, may have to face just the same problems in the forthcoming occupation of Germany. And I wonder how he will cope.

25.10.44. I am kept much under the pressure of my multifarious responsibilities. When I steal five minutes before lunch to go into the grounds of Langford House and look out over the wide prospect of the town and St Aubin's Bay, my thoughts keep reverting to the morning's business, to the six different places I have rushed around, the strings I have pulled, the tangled skeins I have sought to disentangle, and of how much the welfare of this little state and its people depends on these complicated labours.

Yet I fear I have still failed to exercise enough personal supervision, left too much to others. Woelken, that brainiest of fellows, who had thrown himself with his customary zeal and conscientiousness into the work of the section in control of grain supplies, now finds himself 600 tons short on his estimated production of oats. I had an uneasy feeling that his returns were erroneous, but left it to his clear head. Now, I no longer know on whom I can rely. A bitter blow, it has left me shattered.

At lunchtime the two Red Cross sisters Karin and Else called on us. After a few drinks we all cheered up and fell into light-hearted badinage, Karin and I capping each other's sallies. Such a relaxing hour is a welcome oasis in the grim desert of present-day life.

Am spending a pleasant hour reading an excellent English book on *Woman and the Rococo in France*, which gives a detailed and entertaining account of the rise of women and the role played by them in this most attractive century of French history. I note some of the charming bon-mots in my scrapbook, such as Madame Necker's *'Être aimé c'est recevoir le plus grands de tous les éloges'*. Such lightly mocking but pertinent observations are part of the Gallic heritage. What heavy weather, in comparison, the northerner makes of a love affair, in which he seems to find the greatest pleasure in its tragic aspects.

In the late afternoon Mrs. Riley called on me and stopped to chat for an hour in the twilight. She wore an impossible get-up, a hat like a child's clapped on her head and a dirty old trenchcoat over a well-worn riding habit. Her costume made not the slightest concession to feminine pride. The fanciful thought crossed my mind, that here, in the fifth year of the war, when such bizarre dress, if still uncommon, should excite no surprise nor condemnation, I saw in this Englishwoman who sat totally unconcerned at my desk in her scruffy masculine attire, a vision of Britannia herself, ageing and battle-worn.

26.10.44. The Russian invasion of East Prussia and Norway, the daily heavy bombardment of German towns, our armies' defeats in the Baltic and the Balkans, are all crushing blows which bode little good for the future of Germany. Family, home, possessions, all are in jeopardy. The only thing one can fall back on is a resolve to see it through with such decency and courage as one can muster. And never to lose one's joy in the beauty of this world – to take that much at least home with one from these beguilingly beautiful islands.

In the morning the Attorney-General, Duret Aubin, brought me a list of the Jerseymen still in gaol for owning wireless sets. Their pardon has already been requested and in effect granted. Unfortunately, in the night, the houses of many local people who are friendly towards the Germans were smeared with tar and swastikas, and this could, at the last moment, unfavourably prejudice the case.

Duret Aubin's constant demand is for news, the latest news, above all, when is the Red Cross Commission, anxiously awaited, due to arrive, I wish I knew myself. I jolly him along and say I feel like a debtor who keeps putting off his pressing creditors with a yarn about a rich uncle in America. This little witticism will soon go the rounds and do more to reassure local officials, at least temporarily, than any high-sounding promises.

Helldorf rang me up and asked me to get the Bailiff of Jersey to compose a note to the International Red Cross in Switzerland. This is at least an acknowledgement that Coutanche is a more dynamic political figure than the officials, now obviously out of favour, in Guernsey. This appeal will strengthen his position here and pacify the public for the next couple of weeks. Also of course, if there is no reply, it will be the Bailiff's responsibility, not ours.

The German authorities are again obsessed by the idea of evacuating the civilian population to England. I am to make out a new list of the people whom we positively cannot do without here. Helldorf is ready to provide me with a whole posse of agricultural workers from the troops, to help out in case of need. Now that the harvest has been brought in and fruit gathered, this would only mean letting loose a lot more peculators among the farmers. As far as I am concerned, the Field Police are already enough and more than enough, with the good tenth which they certainly put aside for themselves from the goods they impound.

Even my own commanding officer, Heider, is always pestering me to divert a bit from civilian supplies for the benefit of our own unit. Personal probity has certainly become the exception rather than the rule. With his mercantile approach to life, his shortness of vision and his obsession with any misplaced notion once he gets it into his head, Heider makes life difficult for me. On the other hand, his indolence and basically obliging nature enable me to circumvent his more outrageous demands by a policy of silence, forgetfulness and postponement. Well, I could hardly expect to have a commander who would in the long run leave absolutely everything to me. I could be worse off than with Heider.

27.10.44. I am overtaken by the zeal of the chronicler to put it all down on paper, to the bitter end, if I am then still in a position to write in this secret diary. Perhaps, whatever the end may be, some happy chance may someday bring these pages into the hands of my wife. This urge to commit it all to paper cannot, I am convinced, arise from any personal pride or wish for future fame. I have debated with myself about this in all too many lonely hours. It is only this communion with my secret diary that brings me into some sort of spiritual communion with my wife and family. It is my way of sharing my present life with them, and even inspires me – futile as this hope may at present seen – with the hope that I may, at some future date, join them again in reality and share all the joys of home.

Not many people can stand up to complete frankness and trust. It is dangerous to reveal one's chain of reasoning; a careful weighing of the pros and cons can all too easily be taken as a sign of weakness and indecision. An old Arab proverb says that if you joke with a slave, he immediately assumes the air of master. In my case this might be adapted to read: explain the difficulties of any matter to the petty official and he will immediately instruct you on its actual simplicity. In both cases one is made to feel a fool.

Today Inspector Pokorny, who has all the virtues but also all the overweening self-righteousness of the typical civil servant, saw fit to instruct me on a whole range of subjects, including those which are my particular professional province. This assumption of the airs of the master by the subordinate brought me up with a jolt and taught me a lesson. I should never have taken him so much into my confidence and discussed matters so freely with him. I have made too great use of him as a sounding-board for my own ideas. In future I shall keep these to myself and make my decisions independently.

The proposed note from the States of Jersey to the Red Cross was the subject of two conferences today. The Bailiff, generally so cool and astute, advanced the dramatic and unlikely view that the British Government would send no supplies whatsoever to the islands; that it intended to starve us out, even at the cost of its local British subjects. I could see that Duret Aubin, for the first time, strongly disagreed with him. The Bailiff had once before and with great conviction expressed a view which turned out to be mistaken. This was when he declared that Britain would certainly attack the islands before the autumn, and on precisely the opposite grounds to those which he now put forward, i.e., that the British would not allow the islanders to suffer want. It is interesting to observe how such a talented man can fall into such errors of judgement. Such a chopping and changing of opinion seems to reflect a lack of intuitive feeling and a basic instability. But a man may be deluded by his own brilliance of mind and his vanity gives force and weight to his argument. In such crucial times as these, one must learn to adjust to foreign modes of thought and reasoning and watch out for cracks in the interlocutor's psychological armour. While this cannot lead to any accurate forecast of how matters will turn out, it does help one guard against the numerous possibilities of deception.

In the afternoon Wegner came to see me, obviously in a great state of agitation, to impart to me a 'most delicate and embarrassing affair'. It seems that the notorious Miss Langlois was suspected of possessing arms and when the Secret Field Police made a search of the house, they found not only the suspected revolver but a number of letters from a high-ranking officer. Miss L. may well be described as the most active and experienced girl in the island in the field of amorous adventure. With her considerable sexual allure and her indefatigable quest for male scalps, she must have quite a series of romances behind her since the occupation began. In the early days she used often to drop in at my office, but such an open merchandising of sex leaves me cold. I am susceptible only to genuine feminine charm. Wegner feared a dreadful scandal if this matter should be brought up before the Military Court. Fortunately, on my immediate intervention, our worthy and much feared chief of the Field Police, Captain Bohde, tactfully left the letters in Miss Langlois' possession.

After the scarifying experiences of the last few weeks, I find myself obliged to take still more work on my own shoulders. Certainly I have far more to do them anyone else here and am often conscious of the heaviness of the task which now leaves me no time for any personal life or relaxation. In fact I feel myself depersonalised into a sort of administrative automaton, created by the special circumstances of this occupation and existing only to deal with them. My colleagues adapt according to their age and disposition, mostly into a personal dream-world which is far removed from mine. If the natural law of passing time and worsening conditions did not drive me on, I could ruefully chide myself – and laugh at myself – for becoming so wedded to my work, such an administrative beast of burden.

In Guernsey Admiral Hüffmeier has succeeded in getting himself appointed Chief of Staff. The General will now be more than ever pushed into the background; he is no match for such a ruthless ambitious man. Helldorf's confident assumption of the imminent arrival of the Red Cross Commission proves, on investigation, to be a myth.

28.10.44. There are very few Jews in the islands. The two Jewish women who have just been arrested belong to an unpleasant category. These women had long been circulating leaflets urging German soldiers to shoot their officers. At last they were tracked down. A search of the house, full of ugly cubist paintings, brought to light a quantity of pornographic material of an especially revolting nature. One woman had had her head shaved and been thus photographed in the nude from

every angle. Thereafter she had worn men's clothes. Further nude
photographs showed both women practising sexual perversion, exhibi-
tionism and flagellation. I declined with distaste the loan of a book on
cubism written by the father. At the moment pronouncement of
sentence is being postponed. Normally, on the charge of inciting the
troops to rebellion, they could be condemned to death, but women
cannot be executed here.

Just now the nights have a special enchantment. Under the clear
moonlit vault of the sky, low-lying squally clouds scurry past, making
rings round and sometimes obscuring the face of the half-full moon.
The dark sea mirrors the sky in changing patterns of golden light. The
swift passage of the clouds conveys a sense of cosmic movement, of all
the suns and planets wheeling in space, as they have done primordially,
long before the coming of man.

Heider must be the world's most tone-deaf man. His perpetual
tuneless whistle, the way he turns the radio on at full blast and
continues along the wavelength without adjustment and his total
inability to drive a car without crashing the gears, are at times enough
to drive one mad.

Today Lieutenant John, of the Field Gendarmerie, took me into a
room piled to the ceiling with black market goods found in the
possession of a French doctor here. I was furious. A basket of huge
hams, a ton of salted beef, boxes full of flour, a hundredweight of potato
flour, sugar, groats etc. by the sack. And in addition 20 hundredweight
of potatoes. Something exceptional had to be undertaken here. This
sight, looking like the stock of a delicatessen shop in peacetime, must
be shared by as many people as possible. I had an idea. We would put it
all on show in a big shop window in the town this afternoon, on
shopping-day, with appropriate notices. The Colonel gave his permission, the military court had no objections. The Colonel made only one
proviso and that a very wise one: that the man should not be named at
the exhibition and that the food should afterwards be handed over to
the public kitchen at the express order of the Colonel and in his name.

I had the placards made in the morning. The first read 'This hoard
was confiscated from a local resident', the second 'All the goods will be
handed over to the Public Kitchen on the orders of the Fortress
Commander', and the third 'Help defeat the black marketeers'. The
Field Gendarmerie's lorry was scarcely large enough to carry it all. I
had commandeered a large empty shop in the main street for the day,
and we had to open the back partitions of the three windows to get all
the stuff on display. Even as it was being set out, a large crowd started
gathering in the street. The people did not disperse until the evening,
when the goods were picked up by officials of the Food Control
Committee. The effect was shattering. I could not resist looking on at a

distance, and felt rather shattered myself at having stage-managed such a production. But the penalties we impose for black-marketeering and hoarding – fines and imprisonment – are no longer a deterrent. Money is of doubtful value and long prison sentences are hardly likely to be served. There will be an article about it in the local paper this evening.

Amid all this excitement, I also managed to attend a rowing regatta held between the naval flotillas in the harbour, to which Captain Breithaupt had invited me. I always feel at ease with the navy. In spite of an outward show of rigid discipline, the personal atmosphere is relaxed, in pleasant contrast to the ever stiff and hidebound army.

29.10.44. In the sleepless watches of the night the hungry faces of all those poor people gazing so longingly at the unimaginable piles of foodstuffs again passed before me. Yesterday I was called on to play the part of producer in a sensational show, and I wondered if any theatrical producer had ever experienced a similar moment of power as he observed the rapt faces of his audience.

This afternoon I watched the pigs belonging to our unit being fed. There is a grim fascination in such a display of greed, the fleshy pink snouts rooting tirelessly after sustenance, especially when we are fighting a rearguard action against starvation, by which, according to the Bailiff, Britain intends to bring us to our knees. We were joined by the paymaster-general, who told me how, at a conference at the Officer's Club which he had just attended, all the officers agreed it was no longer possible to provide the men with adequate meals – they constantly complained of always being hungry.

Spoke at great length with Helldorf on the telephone about how long supplies will last out. New viewpoints are constantly being advanced and the situation is tense in the extreme. And what will happen if the Red Cross Commission does not turn up? The fact is that, no matter how far ahead we set our sights, how much we try to eke things out, we shall never achieve our target – holding out until the next harvest.

30.10.44. I have now had the third letter from my mother, but still no word from M [the author's wife]. For an old-fashioned person like my mother, it must be much more difficult to conceive of a connection by air with these far distant islands than it is for us younger folk, and I am all the more touched by her steadfast loyalty in still writing to me.

There was also a letter dated last August from my sister Anni. She tells me that Schloss Greifenstein[1] has been expropriated by the State. This deeply grieves me. A photograph of Greifenstein always stands on my desk. Whatever may now transpire, whether it becomes a youth hostel or whether it is eventually restored to the Stauffenberg family[2], it will never be the same again; well-loved family home, permeated with the culture and tradition of generations, a symbol of the old world.

My sister enclosed two picture postcards of Franconian peasant women. I studied them nostalgically. All decked out in their Sunday best, they still conveyed that impression of sturdy self-sufficiency and independence, allied with native pride and wit, which is so typical of their kind. How awkwardly they pose for the photographer, holding out their work-worn hands to each other in a way they would never do in real life. It cheers me to see them, I know them so well, the 'Kunis' and 'Marchrets', I can almost hear their robust dialect. How I wish I could join them in the local train, on my way home, and enjoy their parting witticisms as they climb out at Kirchehrenbach and Pretzfeld.

Today a big military exercise was held at St Ouen's Bay and all officers were invited to view it, especially the many naval officers now in the island. A sharp north wind whistled across the sand dunes. Beyond lay the severe blue immensity of the sea, broken only by sparse glints of sunlight. It was an impressive artillery display, demonstrating all the tactics of modern warfare. Again and again the low-lying profiles of the guns sprang up to sweep the sea and shore at an ever-decreasing range and to an advancing cloud of gunsmoke. A very well planned and conducted performance. All that was lacking was the tanks and 'planes which would have lent reality to this earth-bound battle and in reality borne the brunt of it. Formidable as the defences of the islands may be, we are lacking in these two essential weapons of war.

Afterwards we adjourned to the Soldiers' Home in St Brelade's Bay, where we joined Sisters Ruth and Karin round the fire. But the company was too diverse to engender the companionable atmosphere proper to the fireside. How much I still miss Dr. Auerbach;[3] since he left I have never encountered such a similarly congenial spirit. Ruth chattered away with her usual fund of wisecracks and aphorisms. Karin flirted with everyone; in her element. The only thing she does better is to dance. The exchange was confined on my part to suitable back-chat and an avoidance of her ardent eye. But her vitality and joie-de-vivre and robust femininity are pleasing to many men, if not to me, and these attributes also deserve their meed of praise.

31.10.44. There is a special fascination in reading books in a foreign language. The concentration needed claims one's whole attention. I have often found myself so absorbed that I have gone on reading in the midst of noise and movement. The familiarity of one's own tongue allows one's thoughts more easily to stray. In a foreign language one advances step by step, as over a narrow footbridge, with no attention to spare for the world on either side. Many words are not clear to the reader and in relating them to their context, he begins to construct his own meaning, like the child who sees behind the printed words his own vision of the events portrayed. To the well-read man his own language is so familiar that he may well reach a stage when its well-known cadences fail to convey their full power of meaning and expression, whereas in a foreign language he can still discover a childlike wonder and surprise. For this reason alone everyone engaged in intellectual pursuits should study foreign languages and read foreign books. His greatest reward will be that he will return to his own language with a heightened appreciation of its own unique power and appeal.

At the moment I am reading a delightful French novel, *Axelle,*by Pierre Benoit. It is the love story of a French prisoner-of-war, exiled on a remote East Prussian estate, with the daughter of the house. The enormous distance separating the child of this old military family from the rankless and despised representative of the enemy, gives rise to conflicts delicately portrayed and in the end touchingly resolved.

I fear that many of the States' officials do not, in their position, set the example they should. Current rumour credits them, with the exception of Duret Aubin, of generally dabbling in the black market and taking advantage of their privileged position. If this is true, the show of black market goods in St Helier yesterday must have given some of them a jolt. At all events, Jurat M., reputedly the worst of them, has just been to see me and enquired in aggrieved tones, what may one then legally retain on one's premises as family stores. Viewing his well-nourished appearance, I surmised he must have a well-stocked larder. Tomorrow I shall have a notice published in the paper, defining such stocks as the normal householder might still be expected to possess. After that, it is up to the individual conscience.

Chapter Three

November – December 1944

1.11.44. Another new month which will doubtless bring many new problems, but the first day at least has passed agreeably enough.

The Bailiff and Attorney-General brought me their latest note to the Protecting Power, incorporating a reminder of their previous appeal and of the seriousness of the situation. After their experience of the furore caused by their former memorandum, they presented this one in draft form. I thought this very sensible. At our last meeting I had touched on but not directly discussed the vital question of the requisitioning of all remaining civilian supplies before the arrival of the Red Cross ship, it seemed to me marginally and merely as a possibility. They now took up my feelers on the subject and I am hopeful that we may be able to work out some agreement, feeling our way in time-honoured diplomatic fashion. At least today no contentious subject was broached. On the contrary our mutual interest in this Red Cross business seems to unite us in an almost family feeling. And our press announcements of the freeing of all prisoners held for possessing wireless sets and of a quite generous allowance of tins and foodstuffs which may be held in private possession, should add further oil to troubled waters. So I hugged my trump card – an impending considerable increase in paraffin and petrol rations – to my chest, to play against the States' inevitable protest at our coming demand for more oats (arising from an error in their own returns) when we engage on the next round.

In the afternoon I took Colonel Ziegler and the two naval captains, Lentsch and Breithaupt, on a tour of some of the island's interesting spots, including a big farm where the famous Jersey cattle are bred. I had read up on the subject in a book on cattle breeding and was also armed with facts and figures from our own campaign to step up milk production. My guests, however, became so absorbed in the attractive calves and the way the stalls were fitted up, that my hard-won knowledge had to remain unimparted. While the poor cows, bred solely for milking, but now, through the lack of an oil-rich diet, appeared pitifully emaciated, the eight great bulls, isolated on their tree-surrounded pasture presented a formidable picture, true representatives of the native breed. They resemble bison, heavy of body, wild of eye, but with a native majesty. As we entered the meadow, low grunts of displeasure arose, doubtless to alert the herd and warn off trespassers.

We approached the most massive bull, which lowered its horns at us. An iron ring through its nose, attached to a chain restricted its grazing to the circle of the chain's length. The black-brown marking of the head increased its ferocity of expression, as did the thick shaggy fell. In its rage and powerlessness, the bull drove its horns into the earth and hefted up a great clod of turf. I should not like to be at the mercy of that powerful skull. My guests were much impressed.

Afterwards we went on to pay a call first at Rozel Manor, then at Samarès Manor. Here the cypress trees were decked in palest fawn and the other deciduous trees still bore some lingering flags of gold. It is the trees in the park which make this manor most worthy of a visit. Inside, the house is furnished with a museum-like miscellany of pieces which bear no relation to each other, although the individual objects are mostly both beautiful and costly. Miss White recounted in her usual charming manner those tales of her travels which have long since become familiar to me, but to which, to our mutual satisfaction, our naval guests paid flattering attention.

In the evening Heider brought along Sisters Erna and Karin to join the party and we spent a cheerful evening chatting round the fire and dancing. Karin was obviously gratified by my crack that she was 'a young witch, possessed by the spirit of the dance'.

2.11.44. According to the precepts of drama, as perhaps in everyday life, the ultimate tragedy is often artfully postponed by the introduction of scenes of normalcy that lull one into hoping there may still be a happy end. We seem to be in such a period now. For the moment my pressing problems seem solved. Our relations with the States are good, the population quiet and my own conscience clear as far as work is concerned. But I fear it will be a short-lived period of calm. Tomorrow I must ring Helldorf and ask for his latest news, of which I have already heard disquieting rumours, but this evening I shall indulge myself in a quiet hour by the fire with a book.

3.11.44. Pokorny, with whom I had remonstrated, as tactfully as possible, about his recently taking me to task on matters outside his competence, has to his credit shown equal tact and withdrawn entirely into the affairs of his own unit, with which he has become completely identified. If a turbine at the power station breaks down, one can deduce as much from his troubled mien. When both turbines broke down last night and we had to use precious diesel oil to get the other power plant working, he did not sleep all night and now his drawn and suffering face is more than ever reminiscent of the martyred St Sebastian. His own state of health is so precarious that he really needs as much cosseting as his decrepit machines.

In dancing with buxom but lightfooted Sister Karin, I am surprised by my own primitive reactions. Thought vanishes; the subconscious takes over, there is only music, movement, rhythm. I would never have thought myself capable of such a surrender of the mind to the senses. But perhaps, too, only the highly-imaginative intellect is capable of recognising this half dreaming state – half way to sleep – and appreciating the mental imagery and release of tensions, which, like sleep, it brings. The subconscious exercises its own power and mind and matter must be indissolubly linked.

In the afternoon I accompanied Woelken on a tour of inspection of the threshing. Our idea of putting German landworkers to supervise this process does not appear to have met with much success. In one case a German superviser himself made off with 30 lbs. of grain. In another, a neighbouring German unit, watching the work through binoculars, had seen the Jersey workers stashing away quantities of grain under the nose of the German soldiers and had reported this.

Afterwards we returned to Linden Court for a cup of tea and got into a discussion on the inevitability or otherwise of war. The mere posing of such a question involves premises of doubtful validity, from which there can be no escape and no logical deduction: one could argue all night. Our conclusions were predictably at variance. Woelken maintained that war was avoidable and should be rejected and as an instance cited the Quakers in North America, who, by refusing to fight and accepting all that happened to them, in the end gained a greater victory over the Indians. I advanced the contrary view that history showed the advance of mankind as a vast process of Nature, and that Nature, in eternal re-creation, used all means, including death by war, to accelerate that advance. In the one case the belief that man is master of his own fate, in the other a more intuitive reliance on Nature's grand design.

My forebodings yesterday about the state of apparent tranquility have proved amply justified. I heard today from Lt.-Colonel von Helldorf that England has refused to give any support to the islanders. This scarcely bears thinking about. It looks as if we are nearing the end of the drama. Certainly the end of all our hopes.

4.11.44. Yesterday morning von Helldorf authorised me to inform the States that Great Britain had received their note via the Protecting Power. About the rest I was to keep strict secrecy. The States could, however, now write another note, independent of the first, and send this directly to the International Red Cross in Geneva, urgently requesting that body's help. I was unable to elicit any details of the text of Great Britain's reply or the date of its reception, although in such a delicate matter the exact wording is of paramount importance. Von

Helldorf spoke of a 'provisional' refusal. When I asked for further explanation, he withdrew behind the veil of official secrecy. This damned propensity of his to deal only in half truths or veiled allusions is exasperating and could be dangerous. It makes me anxious about every word I say to him, in case it should in future be twisted out of context. But in our present situation consultation is possible only by telephone.

While Duret Aubin received my news with a thankful but rather troubled air, the Bailiff, after a few suitable words of acknowledgement, launched into a self-satisfied speech which had little to do with the matter in hand. Naturally, after being informed by me that their note had arrived in Great Britain, neither could see, logically enough, the necessity of addressing another note to the International Red Cross.

When I acquainted Helldorf of this in the afternoon, he was furious, completely blew his top and threatened, most unjustifiably, to put a notice in the papers saying that, if the Red Cross Commission did not turn up, it would be all the fault of the States of Jersey. He is lacking in legal training and has no conception of the legal aspects of the situation. Of course he calls the tune and as long as everyone follows he is kindly and benign. But any opposition meets with a very different reaction. It is clear that the States, as loyal subjects of the British Crown, must profess themselves content with the fact that their message has reached Great Britain and await the reply with patience, and cannot be held accountable if the ultimate reply should turn out to be negative. As small members of a large family, they can only acquiesce if there should be no soup on the table for them. Still, I hope to get over the present impasse and avoid further friction, by suggesting to the States that Great Britain might have some misgivings about their note, as having been sent via the Protecting Power, from Germany, and it thus might be politic to follow this up with a further appeal to the International Red Cross in Geneva, to whom Great Britain might be more disposed to listen. Helldorf seems to think that the Red Cross in Geneva would send help of their own accord, but I am sure they could not do this without the concurrence of Great Britain, otherwise there would have been no point in addressing the note to the British government in the first place.

Another depressing item of news has just come in. The HUV[1] in Jersey seriously overestimated their coal stocks when making their last return. The latest assessment showed the stocks to be considerably smaller. This will mean the power station will have to close down a month earlier.

5.11.44. I composed a note to the States, to inform them officially and in writing that we had received news that Great Britain was now in

possession of the note which had been sent on by the Protecting Power.
At the same time I suggested they should now also address a note
directly to the International Red Cross. To cover myself, I first sent the
draft to Helldorf. He has now sent it back to me with the text entirely
changed. It no longer even states that Great Britain is in possession of
the note, a fact which he had himself authorised me to tell the States
only the previous day. And this is the news to which they attach the
greatest importance. Now he wishes to foist on them a too-clever-by-
half version of the truth, i.e., not that Great Britain is known to have
received the note, but that they must have done so because it is
international usage for a Protecting Power to pass on such a message.
For the time being at least, I shall take no further action on the futile
and infuriating letter. To pass it on to the States would serve no useful
purpose. It is really intolerable to have to work with such a volatile
character, who chops and changes and reverses his own decisions from
day to day. I shall put the whole matter aside until next Monday, when
he and the General are due to visit Jersey.

I am reading a well-written book, F. Friede's *Wende der Weltwirtschaft*
('Turning Point in World Economy'), in which the author presents his
arguments with great clarity and draws some interesting inferences.
The book is prefaced by a quotation from Goethe, which strikes me as
so apposite to our present world in collapse that I cannot forbear to set
it down here.

> There is nothing in the past which should inspire us with a nostalgia for its return.
> What remains is only the present, the eternally new, re-fashioning itself from the
> heritage of the past. So true inspiration must always be creative, must be directed
> towards shaping what is new into what is better.

To this I would add a few words from Stefan Georg, 'The future belongs
to him who can change with changing times'. This I believe to be true.
This is why, in spite of the desperate state of our country, now on the
eve of inevitable defeat, I am still able to feel hopeful for the future.
Through the war, for all it blinds us with insensate hatreds, for all its to
us apparent futility, the world will be brought more rapidly into a new
era of history. The ultimate significance of the war will lie, not in
advancing or overthrowing National Socialist, Bolshevist or capitalist
ideologies, only in sweeping away conditions which had become
unbearable, in wiping the slate clean for a fresh start.

In the evening we sat on the floor round the fire at the Soldiers'
Home at La Hougue. But the intimate setting, with the flickering
firelight, failed to induce an appropriately relaxed mood. Sister Ruth
treated us to her usual wisecracks, and what was worse, insisted on
turning the radio on full blast, with a lot of hissing and crackling,
punctuated by some poor apology for music. I begged her to turn it off,

even quoting Spencer, who said that the quality of a man's intellect could be gauged by his dislike of unnecessary noise, but all in vain. We could converse only by shouting. One of the subjects of conversation led to a heated dispute. This was whether, in the absence of pine and fir trees on the island, the soldiers should be given a free hand to chop down any similar trees for Christmas trees. It is needless to say on which side I stood in this argument: I am strongly against such vandalism. Sister Marie von Wedel was irritating too. She is inhibited in company but rattles on in a forced schoolgirl fashion. With her, everything is 'Prima', from the prisoners of war working on her father's estate to the last log put on the fire.

I escaped early to the solitude of my billets.

6.11.44. Sat with Lieutenant Wetzstein by the open window, looking out over Mont Orgueil Castle and the sea, until far into the night. The evening set in grey and melancholy, with the merest hint of rosy light at sundown. As usual our talk came round in the end to the pressing problems of the present situation and the future. Neither of us was in a mood for weighty discussion or philosophical conjecture. We just spoke of our respective fears and worries in everyday terms, and in voicing them a little lightened the burden. Wetzstein's little spaniel slept trustfully on my knees and a few apples roasting on the hearth diffused a pleasant aroma.

Among other things we talked about why a German possessing the highest qualities of his race still did not fit in with the English ideal of a gentleman. The fact is, German spontaneity and warmth of heart are at opposite poles to the Englishman's self-restraint, studied moderation and much-admired nonchalance. The more obvious German qualities of uprightness and a painstaking thoroughness are incompatible with the English ideals of reserve, tact, delicate feeling and courtesy. So German diligence and dedication to work for work's sake must present something of a challenge to the more indolent and comfort-loving Englishman.

7.11.44 Visited a family in the poor quarter of the town. They had had gas lighting but there is no longer any gas and the house is not connected for electricity. The weekly paraffin ration is so small that it provides them with only a few hours' light from a wretched little lamp. The poor, I have noticed, are never resentful of questioning but quite ready to give information about those pressing needs which seem to them a part of everyday life, but which appear to us exceptional.

The island is again lashed by strong gales, with torrential downpours of rain. The last remnants of colour on the trees are obliterated as the year nears its end. Our spirits are as sombre as the weather as we too face the end and a winter of hunger and distress. There is a daily increase in the number of prosecutions for food thefts, both in the civil and military courts. From tomorrow the daily bread ration will be only 300 grams.

The heavy storms are delaying the arrival of the divisional staff officers from Guernsey. This visit will probably result in some pretty drastic measures.

8.11.44. These long dull days are just the time for books. In an effort to gain some possible insight into the future shape of the world, economically and politically, I am at present grappling with four differing pillars of wisdom.

Pfeffer's book, *England als Vormacht der bürgerlichen Welt* ('England as the Leading Middle-Class Power'), presents us with an outstandingly scholarly if sometimes rather over-written account of Europe's offshore island kingdom, its weaknesses and strengths. He emphasises that England's greatness stems from and is bound up with the 19th century. *Searchlight on Europe*, written in 1940, recapitulates the events which let up to the present war, from the English point of view. Friede's *Turning Point in World Affairs* marshals an array of historical facts and figures to demonstrate that the crisis, the turning-point, occurred with the break-through of technology and the rise of the masses. My fourth book is *Le Genie Francais*, written by a Hungarian. So this chance selection of European writers provides me with mental sustenance in a Europe – that oldest and most civilised corner of the globe – which is itself now being laid waste and shaken to its foundations.

9.11.44. What must the people of Germany be feeling? Indignation, perplexity, disillusionment? This year, for the first time, Hitler failed to give his customary address to the nation. What has happened to him? Has he been taken prisoner by Himmler? Is he still alive? Still in possession of his senses? After all these years of subjection to totalitarian leadership, to the Führerprinzip, the people have a right to know what has happened to their Führer. But now, it seems, in their hour or direst need, he has deserted them. On the same day that Hitler should have spoken, Roosevelt was re-elected as President. Both facts are of more significance than a battle lost.

Helldorf and the General have got here at last. Owing to engine trouble, their party had to transfer from the larger ship to three small ones, which had a rough passage. When they arrived in the afternoon, the seas were so high that a minesweeper had to go out to their assistance. I watched it for some time through glasses, battling with the heavy seas. One of the little ships has brought us two sacks of airmail from home.

At table, Heider was joking in his light-hearted Rhineland fashion, that in the absence of a speech by Hitler, *he* would have to address us. Yes, he said, tomorrow I shall speak to you all. Coming from him and delivered in such portentous tone, this led to much laughter and applause. Encouraged by this he continued in similar vein, saying that the New Testament was just a pleasant novel and *Mein Kampf* the new bible, without knowing or caring whether his remarks might give offence to anyone present.

In the evening he confessed to me, over a glass of his excellent cognac, that after the war he would never enter government service or do any sort of office job. He was a sales representative and would remain a sales representative, even if all he had to sell was shoelaces. Here his stock-in-trade is his cherished stock of cognac and I always enjoy watching him issuing permits for it; he is in his element. He is good-hearted and light-minded; has not much conscience but a great zest for living; his motto 'live and let live'. In secret I have changed his rank from Platzkommandant to Platzkognakdant.

The General soon came round to see us. He was in very good spirits. He gave us a review of the situation in the light of the latest communications from HQ. Their orders seem muddled and lacking in sense. At least the General, thank God, seems to have no intention of following the hotheads' advice and cutting off civilian supplies right away. It seems probable that the British government will have heard from escapees from the island, that the estimated date when supplies for the civilian population will run out is 1 January 1945, and is deliberately holding back until nearer that deadline. I volunteered to fly to Germany on the General's behalf, to give an up-to-date sitrep. This is being given serious consideration. Apart from Helldorf there is nobody for such an assignment but me. The thought that I might also see my family is almost too wonderful to contemplate. But the mission in itself would be interesting and well worthwhile.

10.11.44. Spent a sleepless night. Stocks are again falling far short of our estimates. This time it is a matter of some 700 tons of potatoes. 100 tons have been issued in Guernsey, against my express orders and owing to the negligence of Inspector Spann, who talks too much and pays too little attention to his duties. The remaining 500-600 tons are not there simply because the agreed quota of local deliveries has not been kept. By now these potatoes will have vanished into private stores and it will mean drastic and painful measures to get possession of them.

So if, as now seems likely, those mythical Red Cross ships are not going to turn up with food for the islanders after all, I think it is high time to review the situation once again and revise our estimate of the deadline to which we can hold out.

The military authorities here tend to take an optimistic view of the situation and refuse to face up to the frightful conditions which could develop, although everything depends on the general military situation, which is something they should understand. I will try to consider it from a military point of view. First: is there any possibility of these beleaguered islands being relieved? In view of the statements by Himmler and Goebbels that our policy is now to hold the enemy on Germany's frontiers until he is ready to make peace, even the military must rule this out. Second: can we hold out here indefinitely, with or without also supporting the civilian population? No. There is not enough seed left to provide another full harvest, nor could we last out until the next one. Third: what is the minimum ration on which the troops could still bear arms and the civilian population still exist? This must be decided by the medical men. Four: in the event of a prolonged hunger blockade, should the troops be fed and the civilians allowed to starve? The validity of the question depends on what time could be gained and what purpose would be served.

If all civilian rations were diverted to the troops from 1.12.44, we could hold out until the beginning of August 1945; if from 1.1.45, until the beginning of June 1945 and if from 1.2.45, until the beginning of April 1945. Accepting, for the military argument, that Germany may be able to hold the enemy on her frontiers until he is ready to make peace, this will certainly not be until next autumn or the following winter, a deadline of which all our estimated dates fall far short. And the last date to which we could hold out (August 1945) would mean surrendering the islands with the population extinct.

So the question we are again facing is whether the doubtful gain of holding out in the island fortresses for a few more useless months would be worth achieving at such a frightful cost in human life. Never must the German soldier be made the instrument of so hideous a crime, totally irreconcilable with his military honour or his duty to his country, as the wiping out of the island population. We could not in all conscience carry out orders to this effect. The soldiers here, I am convinced, would rather tighten their belts and go hungry with the islanders. Not to mention, if the Nazi hotheads are deaf to humane reasoning, what might be likely to happen to a garrison surrendering the islands with all the inhabitants dead.

I am therefore going to propose that all rations, for troops and civilians alike, be reduced to an agreed subsistence minimum immediately. Thus, without outside help, we ought to be able to hold out until April 1945. After that there will be no alternative to surrender.

11.11.44. After mulling this over all night, in the morning I called my staff officers together to acquaint them with my assessment of the situation and my determination never to serve as hangman's assistant in the annihilation of the population or lend my name and responsible position as head of civil affairs to any orders to that effect. If such a barbaric measure as depriving the civilian population of all food to enable us to hold out longer should be carried out, I should certainly not be here to witness the final surrender of the islands minus islanders, as I should long since have been dead myself, as a preferable choice.

(As a child of nature, grateful every day for all the beauty of the world, I believe I could meet death with equanimity. All the beauty of the world, of which I have glimpsed only a fraction, will still be there. The sun will still swing over mountains, tops capped with snow, spring will break through in delicate green and autumn go down in gold and orange glory. What matter if I am not there to see it? The memory of all this and above all the memory of the happiest hours of all with my family, would sustain me in the hour of death.)

To return to my officers and their response when asked for their comments. Pokorny was the first to express absolute agreement with my views. Sonderführer Ten Harmsen declared that he was an old National Socialist; for him all that counted was the Führer's orders. Incredible that there are people who can still believe in the Party's insolent claim, as it was posted up on the frontiers of occupied Alsace Lorraine, 'The Führer is always right'. Even for them, one would think, Hitler's recent failure to speak to his people would have disqualified him from their leadership. Woelken swiftly countered Hermsen by saying that the German soldier has his own standard of honour and it would be senseless to give him orders against his conscience to carry out. I heartily agree. For me the final arbiter must be my own conscience.

In the late afternoon, after a protracted session of discussion with Helldorf, I got in the car and drove off at random for a change of scene and breath of fresh air. The storm had blown itself out at last. All was quiet and still. Against the sky the sea showed up in sharp definition, like a dark ring around the island. Long ragged streamers of storm clouds drifted down towards the horizon uniting in a final sombre threat before dispersal and the setting sun, shining through the lattice of cloud, reawakened the grey sea to shades of deep green and blue. The clean exhilarating air blew in through the open windows of the car. I was grateful for this solacing hour alone with nature.

12.11.44. Woelken (in Jersey) and Spann (in Guernsey) have, it turns out, made many miscalculations in their advance estimates of supplies, naturally always to our disadvantage, which costs me many sleepless nights as new examples come to light. It is impossible for me to conduct all the minor negotiations and check all the figures personally. I am disappointed in the final figures for the harvest, but even more so in the miscalculations which led me to expect them to be higher. But on the whole, I suppose, taking the circumstances into account, this harvest in enemy territory, sown and brought in during the seven months that the islands have been under siege, may still be regarded as a major achievement.

19.11.44. After three long months without a letter from my wife, horrifying news has reached me. My darling wife was arrested by the Gestapo on 19 August 1944 and is now to be brought before the People's Court.

It is useless to try to put my feelings into words. I am utterly overcome and shall never know another minute's peace. She, my lovely, sensitive, delicate young wife immured behind bars, in the squalor of a prison cell. Even if it is proven, as it must be in the face of all malicious gossip, that she is politically totally uninvolved, can she survive the cold and hunger and the ignominy of the situation with her health unimpaired? I cannot set down here all that I feel. One's every utterance, spoken or written, is subject to misinterpretation and the petty informer haunts us all.

After a week of numbed silence, I return to my diary again only as an occupation to blunt the edge of pain and a means of keeping in touch, at least in thought, with my poor wife. I hope that she too will have the strength to carry on and survive, although for her, snatched away from the care of our three young children and with no means of diverting her thoughts from her sordid surroundings, it is all so much more difficult.

Never before in the history of our family or our country has such a thing happened to a woman of our line. I recall Bismarck's dictum, 'A state which refuses to recognise my possessions can no longer be my fatherland'. How much more strongly would he have felt if not just his possessions had been concerned but his wife! But in those days the state we now live in could not have been even dimly envisaged. My wife has faced the difficult times with fortitude and good-humour and has never uttered one word of complaint to me. If she sometimes likes to criticise wartime abuses it is because, as the daughter of an old military family, she has been brought up to speak her mind freely and fearlessly. That this courageous, honest woman should now be arraigned at some monstrous show-trial seems to me to belong to the dark days of the French or Russian revolutions and to have nothing to do with the true spirit of the German people.

21.11.44. I force myself to read, to write, to take physical exercise. I can find no pleasure or interest in anything. Every day I take this diary from its hiding-place. I now keep it well hidden, as I go in daily fear of arrest. I must assume that my wife may not have had time to destroy my letters before she was arrested, in which case I could be charged as an enemy of the Nazi regime.

It is now a week since the General and Helldorf departed after their recent visit. Helldorf, as usual, consulted his local contacts, a dancing-teacher and a girl of ill-repute, and from their silly gossip gave me the result of his findings on 'informed local opinion'. I listened politely but made it clear that I was not to be bluffed. He did not seem to take this amiss, rather to respect me for it. I was even able to persuade this diplomat of the old school to cease fobbing off the Bailiff with half-truths and to allow him to be informed of the true facts of the situation.

On Sunday 12 November 1944, before the General's return to Guernsey, a meeting took place between him and the Bailiff at Linden Court. This was not intended for further discussion, merely as a conciliatory gesture of leavetaking. But the Bailiff seized the opportunity to indulge in impassioned rhetoric, even rudely interrupting the Attorney-General to ensure that he alone held the stage.

On this visit the General seemed more charming and likeable than ever. Unfortunately he was also more than ever under the influence of Helldorf, who encourages him to hit the bottle and consort with the notorious L. He was also led astray by Helldorf into making some off-hand criticism of an old and tried officer here. This will certainly not have gone down well in the army. In fact I fear that some feeling against him – however unjustified – could build up in forces' circles, which could be all too easily exploited by such an ambitious character as Admiral Hüffmeier.

Fantastic storms are again raging across the island. Nature stages a daily drama as in high opera, with the island as a backdrop.

22.11.44. I am sunk in a morass of despair. Work is a narcotic but not a cure.

Today we received official confirmation that Red Cross ships will be bringing soap, medicaments and food parcels for the civilian population.

23.11.44. The hours of solitude, which used to afford me some refreshment of spirit, are now bedevilled by feelings of hate and fury. All my thoughts are with my wife. For her I have piled my desk with flowers, fir twigs with golden chrysanthemums – yellow-red chrysanthemums interspersed with tall stalks of lavender, late-flowering dwarf gladioli, blood-red against dark evergreens. In the evening I turned on

the desk-light and sat there for an hour, the lamp lighting up the
flowers and illuminating, just a little, my sad spirit.

It is pouring with rain again. At dusk Pokorny and I took a quick run
down to the beach. The storm had thrown up more seaweed than usual
and swept away the sand. Poor Pokorny can never escape the cares and
anxieties of office. Some people seem driven to unload their worries on
each other, instead of making the most of the odd carefree hour of life
that remains.

At the moment I am much involved in ticklish negotiations with the
Bailiff. The States are contesting our immediate confiscation of all
civilian stocks calculated to last beyond 31 January 1945. I doubt myself
whether Helldorf will be able to justify this measure to the Red Cross
Commission. The first reductions in bread and fat rations must now be
implemented and a large delivery of cattle to the occupying forces
imposed. I feel dull and lifeless and it is difficult to summon up the
energy and concentration which these exchanges demand. My preoccupation with my own affairs, and those of my wife and family,
undermines my resolution in the conduct of affairs.

24.11.44. In the night I indulge in all sorts of fantasies about how I
might bring about the freeing of my poor wife from prison. Yesterday I
found the little silver knife she gave me, which I had mislaid since the
news of her arrest. In the absence of further news, I take this as a
favourable omen.

Have just read a good French novel, *Femmes* by Marcel Prêvot. When
in his forties, a lifelong sensualist and woman-chaser finds that he is
genuinely in love again. While still able to recognise all that true love
means, he is no longer able to respond to it except by a heightened
turmoil of the senses. The young woman is equally involved, but
recognises his depraved worldly character and rejects his advances.
There is some apposite comment on the use of the word 'love' and on
the misleading and opposing concepts brought together under this
heading.

25.11.44. Yesterday a young private soldier was married at the
Soldiers' Home by proxy. The sisters arranged a small table as a sort of
altar, decorated with flowers and candles. In the middle stood a
photograph of the bride. Dr. Harmsen, head of the Military Court, read
out in his dry tones the prescribed declaration according to contemporary usage. The Nazi marriage. No mention of loyalty and life-long
companionship, only that the partners were vouched free of V.D., were
not sterile and had no Jewish ancestors. A wretched ceremony, but
Captain Koppelmann raised our spirits a little by a rousing speech at
the well-stocked breakfast table.

Apart from ensuring the bride of her subsistence allowances, there seems no advantage in these proxy marriages. Perhaps the totalitarian state will next invent procreation by post. This would be in keeping with its general policy of the enslavement of the individual. A supply of fresh male sperm to the women's labour camps would obviate the time-wasting act of love and step-up the supply of population for the state.

Sister Gretchen, who also became engaged very young, sat beside the bridegroom to represent the bride. In spite of the prosaic ceremony, she was obviously much moved, quite pale with emotion. Women are often more affected by their own conception of a situation than by its grim reality. That is part of their charm.

26.11.44. I am lately under constant attack by Major Schade, who has taken over from Colonel Lindner as the officer in charge of supplies for the troops, and who in this capacity, can find nothing better to do than to criticise the work of Military Administration in the department of agriculture. I spent an hour today dealing with his complaints. I did not treat these lightly but dealt exhaustively with each item he brought up and again produced printed facts and figures to refute his arguments. All to no avail. With time on his hands and a bee in his bonnet, he obviously finds some satisfaction in 'investigating' all we have done or are doing in order to disagree with it. A tiresome know-all and busybody, but I suppose coping with him at least takes my mind off my own troubles.

I am recovering a little from the numbness of shock, if only in the lower plane of the physical. Have started early morning exercises again and enjoy the physical refreshment of cycling, fresh air and sunshine, but am haunted by the thought of my poor wife, who lives under a different sky, shut up in a dank cell where the sun never shines.

The conference with the Bailiff about a reduction in rations took a surprising turn. After an initial attempt to bypass the subject, he and his advisers disclosed that the 100 tons of grain which we had demanded should be set aside from the production of flour during December and January, for spring sowing, had in fact already been set aside for that purpose. In view of this, I hope we may be able to dissuade Helldorf from the further cut in bread rations although I fear – *l'appetit vient en mangeant* – it may merely strengthen his determination to stretch supplies to the utmost and he may still insist on the cut. A reduction in the butter ration could conceivably be justified, but if we can avoid a cut in the bread ration, we shall be in a better position to discuss the confiscation of all civilian supplies extending beyond 31 January 1945. And we should avert another protest by the States, which, with the visit of the Red Cross Commission now imminent, would be of inestimable value. We must now exercise all tact to win Helldorf over to this view. This should not be impossible, especially as there will soon be a drop in the number of heavy workers receiving supplementary rations, and Helldorf's order, in the first place, did not call for a further cut in rations but for the delivery of 100 tons of seed wheat.

Have also resumed my leisure-hour chats with Wetzstein. He lacks mental discipline and is swayed entirely by the mood of the moment. This tendency manifests itself outwardly in little eyes, too small in comparison with the wide cheekbones and wide but backward-sloping forehead. Yesterday he was praising his wife to me in the highest terms. She is the best wife in the world, but only, it was evident, because she defers to him, has the highest admiration for his achievements in life and never fails to tell him so. I fear this typifies the German pattern of marriage. In his works and aspirations the man requires the uncritical admiration and support of his wife, while she on her part asks nothing better than to look up to him. Thus each loves the other as an ideal rather than as a human being. I am reminded of Moltke's letters to his bride, demanding a similar unqualified devotion.

In the evening, after a couple of glasses of port, this highly intelligent man launched into a nauseatingly fulsome account of his own achievements. No wonder that, so easily borne up by praise and approbation and cast down by misfortune, he should in these difficult times suffer some mental derangement. This has latterly shown itself physiologically in a nervous tic under the right eye. This is particularly pronounced when he is in low spirits or under stress.

In the afternoon we had been to the cimema together. I quite enjoyed the film, as I thought the leading actress was charming in her portrayal of an unsophisticated young girl. Wetzstein thought such naïveté showed feeble-mindedness rather than the innocence of extreme youth. So opinions differ.

27.11.44. On the same day that we put in a protest against being constantly harassed by Major Schade, his regimental commander very considerately arranged a get-together to see if we could not resolve our differences. This went off very well, led to a real reconciliation and a welcome clearing of the air. I think we all left the meeting with a feeling of relief. Major Heider deserves all praise for his tactful handling of the affair; he is very good at soothing ruffled spirits and introducing a note of amity. Our sharing billets together at Linden Court has undoubtedly helped in a mutual understanding and sharing of our tasks.

Mail from home has arrived unexpectedly. I had hoped for, yet dreaded this. There was nothing for me of a personal nature. The others had many letters from their families. I feel an outcast. This exclusion, this absence of news, brings home to me more deeply my wife's tragic fate. And I don't know to whom or to what address to send the one letter we are permitted to write. Nor do I know whether my little son Michael, born last May, is still alive and well, although I have assumed this from references to 'the three little ones' in letters received in the last six months.

Visited the big library at the Jesuit College. I feel that the Father and I are to some extent united in a common interest in European culture. He is in charge of the College's over two hundred thousand volumes. This impressive collection is largely devoted to French literature, art and philosophy, not only over the ages but up to most modern times. The quiet amiability of the two French priests is a pleasant change from the stiffness of military life. I was allowed as a special favour to take out a book on loan, so hope never to go short of reading matter again.

The big operation, conducted by Lieutenant Ambacher on the orders of Helldorf, to search out and confiscate on the spot any illegal food supplies held by the civilian population, has turned out rather a damp squib. The returns were meagre: we could have told them this in advance. At least it has shown that supplies are not being diverted or illegally hoarded, and that the statistics provided by Military Administration are accurate and no longer to be contested.

28.11.44. Tension is mounting here daily. Helldorf's over-optimistic assumption that Red Cross ships woud be arriving shortly and would then take over the entire provisioning of the civilian population has hitherto proved fallacious. When they were here last I warned both him and the General against taking any such possibility into account when advising High Command of the last estimated date to which we could hold out. This would be, under present circumstances, about March. If, out of some mistaken idea of honour, the target date is reported as June, July or even later, High Command will accept this as fact, sweeping aside the pre-requisite or extent of outside help on which such an estimate would depend.

What was actually reported, Helldorf has not revealed to me. His policy is to keep everyone guessing, play his own game and build up an empire of underlings responsible to him alone. The General finds him more than ever indispensable and Helldorf exploits this to denigrate the work of other military establishments and to undermine their authority. What is worse, he foists onto the General the responsibility for harsh measures of which that kind-hearted and chivalrous man could certainly never be the originator.

Recently Colonel Heine, our very decent and meticulously correct fortress commander, received a dressing-down such as, he said, he had never experienced in the whole of his military career, simply because he had not set up his M.P. posts in the exact locations referred to in a talk with Helldorf.

Now orders have been issued to the troops to make a return of any stocks of potatoes or flour they hold additional to the rations issued. Military units had been encouraged to help themselves by tilling the ground around their units and planting potatoes and grain. Many of them have invested their leisure hours and their own pay in doing this. If these wretched supplies are now to be called in, it will scarcely add to the time we can hold out here, but will certainly increase the general depression and perhaps lead to disciplinary measures against these men who will be understandably reluctant to part with their small but hard-won surplus stocks.

On the other hand, the heavy cuts, the blocking of part of the soldiers' pay and of local marketing funds are certainly necessary measures. Everyone is on edge and an unnatural activity prevails. All rather like trying to burn a candle at both ends but make it last longer. Woelken sums it up in what he tells me is an English proverb saying 'You can't stick a sweet on the shirt of a naked man'. That is what we are all trying to do here.

I have just had a confidential and highly important talk with a friend. This has reassured me to some extent. But it is dangerous to name names or to confide too much to paper, so I shall say no more about it here.[2]

Major Schade and another officer have been summoned to Guernsey for briefing. Apparently they are to be entrusted with a social mission in Jersey. The fortress commander himself knows nothing about this. Another instance of his authority being by-passed, which, understandably, he particularly resents. Well, I suppose we shall hear what particular task Helldorf has entrusted them with when they return. In the evening we had dinner with Colonel Lindner, who also could not conceal his mistrust and anxiety about this latest development.

Had awful nightmares about being hanged – appropriate perhaps to this day and age – followed by waking nightmares of all that my poor wife must be suffering. Find I am increasingly inclined to the nervous movement of passing my hands over my face, as if I could brush away all these incredible circumstances which are so difficult to accept as facts. What is happening to my children? They are constantly on my mind. Is Uta being taunted by the children at her school or ostracised by them?

29.11.44. Helldorf is getting really jittery. We have received a telex from Guernsey asking why we did not instruct the States of that island to deliver the late potato crop to the troops. As if it was within the competence of Military Administration to take such high-handed action! We supervise the harvest and gathering of crops, keep meticulous records and report as meticulously to the office of the C.i.C. Orders for commandeering supplies rest with him, although of course we have the task of passing them on to the States of the two islands. (And at the same time to try to maintain good relations with those bodies.) All this I pointed out rather acidly in my reply. Obviously Helldorf is looking for a scapegoat on whom to shift the blame, as the Red Cross ships have not yet turned up, and when they do they will not be the cornucopia he had expected.

In the evening was invited to supper with Lieutenant John of the Feldgendarmerie, who has just been promoted to captain, and was celebrating with a roast goose. On the way back, I noticed how the sky had cleared of all but a few drifting tatters of cloud. It was a lovely mild moonlight night with air as fresh as a cool wine. I had a sense of rediscovery of the vast vault of heaven, of the infinity of stars shining so remotely and peacefully above a war-torn world. In my bedroom I removed the blackout curtaining, opened the windows, and went to sleep with an odd sense of comfort in being part of this endless universe stretching from infinity to the end of my bed.

30.11.44. Captain Lentsch invited me to coffee in the afternoon. After the second glass of cognac, I remarked that, although I was very well informed on the local situation and well acquainted with most of the leading personalities, there was one man whom I had not yet met, but who might well play a leading role in events in the immediate future. This was Admiral Hüffmeier, who had come to the islands in the few months preceding the siege, when we were cut off from the mainland of France and had taken over command of the naval units. I asked Captain Lentsch, rather diffidently as his own commanding officer was concerned, if he would mind giving me his own personal opinion of the Admiral. To this he readily agreed in his usual pleasant manner. He rated the Admiral's abilities very high. Hüffmeier knew exactly what he was aiming at. He had an excellent grasp of affairs and was the leading exponent of the policy of holding out to the end at any cost,until the autumn or the 'final victory'. In his last posting he had been the chief Party executive on the staff of Admiral of the Fleet Dönitz, with whom he was on intimate terms. He was undoubtedly the driving force behind the measures to cut down rations and conserve supplies, that is since he had consolidated his position and had gained a voice in local counsels by being appointed a member of the General's Headquarters Staff. He was personally an affable and likeable man. As a personal adviser he tended to rely on Captain von Kalckreuth, a small landowner from Silesia, who had put his men to work on a smallholding project and

thus proved, or claimed to have proved, that he had made his own naval
unit self-supporting.

But, I objected, if the Admiral was reporting to Germany that we
could hold out for any length of time, he must, whatever his abilities, be
quite out of touch with the reality of the situation. Yes, agreed Lentsch,
in that sense he was. As a dedicated Nazi, he believed what he wanted
to believe and viewed the situation as he wished to see it, rather than on
the evidence on his own doorstep. This was where Lentsch took issue
with his chief and could no longer go along with his policy. But he still
had to give due acknowledgement to Huffmeier's determination and
singleness of purpose.

Here I interjected that the General, Helldorf and I were in complete
agreement that we could not and would not allow the islanders to die of
starvation simply to prolong the siege by a few months. The military
situation could not justify such a breach of humanitarian principles and
international law. Would the Admiral, then, be prepared to disregard
such considerations? Undoubtedly, in Lentsch's opinion. All he cared
about was holding out to the bitter end, irrespective of whether the
civilian population was wiped out, evacuated or, if they were fortunate
enough, fed by Great Britain.

So it amounts to a trial of strength between the General and the
Admiral. As I saw it, I told Lentsch, as far as Germany was concerned,
it was a political rather than a military decision. The islands were now
of no military value to Germany but still of some political significance.
If we let the islanders starve to death, we could certainly hang on for a
few more months, but this could only lead to reprisals against the
Germans in British hands, who must outnumber the population of the
islands. Ultimately neither General von Schmettow, nor Dönitz – least
of all we little local functionaries with our opposing viewpoints and
internecine strife – were the proper arbiters. It was a matter for
consideration and delicate negotiation by the German Foreign Office,
in consultation with the High Command.

Lentsch shared my appraisal of the situation and also agreed that it
should be handled by the Foreign Office, provided it had men of
sufficient calibre to deal with the Protecting Power as an independent
ministry and not as a mouthpiece of the military authorities. Even in
wartime the forces should be allowed no voice in political affairs; the
strongpoint commander was trained to defend his position to the last
and lead his men to death bravely, but not to think further than that.
That is what worries me. Without knowing the wider implications and
the persons who may be involved, I incline to the belief that there are
few if any officials in the nation's present leadership capable of making
a well-balanced and reasoned judgement. Rather they seem all to be
ruled by military madness and an urge to self-destruction.

At any rate, I told Lentsch, if it should be decided to abandon the local population to starvation, I could not carry on here. I should ask to be relieved of my command, which, as I saw it, meant the just administration of the civilian population, taking into account all the prevailing circumstances, a policy which, whether through a divergence in reporting by local commanders or by a lack of understanding of the overall situation, had never received a proper hearing. I felt vastly cheered that Lentsch, too, like so many of the other high-ranking officers whose views on the subject I had already tested out, agreed with me that to leave the islanders to starve was unthinkable.

Now I can clearly see how the wily Helldorf has been trying to steer a middle course between the two opposing camps and to keep both sides happy. Also how much, in so doing, he has relied and still relies on England coming to the rescue. This was evident when he rang me up the day before yesterday to say that in his estimates for linking up present stocks with the next harvest, he now found himself short by 400 tons of grain. This was because he had discounted the needs of the civilian population for January in the belief that they would by then be supported by the Red Cross. In spite of this, he is still optimistic, in my view unjustifiably so, as evidenced by his conviction that help will certainly have arrived by February and by the order for the retention of 500 tons of seed-wheat for sowing in the spring, this order being no more than a cock of the snook at circumstances. We could hold out until the next harvest only if the entire support of the civilian population were taken over by the Red Cross. This seems to me very unlikely. On present information we can rely only on some strictly limited supplies for the islanders, supplementary to the basic rations. If the General's policy prevails, and the islanders continued to be issued with these basic rations from local supplies, we could still only survive until March – far short of the harvest, even of the early greenhouse potatoes. And the troops on their daily bread ration of 300 grammes, with other foodstuffs similarly short, will not, according to the army doctors, be fit for active service by the spring. I resolve to make another comprehensive report, taking into account all these statistics and any possible further unfavourable circumstances which may arise.

Lentsch and I also spoke about Major Schade's recent preferment to O.i.C. of army rations and food supplies, in place of Colonel Lindner, who has been transferred, with all tact and decency, to another command. Likeable as the genial old Silesian squire is, he was never really up to the job. Nor, for that matter, is Schade, as we learned in our recent skirmish with him, when we had to take issue, as it turned out successfully, with his sabre-rattling tactics. He is a small agriculturist who has come up in the world, has some natural aptitude for farming and a grasp of economics, but lacks in calibre and human understanding. Essentially a decent enough chap and as loyal as they come, rather a second edition of Lindner, but being somewhat younger, rather more aggressive. How far his new brief to 'co-operate' with us on matters in which military interests take precedence over civilian interests will be effective, will depend on whom he has to deal with. I have for my part no fear of him, nor any expectations of him either.

I told Lentsch how much I wished that he had been appointed to this post as commissar of the troops, with special responsibilities. The more so when he confessed that, as only two of his flotilla of 14 ships remained seaworthy, he was virtually without employment and wished only to be flown back to Germany. In fact, with his wide experience of international affairs as a former top-rank foreign trade representative, his natural sagacity and political good sense, he would have been the ideal man for the job. And it would have been a pleasure to work with him. I felt that our frank exchange of views was a tonic to us both, and as spontaneously as I exclaimed that I wished he had been given Schade's job, he as spontaneously poured me a third cognac.

A pleasant afternoon in most agreeable company. Our talk greatly heartened me and left me with a good deal to think about. I made a date with Captain Lentsch for a similar get-together when the Admiral pays us his promised visit in the near future, so that at least I shall have the benefit of Lentsch's practical knowledge and insight of the local scene to lend weight to our side of the argument.

The cuts in bread and fat rations settled, once again in peaceable conclave with the States and as peaceably put into effect. In this respect our personal contacts, built up over the years and the mutual trust and respect ensuing, are of inestimable value. We have built golden bridges in plenty. But I greatly fear that, as everything crumbles around us, these too will be swept away by the pitiless pressure of the prevailing circumstances, so that any future evaluation of the times will fail to make any distinction between these circumstances and the individuals concerned in them.

Have just come across a snapshot of my wife, with an affectionate inscription in her own hand. The sorrow and despair this conjures up are indescribable.

1.12.44. Helldorf rang me up today no fewer than eight times, in tones of great agitation, as if some fresh disaster was impending. Owing to the bungling of Guernsey officials, he has got it into his head that the States still have black-market supplies stashed away and it is therefore perfectly proper to make further confiscations of foodstuffs. With this scraping of the barrel the ever-impending threat of starvation will be brought even nearer.

After a meeting with the Bailiff today, he showed me over the Royal Court and States Chamber, where the island parliament sits. This is fitted out in the heavy, over-ornate style of the last century, but is not without a certain dignity and dramatic effect. Whatever revolutionary spirits the future may bring, this imposing chamber, presided over by the portraits of a long line of past bailiffs, stands guarantor for a long-established tradition of law and order. Any future States assembly inspired by Socialist or Communist ideas might well find itself subdued into compliance with conservative precedent in these hallowed precincts.

Systematic depredation continues unabated. Every garden hose, every old canvas sail, every curtain, tin of paint, roll of paper, old car, old tyres, everything, but everything, is demanded of us which we can still squeeze out of this poor little land. And with the impending failure of electricity, cables and fitments will also be torn out of one house to be fitted up on a makeshift basis in another. One sometimes wonders if a speedy total destruction by carpet bombing would not be preferable to this prolonged process of attrition.

In the evening saw a film in which my brother-in-law, Vollrath von Klipstein, starred opposite the cold and affected Marianne Hoppe. I scarcely bothered to follow the story but watched his face for any likeness in feature to that of my wife. I secretly nurse the hope that my celebrated relative will bring his influence to bear in securing her early release.[3]

2.12.44. In the library of the two Frenchwomen who have been condemned to death I have found more reading material than I shall be likely to get through in the short time that remains to us here. I have become quite a connoisseur of French literature and shall miss the opportunity to indulge my taste for it when I eventually get back to my own country.

In the morning I called a meeting of my staff officers. I explained to them how, in the light of our present situation and its possible outcome, I had come to the conclusion that it was now urgently necessary to produce another and absolutely up-to-date report on this for the superior authorities, and I appealed for the support of the various heads of sections. The response was very gratifying. I had the sense that they were all behind me and anxious to help. Something I appreciate and shall certainly need; and this time, I feel, our report must not be a matter of well-turned paragraphs, but must genuinely convey the true nature of the disaster implicit in the situation, with the support of facts and figures and a sober assessment of the same.

3.12.44. Am reading André Gide's *Pages de Journal*. I marvel at how little this writer, who has many wise and witty things to say about life, seems affected by the day-to-day events in the world about him. He lives in a purely literary world, immersed in new books, periodicals and articles. I am amused by his observation 'Les poissons meurent le ventre en l'air et remontent a la surface. C'est leur facon de tomber'. (When fish die, they float to the surface belly-upwards. It is their fashion of falling.) And how right he is when he says that the only justification for writing is an irresistible drive to do so.

Spent the afternoon (Sunday) with Wetzstein in his cosy little room, as I now generally do. He is gradually recovering from his fit of depression, which made him such difficult company, and we are able to resume our talks on the old easy relaxed basis. We spoke about how the age of free speech has vanished for our generation. The age of mass rule cannot afford the luxury of individual opinion, and those individuals, who still indulge in freedom of expression, pay dearly for it. Experience has shown us (I have only to think of Colonel Knackfuss or of my wife) that it is now sheer madness, almost irresponsible madness, to speak openly to anybody at all. As mad and of as little avail as rushing to the attack in a hail of bullets instead of flinging oneself to the ground. It is dangerous to speak one's mind in public or in private. Discretion must begin on one's own doorstep. Even in this diary, which I keep carefully hidden, I exercise considerable restraint. The time for heroics is past. The wise man who keeps his own counsel is no more cowardly at this stage than the soldier who takes cover from the bullets, and is certainly subject to a much more protracted self-discipline. One must practise silence every day. Perhaps it will prove a power in itself outlasting the demagogues and their rabble-rousing influence.

Wetzstein cheered me up quite a bit today when he advanced the view that, after the bloodbath and hangings following the attempted putsch and the attempt on Hitler's life in late July, things would have quietened down and minor offences be dealt with more leniently. How much I hope he is right.

I have heard from Guernsey that a letter from Linz has arrived for me there. Can it be from my wife, from my mother-in-law, from the court? I dread receiving it, but try to console myself that if it comes from Linz, my wife must at least still be there and has not been whisked away to Berlin or some dreadful concentration camp.

It was really a very pleasant afternoon with Wetzstein. I remind myself how critical I tend to be of my fellow men, how harsh in my judgement of them and how few of them I really like, and resolve to try to be more tolerant.

4.12.44. In bed; have been listening to a lecture on Fichte on the radio. What stuck in my mind was the dictum that the driving force of the sense leads to happiness, that of heroism to self-reliance and that of ethics to the meticulous performance of one's duties. The first and last sum up much of the difference between the south and the north German. I was reminded of a duty trip I once made with Heidi von Wedel from Paris to St Germain. When we arrived in St Germain and walked through the great park of the chateau, with the first breath of spring in the air, all my senses were stirred to rebellion against the iron bonds of duty. I wanted to linger, to savour this new place and new experience, to choose the most devious route. But nothing could hold Heidi back in her anxiety to get to her Soldiers' Home with all speed, although I imagine that her responsibilities were considerably smaller in scope than mine. A graphic illustration of the differing forces which motivated us. I was quite relieved when our ways parted and I could follow my own dawdling course.

7.12.44. In the last few days we have been very busy drawing up our longest and possibly our last report. This, amounting to twenty type-written pages, seems to me to cover all that it is necessary to say, including all possible contingencies which may arise from the situation and to which attention should be drawn. The well-informed can read between the lines. On the knottier points the question posed should lead the informed to the answer. I think that, despite its frankness, the report cannot be contested. Up to now our conduct of affairs in these islands has been reasonably fair and decent. What I fear is that it may deteriorate from now on. Even if I am here to record the last days of the occupation, it is doubtful whether this will be in my present influential position, especially if Admiral Hüffmeier is able to seize power and put through his radical policy. So if this is not the last report of Military Administration, it may well be the last report under my signature.

Yesterday the Admiral arrived here with Helldorf. They brought the news that a Red Cross ship is to leave Lisbon for the islands on 7 December. On the 9th I am due to sail to Guernsey, with Colonel Heine, so that I can take part in the negotiations with the Red Cross Commission there. Tomorrow afternoon I shall meet the Admiral at tea at Colonel Heine's. The next few days will be crowded with new impressions and important decisions. Meanwhile I must clear up all outstanding work, to which I may have no time to return later.

I have now received the letter from Linz. It is from my wife, her first letter to me from the prison there. She writes with a rare and touching courage that her incarceration in a narrow dark cell is only a physical one: in mind and spirit she lives free and unconfined with the children and with me. She omits all shameful and humiliating detail. These brave lines, bringing proof of her strength of mind and a steadfastness of purpose rising above circumstance, bring me some reassurance. But the prison notepaper on which they are written, as a mute witness of all she must be suffering, could reduce me to tears. She must bear the scars of this dreadful experience for the rest of her life. All that I most value in life is gradually being eroded away. Soon I shall have nothing more to part from but a healthy mind and body.

By the same post I also had a letter from my mother, who writes with her usual understanding and tact. She is concerned about my wife's imprisonment in Linz becoming known in Aufsess and thinks it wiser not to bring the children home yet. Their presence there without their mother could give rise to gossip and speculation, possibly leading to undesirable local action. She is right. One has only to think of the neighbouring family in Schloss Greifenstein, every single member of which was arrested after Claus von Stauffenberg's attempt on Hitler's life last July.

In the evening found pleasant company at Herr von Pokorny's. I had just come from a sadly inadequate lecture on art given by a young officer. Pokorny's other guests were Dr. Woelken and two Roman Catholic priests attached to the army. With such an assembly of good brains the talk was correspondingly good, ranging from the logic of Aristotle to the problems of present day society.

Woelken had some interesting speculations to make on modern society's need for industrialisation and increased productivity, from which he drew optimistic rather then pessimistic conclusions. A factory could only compete successfully if its employees were contented and happy at their work. Only contented employees could attain the necessary high output. Similarly, he argued, even the despotic Communist regime must, after an initial period of enslavement of the masses, recognise this truth and adjust its policy accordingly.

He went on to point out how the five of us assembled here by chance, were all motivated by humanitarian principles, with much power for good and how there must be thousands more like us, and spoke then like a delegate to the League of Nations, advocating peace and understanding between the nations, improved living standards for all etc. I agree with him about humanitarian principles; I try to direct my life by them, especially in my difficult task here. I agree with his ideals, but feel a little sceptical about seeing them put into effect in the future any more than they have been in the past. Will nation speak to nation, I wonder, and achieve a lasting peace, and will increased production provide for an increased population, or will, as in the whole previous history of the human race, nature adjust the population by death and history sweep the board clean of outmoded rule and custom to achieve a fresh start by recurrent wars?

We went on to talk about what constitutes a Nazi and the various types of the breed.

First there is the 'Nazi by nature', characterised by a fanaticism impervious to fact and unassailable by reason, utterly ruthless in furthering the 'cause'. He is a dangerous animal to cross, as he regards all opposition as a challenge to be wiped out. Such blind loyalty and singleness of purpose must at least be accorded the respect one would give to the brute force of a bull or an elephant.

Next comes the 'Nazi by ideological conviction', stemming from the times when Germany was bankrupt and prostrate. Among them were some good brains, such as Frick. The best of them, fighting against an old for a better new world, might be compared to the freedom fighters of 1813, with a national outlook related to the spirit of Fichte and Hegel.

The third type consists of all the little men, the petty functionaries who jumped on the bandwagon in good time, who have risen to power with the Nazi movement and would sink back to obscurity with its collapse. And fourthly there is the younger generation, who have been brought up under the Nazi regime and indoctrinated with its principles and are unable, or not yet able, to think for themselves. Both these types are also highly dangerous.

8.12.44. At last I met the Admiral at Colonel Heine's billets. Unfortunately, as the light was poor and he sat with his back to it, I was never able to get a good view of his face. I noticed he seemed to have a similar interest in me. I expect he has already heard a good deal about me, as I have a reputation for being pro-British.

As usual at such gatherings, the talk was mainly on military topics; postings, changes of command, decorations. When it occasionally turned to matters of more general interest, it was not for long enough for me to form any particular impression of the Admiral. He did, however, when there was reference to assistance from the Red Cross, give us for the first time the full background to the negotiations. This showed him to be better informed, or at least more frank about the whole business, than Helldorf. He also kindly passed me a copy of the latest telegram, giving details of the ship now expected. It is the Norwegian vessel, *Vega*, sailing from Lisbon on 7 December, with two Red Cross delegates aboard, one with the delightful name of Rindsbacher.

I passed on as much of this information as was permitted to the Attorney-General. He was much cheered by the good news and seized eagerly on every detail. We have such a close community of interests and natural liking for each other that, in times of peace, we should have become good friends. Woelken confided to me that when he had a

private word with the Attorney-General to express his regret that the
ship was not coming to Jersey first, Duret Aubin replied that if the
Baron went to Guernsey to meet the delegates, he would look after the
islanders' interests as well as any local officials.

Am a little put off by the name Rindsbacher. It reminds me of some
of the stuffy provincials I had to deal with as a junior barrister in
Augsburg, whose pompous manners sometimes almost led me into
unbecoming facetiousness.

Unluckily the weather is still very stormy, with heavy rain and hail.
This means not only that we cannot get over to Guernsey but that the
arrival of the Red Cross will probably also be delayed.

Lt.-Colonel Lindner has been finally, if politely, shelved. This must
be very painful for him. He had the best intentions without the ability
to put them into practice; a stentorian approach is no substitute for
finesse. When I had occasion to telephone him the other day about
complaints against a local building firm for unsatisfactory work, he
bawled down the line in such sergeant-major style, that I jokingly
pointed out he was not addressing the offending firm.

His successor, Major Schade, has now got back from his briefing in
Guernsey, looking, after his few days' absence from his new and already
heavily-laden departmental desk, visibly thinner and rather wild of eye.
I pull his leg, telling him he has the harassed air of an examination
student who could not answer all the questions.

9.12.44. Saw a film with Matterstock in the leading role. I think he is
about the best-looking man I have ever seen. Indulge in a little fantasy
about what fun it would be to be a Swiss, a delegate on an International
Red Cross Commission, and at the same time a well-known painter and
famous skater, with a newly-wed beautiful young wife and a history of
'petits amours' around the world.

Am reading an excellent and witty book by Morand. A quotation: 'les
passions sont les voyages du coeur'. In other words, the best journey in
the world is that from one place to another. Am also reading a book
which I find particularly gripping, *Failure of a Mission*, by Henderson,
who was British Ambassador in Berlin from 1937 to 1939. He provides
the best assessment I have ever encountered of the leading personalities of the Third Reich.

10.12.44. Weather still the same, stormy winds, rain, fog and very cold.
But it has been decided we shall sail for Guernsey in the afternoon.

At the harbour there was a big gathering of officers, mostly naval, as
the Admiral was returning to Guernsey with us. Captain Lentsch was
also taking leave of his command on a posting back to Germany, via

Guernsey. The captain's small cabin was crammed with people and thick with smoke.

Pokorny accompanied me to the ship. Under the lowering stormy sky he looked paler than ever but his dark eyes were full of warmth and sympathy. He is apt to attach a greater significance to such comings and goings than they actually merit. He put this into words when he adjured me to 'Come back safely', as if the fate of the island depended on me alone. How fortunate I am to have such a loyal staff.

The crossing, even on the well-found patrol boat, was very turbulent, but at least this time we were left undisturbed by British divebombers. The bow of the ship plunged deeply, throwing up masses of water over the lower decks. Long banners of spray flew past. I stood on deck on the weather side, protected by two overcoats and a tarpaulin from the flying breakers and driving rain. Next to me two young lieutenants kept up a tiresome exchange of chat until nature drove them to lean over the side and communicate with the sea. I had to struggle against the same inclination, especially as a hellish stink from the engine-room kept drifting across my nostrils.

I kept my eyes resolutely on the dwindling coastline of Jersey, then in the twilight spotted and concentrated on the outline of Sark and finally recognised the harbour lights of Guernsey.

The three-hour crossing allowed time enough to meditate on the might of nature as exemplified in the turbulent waters round us and on the fleetingness of one's own life. My thoughts often turned to my wife, Marilis, in prison, who would at any rate scarcely have cause to envy me now. I was making the journey only on behalf of the civil population of the islands. The military aspect was outside my province and had in any case representatives enough.

In the evening we were guests of the General, whose affability and good humour impressed me anew, as they never fail to do. He was keen to hear the latest news of Jersey and gave close attention and apparently complete credence to all that Helldorf had to tell. This was obviously, due to my inhibiting presence, less exaggerated and venomous than might otherwise have been the case.

11.12.44. The next day I had the opportunity to observe the General's sound good sense and human understanding in action. This was at a big conference prior to the arrival of the Red Cross ship. Admiral Hüffmeier, of whom I had never previously had the chance to form a proper impression, raised a lot of long-winded, basically irrelevant objections, chiefly it seemed with the object of getting the navy a bigger say in affairs. What, for instance, he enquired, if there should be timebombs concealed in the food parcels? But he could not himself enlighten us as to what purpose this would serve.

Unfortunately at this juncture a radio message arrived from Naval Headquarters, with the information that one of the delegates, Herr Rindsbacher, was on the counter-intelligence suspect list. He was therefore not to be allowed off the ship. (How on earth are we to get down to business with these people if we treat them in such hostile and cavalier fashion?)

This inspired the Admiral with a lot of counter-productive suggestions as to how our reply to Headquarters should be framed. But the General's more moderate counsels carried the day.

I fancy the Admiral respects, perhaps even secretly admires, the General, who, with the easy manners of the born grand seigneur, stands head and shoulders above him as a military leader. Hüffmeier himself, podgy and inelegant, is an unimpressive figure. As he sat there, with bowed shoulders, I thought the desk might be his more proper sphere of action. But on second thoughts, surveying his snub nose and fat cheeks, I decided he might well have been a one-time roystering student who, on inheriting his father's prosperous business, settled down to hard work and a successful career, thus acquiring a not unpleasing but still not quite convincing self-confidence of expression. Perhaps his present power still sits a little uneasily on his shoulders.

Hübner, formerly major, was there, in all the glory of the red stripes of a staff officer, with a lieutenant-colonel's star, the personification, I thought, of military arrogance. But this was a superficial impression. When I met him in the evening and got talking to him, I found him to be a rather melancholy romantic, much given to introspection.

In the evening all the conference members gathered more informally round the hearth. I again sat next to the Admiral and again had to modify my former impression. There is something very youthful, likeable and appealing about the man.

Indeed the impression I gained from this pleasant social evening with its animated chat around the fire was that the alarming rumours about the General being ousted by the Admiral could have no foundation in fact. Or was I perhaps the unwitting observer of a scene of reconciliation between the two?

Only Helldorf seemed outside the charmed circle, sitting bent, sour-faced and silent. He lacks the ability to join in on a harmless social occasion. His metier is that of a secret policeman, only at home in a conspiratorial atmosphere of whispered half-truth and innuendo. I felt sorry for him this evening, sorry that he could not enjoy himself with the rest of us but sat there like a weary superannuated old owl, his head sunk between his shoulders.

12.12.44. I have been trying to sort out the trouble between the chief of the Guernsey Nebenstelle and his staff. According to the complaints of

the various section officers, it seems that they are at odds with
Counsellor Schneeberger on account of his dictatorial methods and
failure to share responsibility and promote team spirit. I take both sides
to task and try to pacify everybody concerned. Effected at least a
temporary reconciliation, as they all sat down to dinner again together,
for the first time since the breach, from which, it occurred to me, I had
been the only person to profit, as both sides, in relying on me as a
mediator, had confided in me to far greater extent – and given me a
better picture of the local situation – than would normally have been
the case.

15.12.44. The stormy weather continues to hold up the arrival of ships
and I continue to be dependent on the General's hospitality. This has
included allowing me to ride his horse Monarch, the finest horse in the
island and in my experience as a rider. He soars over the highest
obstacles as if they were no more than matchsticks.

One evening the General took me upstairs to his private study and
showed me a magnificent work which has been produced under his
auspices: *Fortress Jersey and Guernsey*. The best artists and photographers
have been commissioned as contributors to this highly artistic
multi-volume book. He insisted that I sit at his desk and brought me all
sorts of interesting items to look at.

We talked like old friends and even discussed personalities. I was
interested to learn that the General had not been taken in by Helldorf's
less pleasing qualities, but valued him for an attribute I had hitherto
overlooked, his good nature.

The General is undoubtedly an outstanding personality, as an
individual and a leader of men; warm of heart, quick of understanding,
also blessed with much wisdom. I could not wish for a better or more
considerate chief, except for that one little failing, his Achilles heel; he
is bored by and cannot be bothered with all the dull statistics of the
situation. Unfortunately, it is just all these dull details of domestic
economy that must play the greatest role in our state of siege.

The General and I have been twice invited to the home of an English
lady here. On the second occasion her two pretty young daughters
showed us all the decorations they had been making for Christmas and
were clearly delighted by our appreciation of their hard work and
interest in English Christmas customs. I thought with anguish of my
own children and wondered what sort of Christmas they were likely to
have in the absence of both parents.

A book lent me by the General, *The Voice of War*, makes a powerful
impact. The French author, René Quinton, deals with his subject in
simple, direct, even brutal terms, sparing the reader no macabre
details, and dwelling on war as a world-wide and historical concomitant

of human development. This leads him to the conclusion that war is a natural expression of masculinity and man is tempered by war to meet the God who ordained it.

16.12.44. In looking round the defences of Guernsey, I came across an anti-aircraft post where a curious and impressive figure manned the four-barrel gun. A sailor, impassive of countenance, with slit-eyes indicating a Slav origin, scanned the skies for enemy aircraft, completely oblivious of his immediate surroundings, his head turning from side to side like an automaton. He must, I thought, have been engaged on such duties for so long, that his responses had become as natural as that of a polybus shooting out a tendril to engorge an intruder.

17.12.44. My impression of Guernsey is that it is even more like a sanitorium for the weak and ailing than Jersey. The soldiers look pale and undernourished, the civilians even more so.

All is peaceful, but it is the peace of lethargy and lack of stimulus. This was brought home to me the other day by the sight of the ten man crew of a plane which had just arrived from Germany. They looked as the serving soldier should. What a contrast they made, with their rosy cheeks and vigorous appearance, to our own pale and listless men on this hungry island.

The Red Cross ship has perhaps not even left port yet. She can only make 6 knots. I shall return to Jersey as soon as I can. The unaccustomed surroundings, the strain of waiting and the lack of a disciplined working day, leave me more than ever prey to searing anxiety about my wife.

18.12.44. In the morning I called on Sister Barbara at the Soldiers' Home. She is a great lady and a great character. With the exception of Hanne, a sensitive soul, bending to every wind of fortune, the others are all just good housewives. Barbara, who comes of the old Silesian nobility, is the only one with the spirit to address all officers by name, without military rank. This she does with such assurance and authority that all officers concerned apparently take it in good part.

At luncheon with the General, we were joined by a visiting air force officer, who was flying back to Germany that evening. He told us in simple straightforward fashion about all that was going on at home, which to us in our news-starved isolation was of vital interest.

According to him, incredible technical discoveries are now being perfected. The worst and bloodiest stage of the war might thus still be to come. He spoke about the new anti-aircraft shells, about the V-3, which gouges out a crater 150 metres in circumference and 30 metres deep. He spoke too about shortwave rays which ignite and blow up an ammunition dump from a distance and other new-type armaments. There was mention of the advancing Russians trying out their latest poison gas on prisoners of war.

He also gave us the latest news on the political front, which did nothing to allay my anxiety about my wife. When will she be freed, if ever? Political prisoners, it seems, are being treated with additional severity.

The General, Helldorf, Hübner and all of us listened practically open-mouthed to this account of all that was going on in the big wide world outside our isolated islands. It seems to leave little hope of ever enjoying another carefree hour.

Spent the evening with Countess Blücher. She has a keen wit, an open mind and the rare gift of being a good listener. I talked more than I had done for a long time, such a happy atmosphere lending wings to thought and thought to apposite comment and witty observation. My unaccustomed eloquence was only checked by the timely recollection of the French saying that the clever man knows when to stop showing how clever he is.

19.12.44. Have written an essay on the 'chivalrous gesture' and dedicated it to the General, who is the *chevalier par excellence* and has shown me so much kindness. The bond between us stems not so much from an intellectual affinity as from the deeper roots of heart and feeling, like that which united the knights of old.

Visited Seiler, holder of the Pour le Mérite award, at his invitation. He is a very likeable, upright man, with a great reputation as a classical scholar. He advanced the astrological theory that the sun, after being in the constellation of Pisces for 2,000 years, covering the period of Christianity and western culture, is now moving into that of Aquarius. Hence the wars and world crises, as the earth adapts to this new cycle of existence. Well, it is nice to be able to shift some of the responsibility onto the stars.

20.12.44. On this unexpectedly warm and sunny day, took a trip across to Herm. Schneeberger and Spann accompanied me in the little fishing control boat. The sea was flat and calm as a mirror.

We berthed at the steps and divided the island into three shoots. I chose the southern one, which is scenically the loveliest. The ferns glowed golden-brown. Stalking through the prickly underbrush, I put up two pheasants, but almost regretted this diversion of my attention from the wonderful sight of the sea and the chain of islands all around.

Sark lay before me. Bathed in golden light, the whole of the island was clearly visible and seemed like a model of the island of one's

dreams; its tall cliffs fissured by deep bays and its upland plateau of
lush verdant land etched in tapestried detail. I could hardly tear myself
away from the sight and in doing so almost stumbled over and missed
two rabbits.

At the southern end of the island I sat down on a block of granite and
divided my attention between the beguiling view of Sark and the
avowed purpose of our trip, to bag some game. The sea was marbled in
contrasting colours, caused by sun, cloud and currents and little waves
lapped softly.

I pushed on through the gorse, and there bagged a fat rabbit. In a
marshy thicket put up two pheasants. Felt a prickling of the spine even
before they flew up before me, the old instinct of the hunter I suppose.
In the confusion of the moment and hampered by the tangled
undergrowth, did not even manage a shot, but was well satisfied with
the encounter.

21.12.44. In the morning went for a ride along the south coast of
Guernsey with Major Albrecht. We were both mounted on the gallant
Monarch. We took a cliff path, bordered by broom, zigzagging
precipitously up and down and affording wonderful views. We might
have been in Corsica, except that the sea was a northern grey, only
occasionally flecked with colour by the sun. Monarch was at his best
and most mettlesome.

On the way, even at a gallop, Major Albrecht confided to me his life's
history, a not very interesting but perhaps not unenviable one, as it
emerged that in civilian life he had been a wealthy director of
coalmines. I confined my part in the conversation to that of the polite
listener, which was all he clearly required. Not, to do him justice, that
he seemed so much concerned with his own importance as gratified by
all the honours and offices which had been piled on him. He would have
been much at home at some 18th-century court, collecting awards and
keeping its ruler amused.

In the afternoon took leave of the General and Helldorf on my return
to Jersey. We parted on the best of terms. I think Helldorf has a greater
respect for me than he has for most people, although this may be at
least partly due to my good relationship with the General.

The crossing, in our swift naval control boat in still glorious weather,
was at first a sheer delight. The sea was calm with only a slight swell.
The sun, low in the sky, appeared now and then like a golden ball
between the rifts of cloud and made a luminous path across the sea.

As we approached Jersey, banks of dense fog suddenly rolled up. We
soon lost all sense of direction and had to steer by compass. Now we
could hear the booming of the foghorn on Corbiere Point, but owing to
the blanketing effect of the fog, had no idea whether the sound came

from behind or before us. There were only three of us on board and we stood round the helmsman straining our eyes for the rocks which surround Corbiere.

Suddenly the lighthouse foghorn boomed out right before us. This was followed almost immediately by a terrifying crash. And there we were, run onto a reef of rocks, our ship undamaged but stuck absolutely fast.

The tide was rising with another hour to go. The boat was soon swamped and as the heavy swell swept over it we were soaked to the skin.

There was nothing for it but to climb out and take refuge on the highest point of the reef. We took our luggage and valuables with us and settled into our eyrie as best we could. By this time it was pitch dark and, with the thick fog, visibility was reduced to less than a yard. The mate let off distress rockets at intervals, but it was doubtful if they would be visible from the coast of Jersey.

After what seemed an age the tide at last began to turn, but according to our watches it was still only seven o'clock in the evening. So we should have to sit on that rock in our wringing wet clothes all night. Fortunately it was comparatively mild and quite windless. We passed the time in an exchange of grim jokes.

When morning at last dawned, we could see with the first light that the fog had completely disappeared. Our ship lay beneath us, water-logged and still firmly wedged between the rocks. Even the full force of the heavy seas had not dislodged it.

Meanwhile boats had already left St Helier to look for us. It was not long before we were able to jump off our reef onto the deck of a coastal patrol boat.

Pokorny and Heider were at the harbour to meet me. They had been greatly concerned about my safety and we were warmly welcomed as castaways already given up for lost. Then the funny side struck us and we all burst out laughing. In my borrowed sailor's uniform, which was much too small for me, and a bit unsteady on my feet after all the schnapps I had taken to keep out the cold, I must have seemed a comic figure. In fact, I did not even get a cold in the head after my 14 hours soaking in sea water.

22.12.44. Captain Breithaupt has left the island on a posting back to Germany. His departure was attended by all the usual naval fuss and to-do at the harbour, with officers being piped aboard and piped ashore. I had known him as the congenial host and sympathetic listener and had taken a great liking to him as a man of outstanding integrity and ability. But he must also have been a tiger for discipline and a hard taskmaster, necessary attributes perhaps of the successful commander.

Between the to-ing and fro-ing at the harbour I gave Colonel Heine an account of my stay in Guernsey. For some reason or other this did not seem to go down too well, although I could not tell what it was that ruffled him; whether my encounter with the well-fed Luftwaffe officers, or my privileged reception by divisional staff – he is very touchy about the niceties of military rank and precedence – or simply my innocent remark that it was good to have an occasional change of scene. At any rate, he took leave of me rather frostily.

On the first day back found it hard to come to grips with the accumulated papers on my desk. On the second was completely immersed in them and found it hard to tear myself away.

22.12.44. Have had a clash with Inspector Bohde of the G.F.P. (Geheime Feld Polizei). He was threatening to arrest an islander unless he handed in some pre-war tinned goods (which, according to the published regulations of Military Administration the man was perfectly entitled to hold), while at the same time proposing to overlook a genuine contravention of regulations in a case of black-marketeering.

Bohde was furious at my intervention. He tried to justify himself by referring to special S.S. briefs and his own obligations as a good National Socialist. At this, I went to town, told him roundly his methods were those of a gangster and blackmailer and such misuse of police authority was unlikely to further the cause of the Third Reich.

He not only swallowed this but apologised profusely. Poor Heider, who had been anxious for the interview to go off smoothly, was at first almost as startled as Bohde himself by my wrath and savage attack on the feared secret police. Such tactics prevailed, today at least. But I must be on my guard against the Inspector. Although we made it up and parted on amicable terms, afterthought on his part could breed resentment and lead to further trouble. Some conciliatory gesture, for which the festive season will provide opportunity enough, may help to restore his *amour propre*.

23.12.44. Jot down six basic rules for survival under state of siege. Muse on how much life has changed. Have noticed that those who do not take it too seriously – and this applies particularly to the young – are as little concerned with its ultimate outcome. This was first brought to my attention when seeing young people as portrayed in a film, and later when watching cheerful young sailors on board ship. Wonder if one will be able to adapt as well to the even greater changes the future will inevitably bring? Or will one be too rooted in the old values of a vanished Europe? Certainly there will be some too rigid in outlook to accept new ideas; Albrecht occurs to me as an example. But I hope I shall be able to go along with the new age at least to the extent of enjoying what it has to offer without too much bitterness or nostalgic regret.

I detect in myself a growing hardness of mind and spirit. I am becoming less patient and accommodating; more resolute, unyielding and determined on my own ends. I chide myself as a dangerous dog; no question of my bark being worse than my bite; I bite and do not bark at all. This is due I suppose to the pressure of the times, not least my constant, grinding preoccupation with what my poor wife may be suffering. Life no longer revolves round the happy home and the peace and joy we celebrate at Christmas; it is a battle for existence in a hostile world with no refuge place.

Another conference with the Bailiff and Attorney-General was conducted in our usual open fashion. They know that by 31 January 1945 supplies for the civilian population will be exhausted and after that all will depend on the Red Cross. The frankness which exists between us precludes all rancour. Rather, with each side aware of the other's point of view, it makes for objectivity and an almost friendly community of interest in forming an accurate assessment of the overall situation.

This is grim and problems proliferate. In this sad siege by starvation, it is no easy task to hold the balance between the just claims of two suffering sections of humanity, our so-called enemies the islanders and our own troops, and still do justice to both. What a pity it would be if I am unable to put the experience thus gained to more constructive use in the happier times of peace.

There is nobody to wrap presents for at Christmas but Stella and Ella. For my darling wife and our three little ones I can do nothing at all. Instead I make what gifts I can to as many people as possible.

Over a hundred Christmas trees have been felled for the troops. Such official action was necessary to prevent a free-for-all which would have resulted in wholesale destruction.

24.12.44. In the morning went riding with Wetzstein. We careered around the football ground like cowboys. The weather was continental rather than insular, with an invigorating bite in the air and the sun shining in a pale blue sky shading to gold on the misty horizon. We afterwards adjourned for a cup of tea. Winnie, Wetzstein's spaniel, lay drowsing and contented on my knees after her strenuous outing. We exchanged gifts appropriate to the times; Wetzstein gave me a jar of sugarbeet syrup, I gave him some saccharine.

In the afternoon called on Mrs. Riley at Rozel Manor. The owner of Vinchelez was there; a boorish fellow, full of his own importance. I find him most irritating. With the old ladies hanging on his every word, he is obviously accustomed to playing cock of the walk.

As in the previous year, Mrs. Riley gave me what must be the loveliest Christmas bouquet produced in the island. Not the now long customary chrysanthemums, nor early camellias, but sweet-smelling mimosa, mixed with pale yellow orchids, coral-coloured berries and red-gold foliage. From Miss White at Samarès Manor, I received a well-illustrated book about horses.

Christmas Eve, celebrated together with the whole of Military Administration staff at the Soldiers' Home, was a moving and uplifting occasion, although depressing thoughts of home much saddened me. But still it was the first quiet and holy night I had known for many weeks, as I slept right through the night and woke up refreshed.

25.12.44. On this first tranquil day of Christmas, have been immersed in a delightful book describing the life of a wild goose and her mate. Find in this simple tale, imbued with a love of nature, a welcome diversion from the more complicated and generally less pleasing affairs of men. Only this morning, the sight of a V-shaped formation of about twenty grey geese flying overhead lifted my heart and struck chords of memory. Even as a child, I could stand for hours in a cold room, watching the hordes of birds which descended in fascinating variety on my bird-table. How enviable to be so free and unconstrained.

The winter weather continues more continental than insular, with the ground frozen hard and hoar frost covering the meadows.

Over these Christmas days our meals are as opulent as in times of peace. Over 2,000 chickens have been requisitioned for the troops; an unpopular measure, implemented with considerable difficulty and attended by some farcical scenes. In one case the tarpaulin covering a lorry came adrift and the fowls fluttered off squawking in all directions. Heider even managed to get hold of a goose; what a gastronomical treat.

Am reading a novel by Stephan Andres, *The invisible Barrier*, which recounts the story of a miller in a high mountain valley who lost his mill and his livelihood when the stream was dammed. The style is original and poetic: 'The powerful stream tumbled down from the high forests like an overflow of their grace and majesty'.

In the evening was invited to a party at the Officers' Club by our good Sister Marie. She had set up a toy electric railway and, clad in an unsuitably youthful ballgown and tall paper hat, appeared as a fairy to recite some lengthy guileless verses. An entertainment perhaps more appropriate to a village hall than to an officers' mess in a former elegant British seaside hotel. But we all recognise her goodwill and appreciate her good cooking.

26.12.44. The Red Cross ship has still not turned up. One grows suspicious. Is this delay intentional?

At the Soldiers' Home in St Brelade's Bay, the sisters have exercised great artistic skill in constructing a model of a Christmas fair, with a picture of a typical old German country town as a backdrop. Am much impressed by this example of German ingenuity in constructing something of beauty out of nothing.

In the afternoon, in exhilarating winter sunshine, went cycling with Wetzstein on the beach. The hard-packed wet sand was smooth as a carpet, and our tyres traced fantastic patterns in spirals and curves. Swarms of sandpipers, hidden in the stranded seaweed, rose at our approach and flew off, their bellies glinting in the sunlight, to settle again a few hundred yards further along the beach. Far overhead a flight of well over a hundred lapwings flapped ungainly on their way. The unusually hard and frosty weather has stirred the migratory birds to unusual activity.

Breithaupt, unluckily, did not reach Germany. His 'plane was shot down on the way and all on board, including the four German prisoners-of-war who made such a spectacular escape from Granville, lost their lives.

27.12.44. At 11 o'clock we at last had news from Guernsey that the Red Cross ship had arrived there. By 1 p.m., the Bailiff and I had embarked on a fishing-smack for Guernsey. The sun was shining and the sea as calm as a millpond.

We made slow progress as far as Corbiére, on account of the strong currents. Felt sure I could recognise the reef on which our ship had been stranded. The gallant little *Swallow* is now afloat again, the relatively minor damage having meanwhile been repaired.

Chatted with the Bailiff on the way in that light, half-ironic style, polite but non-committal, which is his normal mode of communication and typical of his cold and matter-of-fact nature. I doubt whether he could conduct a conversation in any other manner; he is not a man of deep emotions. For me it is an acquired art, a useful way of masking my true feelings in a socially acceptable form.

The calm winter sea was unbelievably beautiful. We passed near to Sark, which, with its girdling rocks, its deep bays and the causeway dividing Sark from Little Sark, must be the loveliest island in the archipelago. What ill-luck that, situated so far to the north, it remained unsung by Homer. Then Jethou appeared and Herm, with its modest crown of trees.

As we approached Guernsey, I suddenly glimpsed the looming contours of the white-painted Red Cross ship. Noticed, with some pride, how much sooner I could identify distant objects than the Bailiff, a born islander. He had already mistaken a dark streak on the horizon for Guernsey, an oyster-catcher for a seagull, and, at first, the Red Cross ship for Castle Cornet. It seems that only the nature-lover is gifted with any special power of observations.

Seen from a distance, the ship looked huge, only an optical illusion of course. We joked about this at last visible manifestation of all we had planned for and dreamed about for so many months past; this unlikely salutation from a far world still at peace.

It gradually drew nearer through the winter haze. Our journey was nearly over. The scene had a legendary quality, the islands hovering round us and ahead the white ship bringing succour at last.

We sailed through an undersea whirlpool of strong cross-currents, where, curiously, in the centre of the vortex, the surface of the sea was smoother than the gentle swell of waves around it. In this area the current can reach 13 sea-miles.

The Red Cross ship was tied up to a buoy at some distance from the harbour. We were able to decypher the word *International*, to admire the newly-painted red cross and recognise the Swedish flag.

We had scarcely passed her when a naval control boat darted out from the harbour and fell in behind us. I chaffed the Bailiff that he, as a Jerseyman, had already a closer view of the ship than any of his Guernsey colleagues. He later duly reported this when telephoning the Attorney-General in Jersey.

The Bailiff had been put up at Camplett House, where our Nebenstelle officers are quartered and where I have also been billeted. So I am host and guest at the same time. But he and I are getting used to coping with such abnormal situations with a good humour which our late experience as unlikely companions on the crossing to Guernsey seems only to have increased.

I paid a short visit to the General, whom I was concerned to find apparently very weary and out of sorts. With the compliments of the season, I hung a couple of pigeons on his Christmas tree, where, I could not help thinking, they made a pretty still-life picture. Helldorf had meanwhile joined us and gave his impressions of his first visit to the ship, which had been very satisfactory and had already led to the dispatch of a telegram asking for more flour.

In the evening, the Bailiff, Schneeberger, Mouthe and I enjoyed an excellent meal together at the *Royal Hotel*. We were later joined by Helldorf and soon reached agreement on an agenda for our discussions with the Red Cross Commissioners.

28.12.44. Today the Red Cross commissioners were made officially acquainted with the Bailiff and members of the States of Guernsey. For this ceremonial occasion, a Guernsey 'bobby' was stationed on each of the steps leading up to the Courthouse.

In the Bailiff's cold and spartan chamber, the assembly of white-haired men lined up to meet us made a startling impression of old age, if not senility. The Bailiff himself, obviously animated by goodwill and the excitement of the occasion, still seemed, with his slack features and awkward, fumbling manner, not properly to understand or be in command of the situation. His secretary Guillemette, on the contrary, although he was not strictly speaking entitled to be there, was very much to the fore. He is a rather pushing, but very able and intelligent young official of the Court. I exchanged greetings with various leading personalities, with whom I had long been acquainted.

Then the General, Helldorf and the Red Cross Commissioners arrived, and we all stood up for official introductions and greetings, uncomfortably prolonged as the speakers floundered on until they ran out of words. Only the Bailiff of Jersey, with his customary eloquence, acquitted himself well and even raised a laugh.

In the afternoon we all met for our first conference at lovely old Rosel House. The States of Guernsey appeared extraordinarily bungling and ill-prepared. By and large we soon reached agreement that the *Vega* should visit the islands once a month with 500 tons of flour and a 10 lb. food parcel per head for the population; also that an additional ship should later bring other necessities. Coal, etc., would be requested from England.

The two Red Cross commissioners are entirely unlike in character and appearance.

Colonel Iselin, the senior and head of the Red Cross Delegation in Lisbon, is of middle height and lanky figure. His leathery and deeply-lined face conveys an impression of great strength and tenacity; perhaps too of overwork and suffering. In his tightly-belted mack and wide-brimmed trilby, he at first appears a rather incongruous figure as an international delegate, but one soon senses his absolute integrity of purpose and his determination to see that purpose through. He is punctiliously correct. His Red Cross work has taken him to Mesopotamia and India and he has a fund of stories to tell about these places. In talking he tends to an over-emphasis of gesture, waving his arms in a forceful but also, one feels, forced way, rather like a university professor trying to infuse life into a dry subject. There is something rather dry and pedantic about him; inflexible, too. One has the impression that all he achieves is only by great personal effort and dedication. He is not the less to be respected for that.

His assistant, Callias, has nothing like Iselin's experience and personality. Callias is a good-looking young man, coming from the French-speaking provinces of Switzerland, obviously with a good

French upbringing, pleasant, modest and well-mannered. A much easier man to establish personal contact with, but without any particular intellectual interests. He could as easily have slipped into any job in the civil service or industry.

The General opened the meeting with a few felicitous words. Whatever the occasion, one can be sure that, speaking in his usual quiet confident manner, entirely without affectation, he will grasp the essentials of the situation, strike the right note and capture the sympathy of his listeners.

After his introductory address the General withdrew. Admiral Hüffmeier then took the chair. He would have been better advised to concede this to Helldorf, as being better acquainted with the business in hand and able to follow the proceedings, which were conducted in English, of which the Admiral has little if any knowledge. As it was, he could only sit there, an ineffective figurehead, straining but obviously failing to grasp what was going on. Hunched forward inelegantly, the better to cast a suspicious eye on every speaker, his whole bearing was expressive of mistrust and uncertainty. This attitude is reflected in his general behaviour. I am still unable to get a positive ruling from him as to where the Red Cross ship is to berth in Jersey, although all our forward planning depends on this. He continues to shilly-shally out of an exaggerated concern for military security.

Helldorf, on the other hand, displayed his customary skill and resource, quickly grasping and dealing with the essentials. He is certainly a man of parts and one can always learn a lesson from him, especially from the way in which, on this occasion, he politely deferred to the senior officers present, although he had already made up his mind and was in virtual command of the situation. I must marvel at all I still have to learn.

Of those present, I was probably the only one to let my gaze wander all too frequently to the big window, where the evening sky darkened behind the lovely old trees in the park. I must always force my attention away from nature to play my proper part in the complicated machinery of human affairs, unlike the coolly calculating Bailiff of Jersey, the pedantically correct Swiss colonel, or even pleasant, harmless young Andre Callias.

The Bailiff and Helldorf are wordly-wise types, whose natural bent is for public affairs; each achieves his own ends in his own way. The Swiss colonel I found more than ever stiff and professorial; all his responses, even his friendliness, seem constrained and geared to the occasion. But it is of course for him a difficult occasion. Two such disparate characters as he and I are hardly likely to hit it off. He probably regards me with some suspicion as over-liberal, unworldly and artistically inclined. True enough; true enough, too, that his strait-laced attitude moves me to rather schoolboyish derision for the stuffy old Head, while in no way detracting from my genuine regard for his unimpeachably correct behaviour and conduct of affairs.

In the evening had supper with the Bailiff and Schneeberger at the *Royal Hotel*. Conversation was restricted to the social and superficial, avoiding offence to either side. Schneeberger is a clever and courteous man, who improves on closer acquaintance. He has a curiously elongated face, reminiscent of those of Charles V and Philip II in old Spanish paintings.

Finished the evening with Helldorf at his quarters. All talks with him take place in a pleasant atmosphere of common sense and liberality, leading to swift and practical decisions. In fact I would like now to record that, in view of recent experience, I must retract much of my previous criticism of him. He is a gentleman in the best sense of the word. Also, in appearance, the smartest and best-looking officer in the islands, which, plus his undoubted ability, in itself gives him a certain ascendancy.

29.12.44. Took Callias on a drive through some of the main streets of the town. He was quite struck by the girls' silk stockings and the rosy cheeks of the infants. We soon established good relations and I felt he was convinced of my honesty and plain dealing. He even offered, quite spontaneously, to bring me anything I wished on the next trip from Lisbon, an offer which I declined, apart from newspapers. After the horror stories he had heard about concentration camps, deforestation, mass shooting, etc., in the Channel Islands, he was clearly surprised and favourably impressed.

Indeed, the Red Cross Commission seems to have been so much impressed by the good relations between the German troops and the civilian population, that they invited us together with the Bailiff for a meal aboard the ship. I would personally not have had the slightest objection to this, but of course war is war, and we could scarcely sit down to dinner, on the invitation of a neutral power, with our enemies, even if, living among them, one tends to forget they are enemies at all. So the invitation to the Bailiff had to be cancelled at, I am afraid, rather short notice.

So the General, the Admiral, Helldorf and I, together of course with the two Red Cross delegates, were entertained aboard the *Vega* as guests of the Swedish captain. His small cabin was impressively furnished with polished wood and well-burnished brass. The meal offered was out of this world, certainly out of our world, as castaways on these islands: French piquance supplemented by Swedish liberality. First hors d'ouevres, ten sorts, with white bread and mountains of butter. Then fried frankfurters with omelette, then asparagus with butter sauce. And then, after an hour and a half the meal proper began, with six courses, champagne and real coffee and liqueurs to finish up with. Such plenitude bordered on the ridiculous and I could often have laughed aloud, especially at the sight of the well-nourished captain in his fine uniform, playing host in his cosy shining cabin, epitomising a second carefree generation untroubled by war, That such living conditions still exist in this world is astonishing. One's stomach must also have been surprised at receiving such quantity and quality of sustenance for the first time in many years, in fact since before the war. The meal lasted four hours, so that we had to postpone the time for our afternoon conference.

In the evening a return dinner-party was given by the General; very spartan and of necessity lacking in peace-time delicacies. I sat next to the Swedish captain, whose bonhomie is rather that of the good businessman. The Swiss colonel entertained us with an account of his hunting adventures in India, with a great deal of wooden gesticulation. Callias appeared in his customary daytime apparel of sports jacket and flannels. One would have thought he would have equipped himself with clothing more appropriate to the social obligations of his mission.

30.12.44. Leave-taking of the *Vega* at the harbour. Again all the highest ranking dignitaries were present and I – I am afraid exciting some envy – was again among them. Reminded myself of 'lieber Augustin', a character with whom I have much in common, who was also once called on to play a role in high diplomacy and fared badly at it.

Have had a bit of a set-to with those stupid security people, who disapproved of my having taken Callias to Cambridge Park, not because Cambridge Park has any military secrets to hide, but because they had not been aware of this visit. As I knew they might report me to the General, I went over to the offensive. Had they been aware, I asked, that at the departure of the *Vega*, that smart young chap Guillemette, the Guernsey Bailiff's secretary, had somehow got into the strictly guarded harbour area, with some papers in his hand which he obviously intended to hand over to the Red Cross commissioners and would have done so if I had not been keeping an eagle eye on him? Completely nonplussed, the Abwehr let me off with a caution, in the shape of the usual long lecture on the security of our defences, to which I listened with a sardonic grin.

In St Peter Port, the Red Cross parcels are already being distributed; a scene of happy activity. The Bailiff has published a warning that the contents must be made to last and on no account be employed for black market purposes. Blackmarketing aside, I fancy that by evening many a German soldier, who has become friendly with or given a helping hand to an islander, will have been given a taste of the goodies.

In the afternoon, under a dull overcast sky, returned to Jersey with the Bailiff on a small warship. Owing to the odd situations in which we have recently found ourselves together, calling for tact and good humour on both sides, our relationship has become much more cordial and we passed the time in a frank exchange of views on all sorts of subjects.

On arriving in Jersey, found a number of officers awaiting me on the quay, with an interest due no doubt more to my mission than my person. The Harbour Commandant expressed the view that I could be the only person to make the arrangements for the Red Cross commissioners' stay in Jersey, on account of the social responsibilities involved. Very flattering for a person generally avoiding rather than seeking the company of his fellowmen to find himself so suddenly a social lion. But if I had had any inclination to preen myself on this newfound popularity, it was quickly dispelled by the sight of the rest of the faces around me. Wegner enquired in half jocular, half sour manner whether, after my 'distinguished mission', I should be able to find time for him. Another bespectacled grammar school type extended a flabby hand. The Head of I.c. (military security) was obviously gratified to be handed some top secret documents, 'hand of officer' from Guernsey HQ.

Colonel Heine wished to speak to me immediately and I gave him a brief report. He is interested only in the nuts and bolts of procedure and was fussily and longwindedly concerned about keeping the reception to the precedent already established in Guernsey.

Later returned to the harbour for the arrival of the *Vega*. Went on board with Cleve and Schade. The Captain reported with a glum face that his ship had been damaged on entering the harbour owing to insufficient draught and would need a long time in the dock for repairs. So the navy has managed to make a mess of the only task they have been called upon to perform in this vital operation. If the ship is laid up, it will be disastrous.

Spent the evening quietly with Pokorny, Woelken and Heider in a desultory exchange of news and views. They have meanwhile been making all arrangements for transport with regard to the *Vega* and its cargo. Then fell into bed, dead tired after all the new experiences and impressions of the last few days, which had even temporarily driven my constant worry about my wife to the back of my mind.

31.12.44. This morning went through the performance of formal introductions between the Red Cross commissioners and the island military and civilian authorities once again. This time the venue was the office of Colonel Heine, the Island Commander.

Heine spoke a few stiff, rehearsed sentences, obviously dictated by duty rather than by feeling or any involvement in the situation. How well our General manages these things, always with the right word in the right place, adapting to the occasion but remaining master of it and always speaking with warmth and sincerity.

Heider too showed an embarrassing lack of tact and sense of occasion. Could not help feeling that his concern for the well-being of the commissioners was not unconnected with the speculation that he too might be invited to that mouth watering midday meal aboard the ship for which the Colonel has already received an invitation for Tuesday next.

Following Guernsey precedent, our first sitting was held in the afternoon, with the Bailiff of Jersey adroitly conducting proceedings in proper parliamentary style. Heine again spoke a few introductory words, rather prematurely, before everyone was seated and sounding rather stilted and flustered. He is a conscientious military officer, but scarcely equipped to deal with such situations as this.

Now in Jersey too the long lines of trucks carrying Red Cross parcels are rolling into the depots. That it has all gone off so smoothly is due to Pokorny's hard work. It is the sort of job in which he is in his element and he looks so much better that I wish, for his sake, that many more such tasks could come his way. He confessed to me in the evening, however, that his heart had been playing up, so perhaps this accounts for the colour in his cheeks.

A talk with the Swedish captain established that the damage to his ship is nothing like as serious as he first claimed. He also confided, in the course of our chat, that the man who follows the sea should get his first command and his own ship not much over the age of 40, otherwise he would have grown too accustomed to obeying orders and no longer have the self-confidence to issue them. The same, I suppose, might apply to those steering the ship of state.

The Swiss colonel, lacking as he may be in personal charm and social graces, impresses me more than ever as having achieved his pre-eminence by sheer personal effort and integrity. He is formidably well-read and well-informed, austere and irreproachably correct. A man deserving of one's highest respect and regard.

Chapter Four

January – February 1945

1.1.45. Celebrated – if that is the right word – New Year's Eve with other members of the mess in Langford House. Sat next to Pokorny and we mulled over the events of the past year. Was painfully reminded of my poor wife's situation and conscience-stricken that the pressure of work had so often diverted my thoughts from her. Worst of all is the realisation that I am so powerless to help her.

This morning Colonel Heine gave a New Year's Day reception at the Officers' Club. This afternoon I took Colonel Iselin on a drive round the island. First showed him Oakland Farm, with its still impressive if now much reduced stock of bulls. We then went on to La Hougue Bie, Mont Orgeuil Castle, Rozel Manor and St Catharine's Bay. Had to take the greatest care not to make any bloomers in my descriptions, as the colonel is damnably erudite.

Afterwards we went back to the mess for tea, to which the Colonel contributed a snow-white Portuguese cake. I brought up several subjects which had been much on my mind and the Colonel soon warmed to the debate. We discussed the legal complications of the situation here and jokingly agreed that there really ought to be another Hague Conference in Jersey after the war. I spoke of my concern about deforestation in the island and the decimation of the valuable animal livestock, of which he had seen some surviving examples today. I put it to him whether, taking a long-term view of the island's future, something could not be done to prevent this unique breed of cattle being slaughtered to extinction. He thought this was extremely doubtful. But whether he can do anything about it or not, I have at least salved my conscience by bringing the matter to his attention.

The best part of this first long day of the year was the very early morning, when I went for a ride on Nestor, a game and sturdy little horse, undismayed by such a weighty and long-legged rider. On the way paid a brief call on Wetzstein, to be greeted ecstatically by his lovely little golden spaniel, Winnie. Have long been touched by her devotion to me. How faithful and affectionate animals are; no human being would, or perhaps could, be so demonstrative. Lucky those blessed in the cradle with a natural affinity with dogs and horses.

2.1.45. The round of official tours and luncheon parties continues, with the same faces reappearing. This afternoon I showed Colonel Iselin over the grounds of Samarès Manor. He is so damnably well-informed. If one points out a magnolia tree, he enquires whether it is a *magnolia poetica* or a *goliata*. When, on yesterday's drive, racking my brain for some appropriate comment, I referred to Neolithic remains in Jersey, it transpired that he was well-versed in the Neolithic period from early to late. Gladly concede him superiority in the academic field. Quite exhausted by the effort to keep pace with his erudition, I consoled myself with the thought that my more modest scholarship still enabled me to enjoy the world around me, even without such encyclopaedic knowledge of it.

After leaving Samarès Manor, we went on to inspect a baker's oven, where people can bring their dishes to be cooked, and a public kitchen which caters for the poorer members of the community. The meals being prepared in the kitchen were in fact rather better than our own average midday meal.

Not, however, our meal today, when we were again invited to luncheon on board the *Vega*. For details please refer to my previous description, written in the first flush of enthusiasm. Am not such a glutton as to wish to dwell on it all over again.

For the Inselkommandant, Colonel Heine and the Platzkommandant, Major Heider, it was their first experience of the gargantuan meal. The naval captain, von Cleve, was able to make authoritative contributions to our discussion of the various brands of tobacco from his experience as a tobacco merchant in Greece before the war.

Afterwards, well-fed and smiling, we all assembled on the deck to be photographed, in proper conference style. From the quay above, sailors peered down at us, no doubt dreaming, poor devils, of all the good things the odours wafted to them had conjured up. And the photographer's camera clicked to record the slightly flushed and contented faces of this small band of fortunate beings in the afternoon sunlight.

Again the length of the meal made us late for our next appointment. This was a tour of the Royal Court, followed by tea with the Bailiff. In the Royal Court Ralph Mollet, the Bailiff's secretary, showed us the silver-gilt mace given to the States of Jersey by Charles II, in acknowledgement of the island's loyalty to him during the Civil War. He had never shown me this historical treasure before, perhaps out of fear that the greedy Germans might confiscate it.

Tea with the Bailiff was a pleasantly informal but stimulating occasion. His house is full of paintings by Blampied, the local artist, which I find lacking in taste. But he has some lovely old furniture and before we left his wife showed us an interesting and valuable collection of snuff-boxes.

The visit certainly afforded the Red Cross Commission still further evidence of the good relations between the Bailiff and me, as representatives of the island government on the one hand and German admininistration on the other, and could have some effect on British policy towards the islands. In these circumstances it would hardly be expedient to engage in a costly attack on them, and we might continue to hold them as a bargaining factor. But who can tell, in this uncertain world, how men's minds work; even the good reputation we have established here could be held against us.

5.1.45. The past couple of days have been busy ones, between routine work and Red Cross affairs. On 3 January we drove out to St Brelade's Bay in the morning and at midday were invited to luncheon by Colonel Heine.

The guests in general sat around the table with scarcely a word to say. Colonel Heine asked a few commonplace questions. It was left to Colonel Iselin and me to keep the conversation going. Happily we discovered a common interest in waterways, of which we could both speak from experience.

Our next sitting followed at 3 p.m., this time at Langford House and undisturbed by a coffee break. The Bailiff again brought his closest parliamentary associates along, mostly elderly men and looking rather out of their depth.

The painful but vital question was posed as to whether the Red Cross parcels were intended as rations for the civilian population or only as supplementary to rations. Colonel Iselin stated that they were supplementary. At this the Jersey contingent broke into such a storm of applause that they might have been sitting in their own States Chamber, instead of being present, here in Guernsey, only out of courtesy and in an advisory capacity. I had to check this unseemly demonstration and announced that, whether or not the parcels were intended to be supplementary, they would still have largely to replace the ever-dwindling rations available. The Jersey side then demanded what basic rations we could guarantee them.

I appealed to Major Schade, who was chairing the meeting on behalf of Colonel Heine, to call a halt to this profitless discussion, as I was there only to administer the policy decided on by our H.Q., and was in no position to inform the island representatives what that policy might in future be. But poor Schade, unable to follow the proceedings either in English or French and inhibited by his German inferiority complex from asking the interpreter for elucidation, completely missed the appropriate moment to break it up, and the impassioned debate continued.

At this stage there was a telephone call from Helldorf in Guernsey. Heider answered it and gave a probably inaccurate and exaggerated account of our lively proceedings.

As a result I had a telephone call in the evening from an irate General who seemed under the impression that I had initiated renewed negotiations with the Red Cross commissioners, which, after the negotiations already concluded in Guernsey, seemed to him superfluous and uncalled for. In fact, of course, we had kept strictly to the precedent and principle laid down in Guernsey, allowing only for some difference in local conditions, which had been agreed in advance.

In fact too, I feel, the differences of opinion brought to light in today's rather stormy meeting can only be salutary in clearing the air and making plain to both the Red Cross commissioners and to the States of Jersey Superior Council, the extreme gravity of the situation. There is much to be said for democracy, even if I was incensed today by the way in which the Jerseymen briefly but noisily took over a floor to which they had only been admitted by favour.

On 4 January the Red Cross commissioners at last departed. I breathed a sigh of relief. Taking leave of them on board, I caught sight of the Bailiff on the quay, to which he had presumably been admitted in all innocence by a series of security posts, and waved him a polite greeting. At last the long awaited visit of the Red Cross commissioners is over. Both sides were undoubtedly favourably impressed and the agreement reached provides justifiable grounds for a continuance of the policy we had already embarked on.

The ship skilfully manoeuvred its way out of the harbour in a strong north wind to gain the open sea. Watching its departure brought home to me what an important chapter in local history its visit represented; an occasion in which I had been called on to play a not unimportant part. How fortunate for all concerned that the enemy decided not to root out the canker in the body politic, the occupying forces, at sword's point and at the cost of suffering and bloodshed, but instead to send a ministering angel to their compatriots in the shape of the Red Cross ship.

On 6 January I gave a talk at the Jersey Kriegsschule (military academy) on the Channel Islands, taking as my motto Goethe's dictum that men must seek enlightenment in the world around them.

According to a notice in the following day's paper, M.v.R. von Aufsess[1] engaged the interest of his audience in an informed but informal talk on the hundred and one beauties and singularities of the Channel Islands, some of them obvious, some to be found only by the interested seeker: 'a scholarly review, happily lacking in pedantic dryness'.

I noticed that many of my listeners seemed surprised by my view that military service in the islands was not necessarily a cause for complaint, rather an experience to be enjoyed.

I went on to say that we, of Military Administration, had now been 'islanders' for over four years and had amassed a wealth of fascinating information on our temporary homeland. We even had a file on St Magloire, who had founded a monastery in Sark, from which missionaries set out to christianise the countries round them.

This brought me to more modern times. One day a local Jesuit priest had come to me to ask my help. He had devoted his life to researching the work of St Magloire (or St Mannelier as he is known locally) in the Channel Islands, and wished to send the box of manuscripts he brought with him to the Pope. After ascertaining that I.c. (military security) had no objections to raise to St Magloire's activities in the Channel Islands, I took the box with me to Granville when going on leave and from there addressed it to the Pope. In due course, I received an acknowledgement of receipt direct from the Vatican, and as a token of gratitude from the Jesuits, a regular supply of fine pears from their garden.

Other odd link-ups of ancient with modern times provided further anecdotes. Speaking of the discovery of the remains of Neanderthal man in a cave at La Cotte Point in St Brelade's Bay, as a matter of interest to anthropologists the world over, including our own renowned specialist in the field and former Reich Chancellor, Hans Luther, I was able to tell my listeners about a visit this eminent man paid to the island only a couple of years ago. He signed his name in the guest book of Soldatenheim II at St Brelade's Bay simply as 'Hans Luther'. The disappointed Matron of the home begged him to add his titles. He then added to his name 'a.D.'. [Ausser Dienst = retired]. 'Oh but, Herr Reichskanzler', protested the Matron 'You really must add your proper title'. At which Luther appended his entry with 'Wehrmachtsgefolge'. [Forces' auxiliary]. Having been engaged by the Wehrmacht to travel around lecturing to the forces, this was in fact his official designation in his identity documents. Such modesty can result only from a study of the antiquity of man, and Neanderthal man, according to Luther himself, dates back a million years.

8.1.45. With the release from the additional pressure of work with the Commission, all my anxiety about my family overwhelms me with redoubled force. In complete contrast, a gay and entertaining book I am reading, *The Good Life* by Schlagintweit, set in the familiar and well-loved scenes of my own countryside, reminds me of what my own life might have been like if it had not been for the war.

Two American prisoners-of-war have escaped from the prison camp. Kessler, of I.c., is making a great fuss about taking all measures to find them, if only for the sake of taking all possible measures, etc., and without much hope of success.

Our latest orders impose further restrictions on the number of dogs and the amount of reserve foodstuffs the individual householder is permitted to maintain. Harsh measures made easier to carry out, if not justified, by the mood of euphoria induced in the civilian population by the arrival of the Red Cross parcels.

9.1.45. Spent the night in waking nightmares.

10.1.45. It is not commonly realised that a light touch is sometimes useful in dealing with serious matters. We have just had a conference on implementing the new severe cut in the fat ration. The canny farmer Bree, and Le Masurier, the genial representative of Essential Commodities, were both responsive to my humorous, if of necessity grimly humorous, approach and the meeting passed off smoothly, even with a good deal of laughter. The stolid Nazi, Ten Harmsen, looked bewildered; he must have thought I was giving way all along the line, but in fact all our demands were successfully pushed through.

Have again been twice let down badly by the over-clever Councillor Woelken. He has a plausible reason for all he does but no grasp of affairs.

Am reading Karl Schäffer's book on travels in Italy. He writes outstandingly well and with great artistic perception. Botticelli's angels, for instance, he describes as expressive of the sum total of knowledge, from the carnal to the purely intellectual. He finds Raphael's works supreme in draughtsmanship and grouping but lacking in religious awe and human feeling. His (Raphael's) madonnas are about as maternal as a stone and might well have been fructified by the Holy Ghost. They have not conceived and borne the Child in earthly love, travail and joy. Their harmony is negative of human values.

11.1.45. The cold, stormy weather continues. This morning there was snow on the ground. The indiscriminate destruction of the island's timber, by freezing islanders and troops alike, is reaching alarming proportions. In Waterworks Valley, young trees, planted quite recently and not yet grown to half their height, have been chopped down. We shall have to post guards to prevent further vandalism.

All potatoes have been removed from the vicinity of the Russian battalion, as they could no longer be protected from the Russians' depredations. They are adept not only in stealing but in concealing their booty underground or even among the minefields to escape detection by the Field Police.

Requisitioning and the sentencing of offenders continues, while the need to introduce further prohibitions and decrees increases. I am tied to the office desk from morning till night by this unpleasant work. There is electrtic light for only a few hours a day; it will cease altogether this month.

In the lunch hour with Marie von Wedel in the grounds of Samarès Manor. In the icy wind we searched for something to make a birthday bouquet. We found a few camellias, some blossoming witch-hazel twigs and boughs with coral-red berries, which she skilfully interwove. We are like brother and sister together in comfortable companionship.

Now, most regrettably, the felling of timber by the troops will soon start in earnest. In a year's time there will not be a tree left on the island. The last of what one holds dear is doomed to vanish. In the bitter cold, I think with anguish of the plight of my wife and children.

We have been assigned a Superintendent of Forestry, whose job it will be to coordinate the tree-felling activities of troops and civilian authorities under an overall command. He is a first lieutenant and comes from the east of Germany. Such a comic giant of a man could only come from the east, with his Punch-like features and a mouth like that we used as children to carve in hollowed-out pumpkins; a veritable figure of woodland myth. But his grotesque appearance sits lightly on him; his naive confidence in his own ability is so absolute that it commands, if not credence, at least a measure of respect.

Have just seen an avant-garde film, *Symphony of Life*, which correlates the composition of a symphony with the lives of those concerned. Found the leading actor, a Frenchman, unconvincing. He mimes too much, reducing life's tragedies to senseless grimaces. Another instance of our great neighbour's tendency to become trapped in the stereotyped and superficial. The French are no good at drama; their own best attribute of *savoir vivre* precludes them from the expression of feeling.

12.1.45. The importance of the law as an institution is daily brought home to me here, in what is perhaps an unique fashion. Although we have absolute power in the land and the right to exercise it to our own advantage and have in fact been doing that for some years past, it has always been through duly promulgated decrees. The arbitrary exercise of power has never been permitted; to have abandoned the proper processes of the law would have undermined our own authority and led to chaos.

Bohde, the Chief of the Secret Field Police, had confiscated over 300 tins of foodstuffs found in a search of the premises of the antiques dealer Burger, illegally I fear, as there is no law prohibiting the possession of such a number. In our orders defining the stocks which the individual householder might hold, pre-war tins were permitted on the reasonable assumption that most people would have laid in a few, but such large stocks were not envisaged, particularly at this stage. I immediately took steps for the issue of an order forbidding such monstrous private hoards, but returned the tins to Burger. The amount is of course negligible in comparison with the size of the garrison, although I can understand the soldiers' bewilderment at my action, their eyes on the 300 tins and their empty bellies protesting. But the important point is that we could only have prosecuted him on the basis of a law already in force at the time of the discovery.

We have to arrange for the collection of 800 tins of potatoes from civilian stocks, for which a requisitioning order has just been issued. Ambacher lost his head and would have stormed and blustered at Jurat Bree, but I was fortunately able to restrain him. I hope, too, that I made clear to him in half an hour's negotiation with the Jurat, how much better these things can be managed by patience and circumspection, taking into account the adversary's viewpoint, feeling one's way round obstacles and finding the path of least resistance. An open display of power and unequivocal issuing of orders is seldom justified and never expedient.

Our woodland giant is instructing his team of forestry experts in their new duties. They are a sorry-looking lot of soldiers in their shabby field grey, with pale, weary faces and an air of total apathy and exhaustion. Their power of resistance must be low and one wonders where they will find the stamina for the job now facing them, the felling of 6,000 metres of timber, with little food in their bellies or hope in their hearts.

13.1.45. My Jesuit father friend, in whose urbane presence I take increasing comfort in these difficult times, has found me a book I have long been looking for, Keyserling's *America Set Free*. Keyserling has always struck me as the elegant croupier among philosophers, pushing his ideas around as freely as counters on the board, while his confréres tend to part as grudgingly with theirs as the savings bank clerk carefully paying out banknotes. Admittedly, Keyserling may fall short on exactitude, but in general he hits the target and is entertaining in an agreeably sophisticated but intellectually satisfying manner.

Work which involves decision-making, planning and organisation really requires time for taking soundings and for due reflection. If undertaken at a hectic pace under pressure of circumstance, it must suffer. So, although I get through a vast amount of work, I am always left with the uncomfortable feeling that something is lacking or that I must have gone wrong somewhere.

The sight of the havoc wrought by the indiscriminate hacking down of trees is so depressing that I scarcely dare to venture out of doors.

Along the front, ancient and characteristic evergreen oaks have been felled without my permission. These trees had been tossed and bent by the storm winds into fantastic pennant-like shapes which formed a unique frame to the picture of the sea and Elizabeth Castle beyond. The local people are curiously insensitive to the beauty of their island. The capital town of St Helier is a good example of this, with its utilitarian buildings and uncompromisingly commercial air, devoid of artistic merit or natural affinity with the surrounding countryside. Humanly speaking, of course, it is painful to have to check the famished, freezing people in their search for fuel, especially as the cold is abnormal for these parts; tonight it registered six degrees C. below freezing.

12.1.45. Sunday. The townspeople's assault on any trees within reach, in their frenzied search for fuel, today escalated into what almost amounts to a public uprising. Following yesterday's felling of some of the wonderful old evergreen oaks along Victoria Avenue – we had warned the local police to keep a watch on these trees – this morning the people turned out in strength and, armed with saws and axes, descended on the avenue in hordes. By the time I had been notified and arrived on the scene, it was one of total devastation, of hacked off branches and mutilated stumps. The local police were conspicuously absent.

I at once started taking identity cards and confiscating axes and saws. But the numbers were so great and perhaps, too, as my fury abated my sympathy with these poor freezing people increased, and I abandoned the task. The rest of them departed, looking rather crestfallen, some dragging branches behind them secured by ropes round their shoulders, others bent double under the weight of logs or pushing high-piled perambulators, leaving the ravaged avenue as a backdrop to the sorry scene.

There could be no more graphic illustration of the States' failure to meet their responsibilities. In spite of it being a Sunday, I summoned the Bailiff, the Attorney-General, the forestry representative and the Constable of St Helier, and confronted them on the spot with this evidence of their neglect of their duties.

There are plenty of places on the island where timber could have been felled for civilian requirements, without lasting damage. But the decimation of this beautiful avenue is an irreparable loss to the island. It will be 50 years at least before the trees can again reach the stature and fantastic shape which lent the avenue its special charm.

Up to now the troops have not been allowed to fell a single tree. The most they have been permitted is the more onerous task of rooting up the stumps of trees already felled. The States, on the other hand, have been informed by me often enough of sites where they had my full permission to fell trees. We had even backed up this permission by what we hoped were helpful suggestions as to recruiting young unemployed men to assist with felling, issuing felling permits, etc. Their excuses for not acting on this were various, but the chief one was the lack of tools and transport. On this occasion at least, I was able to point out, neither tools nor transport had been lacking, as in one morning dozens of stout trees had been cut down and carted away. This had been brought about by a lack of organisation on the part of the States and a lack of concern for the needs of the people and the conservation of the island's beauties.

The Bailiff made a sour face and appeared highly offended. German soldiers, he claimed, had already started cutting down trees in the park. If this is true and he had witnessed it he should immediately have reported it to me; he must know by now how concerned I am about the possible effects of deforestation and how strictly I have forbidden the felling of trees by the troops. I must have some deep-seated Teutonic devotion to trees and their preservation to have got so worked up on this occasion. My fervour communicated itself to Bleuel, who became so loud-voiced in his protests that I bundled him into the car to prevent any further recriminations.

In the afternoon made a tour of the island and visited the various field police stations. Thefts are increasing at an alarming rate. Found the field police short of everything; no light, little heating, poor food, insufficient clothing, no petrol, no tyres for their vehicles, etc. The effects of the long siege make themselves more drastically felt with every day. I am troubled by the comparative advantages I still enjoy at command headquarters, thanks to the care and forethought of my staff officers.

Have finished Schäffler's book on Italy; very enjoyable. He makes some pertinent observations. One recognises the influence which, as he points out, the Italian renaissance had on French domestic architecture of the 17th century, particularly in the development of the Palladian style, when the classic column was so successfully incorporated into houses of especial charm and grace. And this despite the oft-repeated tag that the column is the prostitute of architecture.

Have also been having another look at Keyserling's verdict on Germany and the Germans. According to him, our imagination outstrips our sense of reality. In support of this he quotes an English writer who humorously remarked, 'Show any German two doors, one marked "Heaven", the other "Twelve lessons on how to get to Heaven", and he would invariably choose the latter'.

13.1.45. The Russians' winter offensive is now gathering momentum on a wide front and they are approaching dangerously near to our frontiers. I have had no further news from home and am desperately worried.

Am reading Morand's *From Paris to Timbuctoo*, the travels of the typical Frenchman as popularly imagined. His interest centres on the charms of the young native women, particularly their bared breasts. 'The Governor of the Ivory Coast' he writes, 'informed me that one could assess the political climate by looking at the women. If they all had hanging breasts they were old women; the young women did not dare venture out and this meant that the white man was regarded as an enemy and one must take care as it was a dangerous situation.'

16.1.45. The incurable optimists among us still profess to believe in an ultimately favourable outcome to the war. If they really believe this, what crises of conscience must they be suffering? Would not an ultimate victory for Hitler now be worse than defeat? My wife can now be freed only by the advancing Russians or the advancing Americans. If Hitler were to triumph after all, we should neither of us have anything to look forward to in our own country but humiliation and prison, perhaps the gallows.

The success of the Russian offensive is so stupendous that it tends to reduce local events to a parochial level. But the situation here is serious enough for those involved in it; deteriorating daily and obviously approaching a disastrous general breakdown. I do my best to cope on half a dozen fronts, but cannot hope to do more than stave off or delay the ultimate collapse.

With the confiscation of butter, the milk deliveries fall short. The farmers have delivered only half the quantity of potatoes they were called on to supply. The glasshouses cannot grow early potatoes without petrol to pump the water. The Department of Transport has no more dry wood for generators to drive lorries. In short all depends on more petrol, just when the petrol ration has been drastically reduced.

For the time being, felling trees has been forbidden for everybody, although the weather continues bitterly cold, with a bone-penetrating damp.

The military authorities are insatiable in their demands for more and more requisitioning in the civilian sector, out of their own desperate need, growing daily more irascible and difficult to deal with, as are indeed the hungry soldiers themselves.

Every day I issue new regulations, with the threat of increased penalties for breaking them. But fines and gaol sentences continue to rise at a fantastic rate. Soon there will be nothing left we can forbid to people, except to live.

The latest demand from the garrison is for 700 axes and 300 saws. No doubt such a quantity is in the possession of the local population, but how to get at them? There must come a breaking point and I do not wish to push our demands beyond this.

I dream up schemes for coaxing the islanders to part with these coveted tools in return for permits to fell timber. But I doubt whether I should get much cooperation from the States. They are like children or dotards in steadfastly refusing to face up to the disaster which impends or to try to do anything about it. Have long since reconciled myself to this state of affairs. I cannot change it and feel no inclination to adopt military tactics by just bawling at them. In the long run I find the German military officer has more of the sergeant-major and primary schoolteacher in his make-up than the attributes of the realist and diplomat.

21.1.45. The Russian offensive has now attained such a tremendous impetus that one can no longer believe that their advance will be held up at the frontier. So perhaps it will be the Russians who will free my wife, if she is still alive, if she has survived the bombardment of Linz. I cannot commit to paper the terrors that haunt my sleepless nights.

Military Administration is pushing on with its campaign of reorganisation in all sectors. Last week we had a meeting of the constables, the dairy owners, the glasshouse owners and the officials responsible for timber. My own state of mind is such that it is difficult to summon up the energy and concentration which the problems involved demand. In two matters on the agenda I allowed the opinion of the others to prevail, although I felt sure that the course of action they advised would prove fruitless. I was too weary to argue and thought, let them find out for themselves. But this of course will only lead to loss of time and of foodstuffs, both of inestimable value to us.

So yesterday I went on a tour of inspection to check how the building of the greenhouses was progressing. It is not progressing at all and it was senseless of Ambacher to have embarked on the project in the first place. In every case work was held up by some problem, differing from one greenhouse to the next. All these matters will have to be investigated in detail to arrive at any solution.

Jurat Bree, the States' astute and wily little farming expert, hurried before me like an eager terrier through the mire of the various farmyards and greenhouses, and between us we soon established that the claims made for the benefits we were going to enjoy from the produce of these greenhouses had been vastly exaggerated. I brought to the exercise, besides my greater height, the backing of authority and Bree the expertise of local knowledge. We must have seemed a comic pair to the onlooker; the long and the short of it. But the long and short of the conclusion we reached is certainly not a matter to be laughed off.

Woelken has been employing his leisure time in writing a lecture on England, well thought out and most apt; worthy I feel of a wide audience. But it is a lecture which must remain an intellectual exercise; impossible to deliver it in present circumstances, when our officers and potential officers are permitted to view the world only through the blinkers of Nazi policy.

23.1.45. Am gradually dragging myself out of a deep depression, which has lasted for over a week and from which, I know, my work has suffered. This will not do; I need all my wits about me to cope with the ever-mounting problems.

Today we had an hour-long session with the Bailiff on the acute shortage of firewood. All felling had been temporarily suspended pending the implentation of the new overall plan now being worked out. Now a fresh calamity threatens; the bakers' ovens have only enough fuel left for three more days. I had to call in our new forestry director and eventually we arrived at a compromise allowing for emergency measures to tide us over this crisis until the new regulations come into effect.

The perils and uncertainties of the situation are increased by the growing hunger of the troops. They are 'kidnapping' and slaughtering cats and dogs everywhere. They made an application for permission to shoot seabirds, chiefly of course gulls, with carbines. Fortunately Heine turned this down on the grounds of endangering public safety. Up to January the soldiers had stolen 900 cwt. of potatoes. House breaking, robbery and the procurement of goods under a false assumption of authority are the order of the day. Furniture is smashed and floorboards wrenched up for use as firewood.

The first cases of soldiers dying of malnutrition have been reported from Guernsey. Soldiers here have told me how, on standing guard for the second time, they could hold out no longer and wolfed down their bread ration for days ahead.

There has been no further news of the Red Cross ship. The stock of flour for the civilians will run out in ten days' time. Helldorf, who is still resentful of the negotiations we had with the Red Cross commissioners here, although he did not fail to take credit for the reports I sent him on this, has already dispatched a telegram about the dire shortage of flour.

It is reported that the state of the Channel Islands has been debated in the British parliament and that British support of the islands has been rejected as being too costly.

A widespread network for emergency lighting is being set up, as the day after tomorrow the two hours of electricity in the evening will also cease. This frightful retrogression in every aspect of the human scene makes one long for the end to come here, even that inevitable end so grimly heralded for us by the formidable Russian advance. No more letters from Germany since November.

24.1.45. The policy of wait-and-see, as against precipitate action, has much to recommend it. Left alone, the problem will either resolve itself or develop to a stage where the course of action becomes clear, in fact inevitable. In this I find myself much in accord with the British.

We have worked out a plan for the emergency supply of electricity to military units and have obtained military consent to this, including 14 essential civilian services. The plan depends, of course, on the plant still being worked by local staff, as it has been in the past.

Now the electricity works manager, Burrell, is opposing the scheme. This was quite unexpected. Pokorny, who has always enjoyed a good working relationship with him, says it is the greatest letdown he has ever experienced. I would myself adjudge Burrell as a rather simple-minded man, a good technician with the technician's narrowness of view. Now, having taken a dislike to the scheme, he is digging in his heels and being thoroughly pigheaded. Perhaps his feelings have been worked on by would-be patriots, or, with the end approaching, he is getting worried about having cooperated with the occupying power up to now. We encountered the same intransigence in the manager of the gas works when that service petered out, and it caused us considerable embarrassment and difficulty. Perhaps the last-minute defiance in both cases was motivated by nothing more than the technician's devotion to 'my gas works' and 'my electricity works' and an inability to reconcile himself to this sacrosanct service petering out to a prolonged and humiliating end and being expected as it were to attend the obsequies.

However that may be, at a meeting with the electricity company this morning, the plan was rejected. Jurat Dorey and Mr. Burrell attended the meeting. I could see from Burrell's half-defiant, half shamefaced demeanour, that he was the prime mover in the opposition. I received them in quiet and conciliatory fashion, expressed regret at their decision, but declared myself still ready to do my best for the civilian population, although of course the rejection of the scheme would render my path in this respect more difficult. This unexpectedly courteous reception obviously put them in rather a spot and there were some mumbled apologies.

The Bailiff had contacted me in the morning to express his satisfaction with our emergency measures to deal with the firewood crisis and to express his thanks for my intervention in the matter. In the afternoon he came to see me again, at my urgent invitation. I put it to him very seriously that if the electricity company refused their

JANUARY – FEBRUARY 1945

assistance in our plan for an emergency supply, which as before was to the benefit of the military *and* civilian population, even if, of military necessity, civilian participation was reduced to the essential services, this would seriously hamper my future efforts to get the best possible deal for the islanders. We could of course part company and each side rely on its own efforts, but it would be of doubtful advantage to either to abandon the policy of reciprocal aid at this stage. We are all in the same boat and dependent on each other and for our part we will, in case of necessity, always try to interpret the regulations liberally and to the benefit of the civilians. Any break in a harmonious relationship now might trigger off a series of repercussions which could put the situation beyond our control. The Bailiff was visibly impressed but said that a decision must depend on a meeting with the Superior Council, which he would convene right away.

I did not attend the meeting myself, not wishing to become involved in the minutiae of the plan, but I sent Pokorny and Woelken along to supply any necessary technical details. They reported that the Bailiff and the Attorney-General seemed in favour, but that after Burrell had been called to give his opinion, his comments turned the feeling of the Council against the scheme. It is always the extremist whose loud voice makes the greatest impression, especially if he appeals to patriotic sentiment. It is just the same with us; the moment the rabid Nazi takes the floor, the battle is lost for the counsels of compromise and moderation.

News from the east is catastrophic. The anxiety of the long nights increases. Not only is all one holds most dear threatened by extinction, but by a more lingering and dreadful fate.

Try to distract myself with a French popular novel, *La paille dans l'acier*, by Marcel Prevot, set in a deadly dull bourgeois background but redeemed by an acuteness of psychological perception which tempts one to read on. The author's conclusion is that a life devoted to pleasure is less harmful to women than to men, because it is a man's nature to strive and his natural element is war. For 'war' I would substitute 'action'. War is the extreme of action ending in terror and death, which must remain abhorrent to the thinking man.

Any worsening of our general situation is reflected by a correspond-ing toughening of attitude on the part of the islanders. People's reactions provide a reliable political barometer.

The Bailiff has informed me that the seabirds perform a valuable scavenging service, that they form a *cordon sanitaire* round the island. The town's sewage flows into the sea at no great depth. In spite of Heine's turning down the application, there has been continued pressure to allow the troops to shoot the sea-birds. So I am delighted to have such incontestable reasons for stopping once and for all such a barbarity. It is the wealth of fine old trees and the abundance of birdlife, including the circling gulls around its shores, which constitute the island's chief charm. This heritage of beauty must not be totally destroyed.

25.1.45. Letters from Aufsess have arrived, dated 12 December 1944. Unfortunately they give me no further information about my wife and children. Our Silesians are now of course also desperately worried about their homes and families, but while they await news of the enemy approach with dread, for my wife this could mean being freed from prison. What an ironical twist of fortune; what a base stab in the back by the Gestapo to my loyalty to my country.

Our plan for emergency lighting has been accepted by the islanders after all. After I had broken the ice with the Bailiff the previous day, Pokorny succeeded by personal effort and with consummate skill in bringing final negotiations to a successful conclusion. With some technical adjustments, a satisfactory compromise was reached. I am happy to think that we all work so harmoniously together in Military Administration and feel our success in diplomacy is in itself more important than the question of emergency lighting.

Success in diplomacy consists in finding the happy mean. Fortunately the British, including the islanders, are the world's protagonists in applying commonsense to everyday problems and finding some sensible solution, some acceptable compromise. The temporary abherrant from this policy, Burrell, received a sweetener in the form of a bottle of brandy.

The General rather tetchy on the telephone again, owing to Helldorf's misrepresentation of events here. I wrote to the General and pointed out how much Helldorf's denigration of other people's efforts damaged our cooperation and mutual confidence. I suppose that one-eyed people like Helldorf tend to take a one-eyed view of things; certainly their inability to see the world in the round must have some adverse psychological effect.

In the evening had Schade and our forestry expert round. As neither is an intellectual giant, the long evening passed in profitless and tiring pub bonhomie, with much exchange of toasts and clinking of glasses.

26.1.45. If comparison is odious, it is never more so than when misused for propoganda purposes. The unscrupulous writer or speaker can find examples enough in history which, with a little juggling of the facts, can be made sufficiently analogous to the present situation to hoodwink the ignorant and unthinking. That is what is happening now in Germany and here. They would be better employed in stressing the gravity of the

Russian advance, rather than playing it down by harping on how often Russia has threatened Germany's frontiers before but has always been repulsed.

On my generally solitary way from my billets to the office, I have for years been encountering two ladies who live in the immediate neighbourhood. The elder, a good-looking woman, is accompanied by a girl who has grown from childhood to a budding beauty. Our exchange of glances had been friendly but, according to the nature of the times, reserved.

Our housekeeper, Frances, a confirmed gossip, had long since informed me that the older woman is Mrs. Fielding, the younger her daughter, English residents marooned here by the war. Mr. Fielding is a professor at a university in Mexico and on the outbreak of war they had been unable to obtain a passage to England to make the further journey to Mexico. The family is descended from Henry Fielding, the celebrated 18th-century English novelist and playwright.

Passing each other every day and obviously feeling some mutual attraction, we would in normal times no doubt have become acquainted and established neighbourly relations. The mother must have noticed my interest in her growing daughter and had possibly warned her to take no notice, as the girl looked rather embarrassed and averted her gaze, even when I encountered her alone. Their reserve has only recently melted a little, after I helped them carry home some firewood on a couple of occasions and even had a whole sawn-up apple tree delivered on their doorstep to help with their fuel problem. But this has still resulted in no more than a polite conventional exchange of thanks and greetings.

Went shooting with Heider. Swarms of migratory birds are making a brief stopover on their long flight. Our sedentary life has obviously slowed up my reflexes, as I missed the first snipe on the wing. But the old instincts soon reasserted themselves and I thought how happily I could take to the country life of remote ancestors, with nothing more to do than hunt, shoot and fish.

Heider showed up abominably as a sportsman. He shot a song-thrush in mistake for a game-bird and could not be restrained from popping off at the harmless peewits through the window of the car. Sickening behaviour. Our bag was sufficient to supplement and lend some savour to rations.

The shoot led us into a quiet country part in the east of the island, which I had never previously explored, through marshy meadows of willows and rushes. Beyond lay the sea and Mont Orgueil Castle. The shifting play of light varied, as so often in the islands, between exotic colour and northern grey.

27.1.45. After a visit to the cinema, went back with Wetzstein to his billets. Winnie, his little golden spaniel bitch, devoted her demonstrations of affection so exclusively to me that Wetzstein became quite jealous.

We spoke about Schade, whose reactions to the taste of power after settling into his new office – tending to a loud voice and table-banging – cause me some misgivings. The raw manners of the small county-town official (he comes from a small town in Silesia) are ill-suited to the delicate situation here. He has ability and the typical shrewdness of the countryman and is not to be dealt with lightly. Fortunately he also has the provincial's innate respect for rank and authority, which may enable us to exercise some control over him.

Pokorny grows paler and more emaciated every day. He must be nearly out of his mind with worry about his family. They are now on the road somewhere with thousands of other refugees (3,000 from Breslau alone) fleeing before the oncoming Russians and seeking refuge in already overfilled towns and villages. The Mayor of Breslau was hanged publicly, as in medieval times, for cowardice in the face of the enemy. His wish to surrender was no doubt motivated by concern for the town and the lives of its inhabitants. The General's home too is in Silesia and he must be equally worried about his family. I hope that they will get to my home of Oberaufsess, which I have offered as an asylum.

Our task of administration daily becomes of more boggling complexity as the commodities to be shared out dwindle towards vanishing point. Soon we shall need special permits not only to allocate petrol and clothing but to decide who may have shoes soled, receive razor blades or collect mussels.

28.1.45. A week ago I asked the Attorney-General to come to see me, and taxed him roundly with the inefficiency of the States' officials responsible for the supply of firewood, Jurat le Quesne and his assistant Rattenbury. They have failed entirely in their duties. For months now the Labour Office has been employing 700 men on felling trees. With such a task force the whole island could by now have been denuded of trees. But owing to a lack of proper supervision, the men have been going slow, appropriating the greater part of the timber for themselves and handing in only a minute quantity of logs. We repeatedly suggested piecework payment, but this was never adopted.

Today I again drew the Attorney-General's attention to the urgent necessity to provide help in the shape of fuel for the civilian population in this coldest of all winters on the island. The new emergency agreement about timber which we made with the States a week ago was in their favour but since then nothing has been done for the general public, although there has been opportunity enough for this.

We Germans would not dare risk falling foul of our own countrymen by such signal failure to concern ourselves with their welfare. I long ago suggested that lighted and heated community centres should be set up to assist the general public. This suggestion, too, has never been acted on. One longs to take more positive action. Bur our role as administrators – besides the ticklish job of liaising between the military and local authorities and trying to mediate fairly between the claims of both sides – is a non-active one. We may advise the island government but not usurp its functions.

29.1.45. The way people greet each other reflects the disorder of the times. 'Heil Hitler' has never really caught on. To the General I say 'Heil Herr General' and he says 'Heil dear Aufsess'. In speaking to Helldorf on the 'phone, I omit any form of greeting, which conforms to his undercover method of transacting business. Lt-Colonel Lindner and I are on friendly 'Grüss Gott' terms. Colonel Heine I greet, with proper caution and circumspection, according to the other people present; not with 'Heil Hitler' if this is possibly avoidable. With the younger officers and with Schade 'Heil Hitler' is expedient; with the Geheime Feldpolizei the iron rule. Almost a pity when this special greeting, reserved for people one dislikes or distrusts, falls out of usage.

Still no news of the *Vega* or her next cargo. At the end of the month the bread ration will also come to an end. And the military authorities will certainly not fork out from their own stocks to tide the islanders over, unless there is definite news or at least a reasonable prospect that the *Vega* will bring flour. We shall by then have reached the potentially explosive state of affairs of which I pointed out the probable imminence in my last report.

30.1.45. The other day a German told me it was a matter of complete indifference to him if all the trees in the island were chopped down. How differently I feel. If I heard of some venerable tree as far away as China in danger of being unnecessarily and unfeelingly felled, I should still grieve. Stupid of me probably. Perhaps I was a tree-sprite in some long-past mythical age.

Available reading matter has become as stale and unprofitable as available food. In the long run one can no more sustain oneself on old books, unsupplemented by any recent additions, than on an unrelieved diet of tinned stuffs. An occasional infusion of fresh vitamins and new ideas is needed to keep one up to the mark.

31.1.45. At last the weather has turned milder. The lapwings, so sadly decimated by hungry Nimrods, are also at last, thank God, swarming for departure. All over the island they gather in close formations, to merge into larger ones. The susurration of their wings, dark above, light below, is like the sound of a sudden wind in the silver poplar. Their departure is attended with less noise and bustle than that of the other migratory birds. My heart goes with them.

Have received the depressing news that the Red Cross reports difficulties in obtaining a supply of flour from England. The present bread ration will last only until 10 February. Then famine, with all its attendant perils, will set in. Our military headquarters, on orders from Reich headquarters, will not release any flour on loan to the islanders until they have the positive assurance that flour will be shipped from Lisbon.

One must always be on guard against Helldorf. I fancy he must have got wind of my letter to the General. At any rate, he rang me up today and in angry tones accused us of authorising a larger bread ration in Jersey than that authorised in Guernsey. As usual the source of his information was an undercover one, i.e., a censored letter. But the information is false, I am fully covered and there is nothing he can bring against us. But, with the present meagre ration extending for a further ten days, he is determined to spin it out further still by reducing it again by half.

The army service corps are giving a series of lectures for regular officers at the Soldiers' Home. Schade inaugurated the series with an impassioned address, obviously somewhat out of his depth but doing his best to put his ideas across. He quoted all the facts and figures already so well known to me. Not a bad thing to let military officers lecture military officers on the situation. One can still try to manipulate things quietly and unobtrusively behind the scenes, if only in an effort to postpone rather than prevent the final collapse.

Schade's concluding sentences were delivered with such facial distortions and belligerency of tone that I guessed, after getting all that off his chest, he might be in a milder and more receptive frame of mind; even perhaps grateful for a word of praise. So I seized the opportunity for a friendly chat to try to make him change his mind on his pet project for growing potatoes in glasshouses, which had always seemed impracticable to me under present conditions and about which the States have been pressing me for a final decision.

1.2.45. The naval Captain von Kalckreuth invited me to visit him. He is a lanky, bustling little man, always on the go. He jumped up at least a dozen times while I was there; was fussily self-important on the telephone. The typical north German, who can never settle down to give the quiet consideration to the matter on hand which we south Germans would find essential for dealing with it properly.

2.2.45. Celebrated my mother's birthday, at a remove, by inviting Woelken, whose birthday falls on the same date, to coffee and cakes. As usual the talk turned to our present desperate situation and its unpredictable outcome. At a recent lecture, Colonel Heine quoted Clausewitz's dictum that a war once lost should not be further protracted.

I am marking the Russian advance on a map of Germany. Once the red arrows approaching from left and right meet, all will be over with Germany. And all will be over with us here, too. Whatever trials that end may bring, I could wish it were here already. What worries me is the horrors we may still have to face here, if the radicals gain power, before the end comes. An early end is now all one can wish and hope for.

3.2.45. News of a sort of the *Vega*; she will also be bringing parcels for the prisoners-of-war on her next trip. At least it is a relief to know that there will be a next trip. From next Monday the bread ration will be reduced to 135 grammes a day. I resolve to put aside half my own bread ration and pop it in to those nice children next door.

4.2.45. Heard today that the *Vega* will not be bringing flour; Britain has refused this request. No doubt she is making clear her intention of abiding by international law. According to this, the occupying power is obliged to share local produce with the civilians and may not seize the last supplies for the exclusive use of the troops. The Red Cross parcels are intended only to alleviate the civilians' extreme need and not to replace basic rations. I had pointed out the legal aspects in a paper I drew up some time ago and have again drawn Guernsey H.Q.'s attention to this, alhough I know there is little the General, himself under duress, can do about it.

Lt-Colonel Lindner invited me to a meal. He is the kindly uncle who always puts the best he has on the table for his guests.

The course of events in Germany leaves one with little inclination to seek solace in books or to follow any private pursuits. Still no news of my wife. Sometimes, in an excess of optimism, I am tempted to believe she must already have been released from her prison cell.

5.2.45. One of the more endearing characteristics of humanity – and one of particular attraction between the sexes – is that resilience which enables one to live for the day and make the most of what it brings. In spite of our worries and afflictions, we must not become totally sunk in grief. I find myself in rebellion against these recent weeks of deep depression and feel an urge to reassert myself and try to regain some of my old cheerfulness and resiliency. Feel, too, I must do this for the sake of my wife; an aged and embittered man would be in no state to make up to her for all she has suffered. The few of us who remain in good health and spirits will have an uphill task of reconstruction before us and it is up to us to keep ourselves in good shape.

Called on Marie von Wedel, who is very anxious about her eldest brother and her home, Schloss Cannenberg in Pomerania, which the Russians are now approaching. It has been in the possession of her family for 600 years. She spoke of her home and of other ancient family seats in the neighbourhood, from which the owners will now be fleeing with nothing more than a few necessities in a suitcase. What a tragic collapse of the whole world. I feel for her most deeply. Only the stability of character inherited from a long line of hard-fighting ancestors can provide the courage to face and overcome such blows of fate.

Also visited Miss White at Samarès Manor. For the first time since I had known her, she showed herself unfriendly, bitter and abusive. But she relented before we parted and pressed on me a large bunch of camellias.

The starlings are now in a great state of excitement, preparing for their journey home, lucky birds. Every now and then they descend in swarms on our garden, and I watch with fascination the zeal with which, hurrying and pecking, they investigate every inch of the smooth lawn. At the slightest noise, they all take off together, as if warned by radar, to rise to an even height or make a circular reconnaisance flight before descending to settle on the grass again. Their discipline is fantastic; not a bird falls out of place. Yet in Germany we regard them as the most independent and individual of birds.

6.2.45. The *Vega* has arrived in Guernsey, in the nick of time, just as the bread ration has been halved and is due to end on 17 February. Demonstrations by the workers have already been threatened. That bread, the basic foodstuff, the staff of life, with its Biblical, almost mystical significance, should come to an end, must be taken very seriously. For the moment the urgency of the problem is postponed by the arrival of the ship with Red Cross parcels of varied foodstuffs. But it has already been confirmed that she has no flour aboard, Britain having refused supplies, and whether she will bring flour on her next trip is still an open question.

Tonight a commando expedition is setting out for Granville, with the object of destroying the harbour there. We still want to give an account of ourselves on the fighting front. But relations between the troops and the civilians are so close that the project has become common knowledge before it has even started. It only needs an islander to have escaped to the mainland with the news, and the fate of the commandoes, already half dead with hunger anyway, will be settled.

Sister Margarethe stopped me on the street and with an air of great concern handed me a pamphlet. This purportedly emanated from labouring circles and, while not directed specifically against us, called for a reduction of working time to four hours a day, with full payment of wages and a supplementary ration for the heavy workers at the cost of the wealthy.

In the afternoon Pokorny invited along a local girl who had apparently been dying to meet me. I have, unfortunately, become a public figure here. I hope I did not disappoint her and that she departed with her pretty little head as turned as she had anticipated. Her name was Leonore, an above-the-average vivacious and enterprising young woman, evidently determined, in her youthfully naive manner, to add some glamour to a hitherto unadventurous existence. In view of my resolve to get back to living and make the most of each day as it came, perhaps too because she had such a pert little mouth and a nice line in repartee, I did not find it difficult to play the heavy flirt. Still, that will I fancy be the end of the Leonore overture.

Our housekeeper, Frances, asked Heider for a permit to buy a bottle of cognac to barter for irons for our household laundry. She in fact returned with two rusty old irons, if also a little tipsy. As the second Red Cross parcel[2] was issued on the same day, she was in high good humour and a mood of maudlin generosity. We had to restrain her from lavishing biscuits and chocolate on us. We remember all too well how, after disposing over-hastily of her first parcel, she had come to us with tears in her eyes and said she would have to give notice as she had nothing left to eat.

11.2.45. The raid on Granville ran into difficulties and was called off on technical grounds, failure of engines and the dangers of running into rocks in the thick fog, and the ships after nearing their objective returned to harbour.

In the absence of Heider in Guernsey, entertained his girlfriend Nancy for the evening. She has a lively intellect but is only 21 and, as the sheltered only daughter of wealthy parents is imbued with acquired prejudices and a preconceived view of the world at variance with her own nature. I talked to her about this and suggested that one's own feelings and experiences were a better guide to life than all the precepts learned in school. She responded with animation and I felt quite the latter-day Pygmalion. The spoiled daughter has the makings of a well-integrated woman.

Last evening I gave a little party. I invited Marie von Wedel, so much in need of distraction from her worries, to a modest supper and asked her to choose a couple of guests to join us round the fire afterwards.

Our first guest was a middle-aged Austrian architect, Kutzer, who is already preoccupied with the town-planning and reconstruction he will be engaged on after the war. He has the genuine artistic temperament, much to be admired, but his total dedication to his chosen profession does not perhaps make him the ideal companion for a social evening round the fire. Luckily I was able, without his noticing it, to weigh in with some facetious comment and divert him from his obvious intention of giving us a brick-by-brick account of the reconstruction of a bombed town.

Our second guest was a former art historian, now wearing a corporal's uniform, a modest and well-mannered man, who obviously enjoyed the company and the talk.

After our little supper, in French style, preceded by aperitifs and cigarettes and consisting of a variety of small dishes more fanciful than filling, Marie von Wedel and I were in a relaxed and hospitable mood and this soon communicated itself to our guests.

The firelight lit up our flushed and happy faces. Formality was banished. No angel passed overhead. The little pauses in the conversation served merely to savour what had been said before to reinforce our community of spirit in sharing silence as well as speech. I had the feeling we were all very conscious of the pressure of the times and the epochal changes facing us; of having arrived at a watershed of history. There can have been few periods in history before, presenting one with the doubtful advantage of such a gloomy foreknowledge of the future.

Heavy rainstorms sweeping across the island prevent the farmers from letting out the cattle to graze or starting work in the fields.

12.2.45. Spent Sunday alone in my small well-heated room at Linden Court, with a large supply of books, a little alcohol and the radio and enjoyed the brief respite from the pressure of affairs.

The *Vega* is still lying at anchor in the roads at Guernsey. The stormy weather is delaying her crossing to Jersey. I have passed on to the Attorney-General the particulars of her cargo, in which he is greatly interested.

While I was talking to Sister Marie von Wedel at the Soldiers' Home, there was a telephone call for her from Lieutenant Hase. Her agitation betrayed the state of her feelings and her inability to bring out a further sensible word on her return confirmed them. She is at last clearly head-over-heels in love. I hope this will dispel her lethargy and emotional tension and bring her the happiness of feminine fulfilment.

13.2.45. The mistrust of each other, the spying on each other and the general ill-will among us Germans is unendurable. Colonel Heine, on his return from Guernsey Headquarters, brought the whole sordid atmosphere back with him. The gravity of events in Germany in no way overshadows the petty jealousies and wrangling over trifles here.

The right of controlling access to the harbour and to the Red Cross ship, which has now arrived again, is disputed between the various service commands, German manoeuvring against German to gain the ascendancy, in a way that is of little credit to any of us. One is denied the exercise of any common sense or *ad hoc* action.

I, it seems, am out of favour with the navy for having allegedly carried the Bailiff of Jersey's bag when we went to Guernsey together on the occasion of the *Vega's* first visit. The suitcase I was carrying was my own, an English one bought in Paris. The Bailiff and I certainly gave each other a hand climbing on and off the naval boat. The German is mistrustful of common civilities. He fails to see that the genuinely prudent man is not so dependent on outward form that he cannot treat an opponent with courtesy.

Captain Rauhbold, whose name does justice to his nature [i.e., bully, rowdy] summarily ordered all the crane drivers and stevedores off the harbour, because a small percentage of them had refused to work on the reduced bread ration. And this at a time when we urgently need the men to unload the Red Cross ship. This fundamental German urge to take action on principle, even to our own detriment and when the need for it has passed – the protesting workers had already changed their minds – so disgusts me that I withdraw from the argument.

Callias brought me a small parcel of chocolates and cigarettes. I called a special meeting of my staff and shared out these delicacies, of a quality long since unknown to us. We consumed them with the solemnity and appreciation proper to the occasion, savouring each delicious morsel with an almost intellectual enjoyment.

In the afternoon, Helldorf, Schade and Callias came to tea with us. The occasion passed in an atmosphere of constraint and mistrust, which I am sure the harmless and likeable young Callias had done nothing to deserve, although of course he has been labelled a security suspect by our know-all security service. And Helldorf always brings with him the ambience of suspicion, intrigue and undercover dealings which is his natural background.

In the evening, I was overcome by a sense of the complete breakdown of all aspects of German life. It is a total collapse. Gone is the extolled German uprightness of dealing; gone the comradeship; gone all goodwill. 'Honest Michel', that popular concept of the average German has been driven out of existence. Not only has he lost the war; he has fallen short of human obligations and dignity. And after the war, I fear, he will be as despised, as cast out and as misused as the Jews.

In the morning I stood for a long time looking at a picture of Hitler addressing the people, the lock of hair falling across his brow. This is the maniac who has led us into this state. Poor German people.

At the conclusion of another excellent meal on board the Red Cross ship, tongues were so loosened by the good food and drink that a lively discussion on the contrasting claims of capitalism, Bolshevism and National Socialism started up. Unfortunately this was dominated by the harbour commandant, von Cleve, who got so carried away that he left no opportunity for us to hear the views of our two neutral hosts, which might have been much more interesting.

14.2.45. In the morning we held a small conference at Langford House with Callias and the States' representatives. The burning question, of course, was whether England would supply flour for the *Vega's* next shipment.

With regard to parcels, Callias confessed that he had overestimated the civilian population figures for Jersey, which had thus received a proportionately higher number of parcels than Guernsey. The Bailiff quickly passed on to another theme.

This was the question of whether foreigners, mostly Frenchmen, working for the Germans in the islands, would also be issued with Red Cross parcels. A painful debate ensued. The two islands are divided in opinion. Jersey is in favour on humanitarian grounds, although not, I suspect, without the idea of a goodwill gesture to France in mind. As the number of foreign workers in Jersey is small in comparison with Guernsey, the gesture would also be correspondingly less costly. The Bailiff of Jersey never misses a chance of making political capital.

At the Bailiff's invitation, Helldorf and I visited him at his home in the evening. Seated round the fire, a glass of whisky in hand, we were soon quite frankly discussing how future events might shape up here. There is no doubt that in such off-the-record talks, in a small circle and a relaxed atmosphere, more is achieved than at all the formal sessions at the conference table. One felt a degree of confidence had been established between us which enabled both sides to disregard enemy status in a common assessment of what had become a common problem.

The Bailiff expressed his fear that the occupying forces might continue to hold out in the Channel Islands even after Germany had been defeated. We assured him that once the war was over, we wished for nothing more than to get home as quickly as possible. Between the two extremes envisaged, there is of course still the possibility of a third factor cropping up to bedevil the situation, such as a desperate last-minute faction of Hitler's still making a stand and issuing orders from some stronghold in the mountains.

The Bailiff also spoke in guarded terms of his second anxiety. This was the possibility of a radical change in the German leadership in the island. It seemed to me that in this respect he was better informed than Helldorf and I.

Towards the end of our talk, the Bailiff's wife rejoined us. It was a stimulating and perhaps a momentous evening. We agreed, in particular, on stop-gap measures to tide over the breadless period. The Bailiff was accorded the greatest freedom of action, subject to his assuming the full responsibility.

15.2.45. Busy all day with negotiations in French and English. No doubt one learns a good deal in the process, in particular the importance of remaining cool and affable, as a happy medium between too great a show of cordiality on the one hand and of cold bureaucracy on the other.

At the end of the day, as it was such a lovely evening, I took Callias out for a drive and a breath of fresh air to Mont Orgeuil Castle. He is a most affable young man, if not an intellectual giant.

In the evening, at Colonel Heine's, all rather stiff and formal. I think the Colonel has a considerable liking for me, but does not know quite what to make of my artistic interests and possibly reputed Bohemian leanings. These are factors outside his terms of reference, fitting into no proper military category. I try to compensate for this by praising books I know he must enjoy (such as Gertrud Bäumer's *Adelheid*). Try also not to offend his equally military-minded Adjutant by avoiding any subject of conversation outside the practical.

16.2.45. Departure of the *Vega*. How the time flies. It seems only the other day when I first watched the ship, with her white-painted sides and the large red cross, gliding out of the harbour.

Have acquired an interesting report from the *Times* on a debate on the Channel Islands in Parliament.

At lunchtime talked over all outstanding problems with Helldorf again and we swiftly reached agreement on all points. This is the best time to take one's leave. Lacking in any lighter social side and with no extra-professional interests to engage his keen mind, Helldorf's concept of conviviality tends to be on the lower rather than the higher plane.

In the evening was invited to supper with Lieutenant Fügen. The meal was too opulent, far exceeding the decent moderation which it is incumbent on us to observe in these times of widespread hunger. Even if provided by going short for weeks in advance and scraping the cupboard bare, such gastronomic indulgence is unforgivable, vis-à-vis the troops, the population and ourselves. Well-meant, of course, in the crude and hearty country fashion of giving a guest a slap-up meal, cost what it may.

There were photographs of Lieutenant Fügen's family in his bedroom. In his smart lieutenant's uniform, lean, well exercised and sunbrowned, he does not look much like them, but I would guess he will soon revert to type when he gets back to the home cooking of his well-nourished family.

The pleasantest part of the evening was an encounter with a well-educated and studious looking young art historian, with whom I soon established a wide community of interests.

17.2.45. I continue to write letters to my wife. There is an airmail service about once a month, although half the 'planes fail to reach their destination. As I was hurrying down to the harbour to see Helldorf off and hand in a letter for my wife and a package for the General, I ran into Heine, who held me up on some trifling matter. When I got to the harbour the ships for Guernsey had already cast off. Running to the end of the jetty, I tied letter and package together and tried to throw them aboard the ship leaving the harbour entrance. In my anxiety not to overshoot my target, the throw fell short and both fell into the water. I could have torn my hair with rage at missing such an easy target, when I had always been so good at pitching.

Thoroughly at odds with myself and in search of a little diversion, I called on Sister Gretl at the Soldiers' Home. She is the girl who stood in as bride at the proxy wedding, a traumatic experience from which she has never quite recovered. I pulled her leg a little, assuring her that she looked just like the star of a naive and sentimental film recently on show here. Half believing, half disbelieving, she unconsciously fell into the pose and became quite coy and flirtatious. But when I appeared to take this seriously, she quickly reverted to her natural role of a good young girl and fled to the kitchen.

18.2.45. Schade is typical of the small-town politician who, with a limited education and a taste for power, has come to believe that a certain facility in rhetoric is the equivalent of or a substitute for reasoned thinking. Also he is shrewd, energetic and single-minded of purpose, and his emotive language certainly makes its appeal to the popular causes and misconceptions of his audience. On the other hand he is basically faint-hearted and inclined to bow to authority. But he is pursuing a dangerous policy of denigrating the work of Military Administration and is certainly convinced that he could do it better. Wetzstein warns me to be wary of him and to use all political and psychological means to counter his undercover attacks on our efficiency.

In the afternoon there was a magical change of weather. The sun broke out through a thin mist on a mild, windless spring day. All the birds were singing madly and the last of the starlings assembled in the tree tops for a last conference on their flight overseas.

Tempted by a lovely tree-lined drive in a remote part of the country, I turned into it and found myself in front of a country house I had never previously seen. A pleasant-looking elderly lady came out to meet me. I apologised for trespassing, saying that I could not resist a closer look at her beautiful property. She broke into a storm of abuse and complained that, without a word to her, Germans had already started chopping down her most precious trees, those she had planted herself. Such rude methods directly contravene my express instructions that the wishes of the owner must be given the first consideration. So on the spot I wrote and handed her an order to the German timber-felling unit to spare her favourite trees. She could scarcely grasp such great good luck.

Have just finished Hillard's novel *Making Game with Reality*, set in the Kaiser's Reich prior to the Great War, in which he skilfully evokes the social scene of the period and lays bare its shallowness and futility. He describes delightfully the supercilious manners of the servants of the great; the gossip, scandalmongering and backbiting indulged in by the great under hypocritical pretence of virtuous discretion, and the lives of the bourgeoisie, devoted to fanatical hard work, sentimentality and song.

19.2.45. The loveliest of early spring days; the birds rejoicing, the lawns of freshest green and a smell of good earth, tangy and aromatic. In the afternoon, Pokorny and I found some excuse to drive out into the country.

Like me, Pokorny is gradually succumbing to a fatalistic attitude to life, to accepting its blows with grim humour. Even now his native city, Breslau, together with the little house he doubtless saved long and hard for, is being bombarded and overrun by the enemy. What use to repine? Better to enjoy the modest pleasures the fleeting moment brings.

We came across a local family engaged on illicit wood cutting. And we all laughed together at the ridiculous circumstances of war which had 'promoted' them to timber thieves and us to big bad gendarmes. Pokorny was quite amused by our exchange, but left wondering I think how his chief, latterly so moody and depressed, could suddenly become so light-hearted.

In the main our work here is finished. The island's resources are exhausted. Electricity, gas, road maintenance, production of supplies, cultivation of the land, deployment of labour, etc., are virtually at a standstill. We have arrived at an interim period in which the best we can hope for is the preservation of trust and good relations. Otherwise we must now await the end with what cheerfulness we can muster, like the labourer who, with an easy conscience at the end of a hard day's work, sits down to face the evening.

20.2.45. In the afternoon I was at St Brelade's Bay. I was looking for a house tucked away in a little private cove. It lay in a tiny valley, well protected from the prevailing winds from west and north and surrounded by lovely old trees. Needless to say my mission was concerned with trees, and I was able to rescue two wonderful old poplars from the threat of the axe. The elderly couple were most relieved and grateful and invited me in to the cosily crowded confusion of their house.

I still encounter the Fielding ladies almost daily. They personify the best of English good manners and tradition. Always discreet and immaculately well turned out. While we cannot disguise our mutual interest and liking, we confine our greetings to the most distantly formal.

In the evening Schade came to see us, to indulge in a lot of tittle-tattle we could well have done without.

21.2.45. The weather is so gorgeous that, like the birds looking for a nesting-place, Bleuel and I went out to look for a bathing hut for the coming season. We were greeted on the beach by a lot of local children who still remembered us and who were again allowed to climb into the car for a short ride. It is not until they reach the age of about twelve that the children learn to recognise and reject us as enemies. The little ones, happily unwitting, still treat us as friendly grown-ups.

Was able anyway to confirm that the children were all looking well, with fatter and rosier cheeks than last summer. Feel that, despite the temporary lack of bread, there can be no danger of immediate starvation. And, although we have had many complaints from the island doctors of malnutrition, our demands for more precise details of the cases involved have so far elicited no replies.

Conditions in Guernsey are far worse. The General told me he had received a letter from the Bailiff threatening him, in effect if not in so many words, with a future sentence of 20 years' hard labour for the starvation of the islanders.

22.2.45. In the night swastikas were daubed with tar on buildings all over the island. The Attorney-General and the Constable of St Helier came to see me and established on reliable evidence and beyond doubt that this idiotic prank had been carried out by Germans and moreover on an organised basis. In fact, it has been established that two German officers were responsible for or rather were the irresponsible perpetrators of this infamous act. Entirely on their own initiative and without the knowledge of the fortress commander, they had issued orders to two companies of men to do the job. They claim that their motivation for this 'political protest' was their National Socialist principles. It was such criminal fools who plotted the 'crystal night' in 1938, which triggered off the storm of hatred against the Jews.

At first the islanders reacted with shock and indignation, but this attitude is already giving way to one of sardonic amusement. On liberation day these swastikas will show what cultural barbarians the Germans were. One humourist has hung an empty picture frame round 'his' swastika; another has written 'England for ever' alongside his; a third has converted the swastika into the type of cross used for British decorations for valour and merit.

The island population has been senselessly provoked and the prestige and good discipline of the German armed forces seriously compromised. It amounts almost to a small-scale mutiny and involves further punishable offences, such as removing and making improper and unauthorised use of military property, etc.

The immediate problem is to get rid of the visible evidence of this night of rampage; this is a big problem, as over a thousand tar-smeared houses are involved. The islanders have no petrol and in the circumstances would hardly be prepared to undertake such a chore.

Every right-thinking German is struck by horror and repugnance at the actions of the Nazi thugs, who consider themselves the elite of the nation, and for whom the whole nation has to suffer and atone.

It has been decided that the tar daubings must be removed by foreign workers of the O.T. (Organisation Todt). It would scarcely be in keeping with the good standing and repute of the troops to employ them on this humiliating task under the derisory gaze of the islanders.

Inspected the electricity works, which is now to function under German management. We had protested at the lack of experience of the Germans appointed to the job, in particular to that of their chief, Captain K., a man unsuited by temperament to achieve good working relations with the remaining local employees.

Captain K. himself had airily referred to this little local works as a mere toy, and enlarged on his own managerial capacities. Faced with the actual machinery, it turned out that he knew not a bloody thing about it and thus immediately forfeited the confidence of the local workers. His unstable character, veering between insecurity and over-confidence, mild acquiescence and wild outbursts of rage, makes him an impossible man to deal with. Now this obviously incapable fellow, appointed against our advice on Schade's insistence, is likely not only to wreck good relations with the electricity board employees, but the installation itself. Of course he excuses his failures with ominous references to sabotage. Another of the Nazi type who discredit our reputation.

23.2.45. Returning from an early evening walk in the neighbourhood fields and woods, I was confronted by an inexplicable phenomenon. In the gathering twilight I glimpsed about fifty metres ahead an elongated object of indefinable character moving in a series of jerks and stops. Was I encountering one of those ghostly apparitions so dear to the Victorian writers? But as I got nearer, the familiar sound of branches dragged along the ground made it clear that this was an apparition of more modern provenance also generally met with in the dusk; some illegally acquired wood being smuggled home.

Drawing abreast, I was genuinely surprised however to recognise the Fielding ladies, generally so soignée, but now dishevelled, flushed and disconcerted. I simply had to laugh. I relieved them of their unaccustomed burden right away, with mock threats, and hoisted the spindly branch of oak on my shoulder, and with much exchange of banter on the way, in which they participated with great goodwill, I deposited the *corpus delicti* at their door. It only needed the punctilious Colonel Heine to see me in such an unlikely procession, with uniform buttons half undone. And having arrived at the door, I could not resist the heartfelt invitation of mother and daughter to come in for a cup of tea.

No sooner was the bough chopped up and the fire stoked, than we were all sitting round the glowing hearth in comfortable armchairs like old friends. The tea was excellent and accompanied by crunchy rusks from the Red Cross parcel. We simply could not get over the comic aspects of our encounter and continued in a mood of high hilarity to exchange badinage. Thus the hours fled.

Inevitably, the talk at last came round to more serious subjects, to the present situation and our individual fortunes. For the first time I found myself relating the sad tale of my wife's imprisonment and separation from our children. The Fieldings too had been through hard times. I could not get over the feeling that the legend of Odysseus and Nausicaä on the island of Phoeacia was being re-enacted in modern dress.

The daughter, Elaine, did not take the seat next to me on the sofa, but perched herself on the arm at the far end, from which vantage point she subjected me to an intense scrutiny, watching my every move and hanging on my every word. My conversation was mostly with her charming mother, but she occasionally chimed in with some witty and apposite remark in a pleasant contralto voice.

When Elaine saw me to the door, it was four o'clock in the morning. I felt deeply moved by this singular experience, by the harmonious hours we had spent together and by my rich reward in having gained the confidence and affectionate regard of these two Englishwomen.

Chapter Five

March – April 1945

1.3.45. Yesterday brought shattering news. At lunchtime Heider informed me that the General and Helldorf have been dismissed from office. From 12 hours midday, today, Hüffmeier takes over as Commander-in-Chief of the Channel Islands. Other far-reaching changes in command have also been ordered. The whole business smacks of a *putsch* or *coup d'etat*. What lies behind it all is as yet by no means clear, but I suspect it is a move long since carefully planned.

As this news was not yet generally known and had been told me in confidence, I rang up Helldorf on the pretext of other business. He asked me if I had a chair handy and proceeded to give me an account of the coup, adopting the only attitude possible to a man suddenly toppled from power, one of sardonic amusement and relief at being freed from his onerous task. I pretended great surprise but refrained from comment, on the suspicion that the call might be monitored.

I had hardly put down the 'phone, when the Naval Communications Centre rang up, asking that an urgent personal telegram should be collected. It was easy to assume a connection; this was either the end of me or of Military Administration. I drove down there at once, accompanied by Heider.

To my astonishment, the telegram announced the immediate removal from office of Heider and the appointment of Captain von Cleve as Platzkommandant. Heider is transferred to Guernsey. He took the news of his posting with the good humour of the old soldier. But ominous rumours are rife and an atmosphere of unease and disquiet prevails in all command offices and orderly rooms.

In the evening Captain von Cleve rang me and asked me to go to see him immediately. He had just returned from Guernsey. I had always liked him very much – he has good manners and makes a presentable appearance – even if I found him a bit of a poseur and over-loquacious. The purpose of his summons was to inform me of my own position. While the Admiral found that there was much which counted against me, he had left it to von Cleve's discretion to sound me out on my willingness to go along with the new policy, which would mean taking a more ruthless line with the civilian population.

So my conscientious work, unassailable I should have thought for loyalty and devotion to duty, is now disavowed and all goes for nothing.

No doubt some biased reporting has something to do with the Admiral's unfavourable opinion of me, perhaps by Helldorf, almost certainly by the unsavoury Hüst, whom I have more than once in the past put in his place. So I find myself, although left in office, quasi suspended, and may expect to be posted from here to some unknown destination at any time.

While I was with Cleve, the General rang up. He was clearly overwrought, worried and angry. With the knowledge that every word we said might be overheard and misconstrued, we could not talk very much. I am deeply sorry for the General, who has certainly never done anything to merit his sudden downfall. On the contrary. It is unfortunate that, from the start, he played into the hands of Helldorf, who pushed him into the background and usurped his power and prestige.

6.3.45. The last few days have been tense and trying in the extreme. I shall try to set down the highlights of events as briefly as possible.

On his second day in office as Platzkommandant, von Cleve had his first meeting with the Bailiff and the Attorney-General. They attended the occasion with obvious mistrust and reserve, and the fact that the subject for discussion was further reductions in the civilian rations was hardly calculated to improve the atmosphere. For all that, von Cleve made a very creditable performance. Speaking in frank and friendly style, with some adroitly introduced comparisons between life aboard ship and poker-playing and our present situation, he soon managed to win their confidence. Which of course happily facilitated the despatch of the business in hand.

The new Platzkommandant also gave me all sorts of useful tips to prepare me for my meeting with the Admiral, for which I was to travel to Guernsey on 3 March. No doubt this visit is for the purpose of giving me another look over and, if I make the grade, of winning me round to participating in the new tough course. Cleve had, he assured me, already sent a favourable report, confirming his opinion of me as being, professionally, absolutely first-class. Whether all his well-meant advice on how to conduct myself at this vital meeting will be a help or a hindrance remains to be seen. One cannot change one's nature overnight. Still, I suppose it is helpful to be acquainted with the more superficial conventions of behaviour, the most important in this case, of course, being to throw up one's arms in the repugnant Nazi greeting.

At the harbour there was the usual crowd of travellers and colleagues taking official leave of them. Colonel Heine, like me, had been summoned to Guernsey on a visit. Major Gebhardt was also there. He has been posted to Guernsey as head of Ia [military counter-intelligence] there, a post he has hitherto held in Jersey. He is one of the more approachable of the radicals but has dangerous limitations. Viewing the world through the blinkers of militarism and Nazism, he is all too apt to 'see red' and can on occasion be stubbornly fanatic. His posting to headquarters in Guernsey is a significant pointer to the course the new policy is likely to take. Of all the shipboard passengers, probably only Colonel Heine felt some sympathy for me. We were travellers on the same boat in more senses than one. No doubt we had both been summoned to the seat of authority for reappraisal and to see if we would fit into the new scheme of things.

The Admiral was already awaiting us on the quay in Guernsey. There was a brief exchange of greetings. Colonel Heine, the soul of rectitude on military protocol, was clearly gratified by the honours accorded him.

In the afternoon I had my first talk with the naval Captain Reich, who has been appointed to Helldorf's post as aide to the Commander-in-Chief. He is a man of about my own age; an affable Rhinelander from Cologne, a banker by profession. He is not of Helldorf's calibre and clearly lacks his perspective on affairs and, above all, Helldorf's practical knowledge of management gained in a lifetime of experience of big business. Reich seems, however, a conscientious worker, taking his job seriously but perhaps over devoted to facts and figures. I suspect he is more at home with figures than with people, although he is easy enough to get on with, and it is not hard to gain his confidence, as the exclusively naval party to which he invited me in the evening only served to confirm. I am struck more than ever by the difficulties of conducting affairs fairly and justly. The facts and figures that come up on one's desk seem easy enough to deal with, the results of acting on them in terms of human involvement less so. I would guess that Captain Reich will be more concerned with the facts and figures than with the human element, or with the necessity of keeping up good relations with the islanders' representatives in the States Controlling Committee.

In this diary of the last phase of the occupation, the months under siege, I have often enough written about Helldorf, largely to his disparagement. In spite of his undoubted achievements, my final judgement of him remains unaltered. He made clever use of his key position as adjutant, while ostensibly smoothing the path for the General, to gather the reins of power into his own hands and to keep the General isolated from his friends, and above all to keep him in ignorance of the most vital factor of the siege, the state of supplies. In this he did a grave disservice to the General, who could scarcely have been so summarily toppled from power if he had not grown so sadly out of touch with the facts of the situation and the people concerned.

No doubt too that naval ambition has been an important contributory factor, ranging from Naval High Command, under whose orders the islands have been placed, down to our own local sea-dog, the Admiral, cast up on these shores by the fortunes of war without a command but still anxious to acquire one.

Small matters have been blown up out of all proportion and the impression has been conveyed and propagated that the General and his staff have failed to provide properly for the troops, thus inducing a mood prepared for change at any cost.

A combination of all these factors, building up over a period, has probably led to the sudden and drastic change in command. But no clear and proper reason has been given for the change and for the General's recall to Germany, which as an outstandingly able, conscientious and humane commander is so clearly his due. Officially, his state of health has been made the excuse for kicking him out.

The following morning I was summoned to an interview with the Admiral in his quarters. He explained to me his ideas for holding out in the islands for as long as possible, while at the same time he was anxious to avoid at least any outward show of any change from our previous policy. His general conception of the situation and his plans for dealing with it seem in no way incompatible with my own. Of course he was buttering me up to some extent, to win me over to his side. He mentioned, for instance, that he had read and been most impressed by my memorandum of 12 June 1944, six days after the Allied landing in France, in which I had been the first to point out the necessity of laying in supplies and preparing for a long siege.

Having established this degree of good understanding, he proceeded to speak very frankly about what was, for me, the other side of the coin. He paid, he said, no attention to rumours and would certainly not base his opinion on them. It had come to his knowledge that I was not a good National Socialist. His subsequent remarks made clear that my essay on 'The Gentle Exercise of Power', which I had lent the General, had fallen into his hands. Referring to specific passages in it, he declared that, as the leading official representative of the Party in the islands, he must be able to rely on his officers' loyalty to the Führer. He could still, however, respect opposing points of view and did not require me to justify mine or to reassure him in any way. All that mattered to him was that I worked honourably with him in attaining the target he had set himself, and on which we were already agreed.

At this point, apparently carried away by his own eloquence and spontaneous feeling, the Admiral jumped up and shook me warmly by the hand. To anyone looking on it would have seemed that two men were settling their differences in manly fashion. But the Admiral's concluding scene was so theatrical that I could scarcely forbear a smile. Once outside, with the curtain, as it were, fallen behind me, I thought over this interview very soberly. Although it seemed I had been absolved of my crimes, real or imagined, I could see that, with a man of the Admiral's impulsive and volatile nature, I should have to tread warily indeed.

Following this, I went to see the General. He was seated at his desk, which was decked in spring flowers among the many portraits and personal mementos. He looked utterly wretched, weighed down by care, but full of angry indignation, which he expressed quite openly, at the plot against him. Having come straight from the Admiral, it was painful to find myself so placed between the two sides.

To cap the situation, Helldorf arrived. Unlike the General, who is genuinely angry, Helldorf seemed subdued, almost tearful, with the harassed air of a man driven into a corner. He showed me an order which forbids him to hold any communication or conduct talks with any local authorities or commands. He is to be brought before a court martial for having failed to carry out orders from Germany. In my opinion he has always behaved perfectly properly in this respect, or at least to a degree which should absolve him of blame. In the changing scene of local conditions and supplies, administrative orders from Germany could not always be followed like the Ten Commandments.

The situation became still more painful when Colonel Heine burst in. He had come to mediate and arrange an exchange of views between the Admiral and the General. General von Schmettow, in his own and impulsive fashion, was at first inclined to reject this proposal out of hand, but after we had lunched together, he asked my advice about the matter. I tried to persuade him to attend the meeting, for the sake of his staff officers, whom he would be leaving behind, and also because I felt that such a talk might relieve the tension and mitigate the General's feeling of bitterness and betrayal.

The meeting between the Admiral and the General took place the next day. If anyone stands to profit from it, it should be Helldorf, and all credit is due to Heine for bringing it about, irrespective of whether his object was to be of assistance to Helldorf or the contrary.

My leave-taking of the General was cordial and mutually affecting. We had become good friends. Now he is returning to a Germany where he will not have a roof over his head, where his homeland has been overrun by the enemy and where his family must be on the road somewhere as refugees.

We paid a final visit to the stables, the General making for his favourite, a graceful and spirited brown mare, a lovely thing. I remembered how, last June, she had galloped with him, as light as thistledown over the flowery, high-set meadows. The General petted and fondled his favourite horse. It is in this attitude I shall best remember him. It is in such a kindly and guileless setting that he belongs, an old pastoral world of chivalry and noble horses. In our present rougher times he has been rudely attacked and unsaddled, something which could never have happened to him on horseback. I paid my respects to Monarch, that incredibly gigantic horse, who nuzzled me and thrust his thick lips into my hands. I shall certainly never in my life ride such a majestic horse as this again.

On parting, the General wrote me a pleasing testimonial of my work here, summing up the essentials in a few felicitous lines of his own inimitable style. He is also having a special shield of arms of the islands sent me in token of his regard. There is little I can do in return. The best I can muster up is a bottle of old port, but perhaps, in his depressed state, this may help to cheer him.

We are all much concerned about his flight back to Germany and hope he will arrive there safely.

Spent the evening at the Admiral's. He entertained us with an interesting account of his experiences as commander of the *Scharnhorst*, and became so carried away by his reminiscences that it was very late when we broke up.

6.3.45. We returned to Jersey in beautiful weather. Talked over in frank and friendly fashion with Colonel Heine our impressions of our visit, which had not on the whole turned out as badly as we expected. Then remained alone on the bridge and my thoughts ranged far and wide as I considered again the peculiarities of our situation and the difficulties of the times, and viewed the soothing expanse of the sea all around me.

There is still no news whatever of my wife. This is so mysterious that I sometimes wonder if there could have been some mishap which they think better to keep concealed from me. It is hard to believe that my wife must, presumably, still be in prison. When the *Palace Hotel* blew up yesterday, as a result of a fire near the munitions store, it brought home to me the terrors my wife must be undergoing, in the air raids on Linz. How remote we are here in the islands from the hell of Germany, which, as was evident at the recent general posting, has almost come to be looked on as a place of banishment.

7.3.45. Went on a tour of inspection with Mollet, the Bailiff's secretary, and another islander who is a man of local standing and expertise.

We first visited an anti-aircraft gunsite near Corbiere Point, where a bright young lieutenant had made a find of prehistoric flints during excavation work.

Then on to St Ouen's Bay, to examine the damage done to the seawall by the high tides. Here we were met by a scene of devastation. Great boulders and slabs of concrete weighing tons had been tossed about in all directions. Two mighty holes had been torn in the eight-metre high wall, through which two buses could drive with ease. I was much impressed by this evidence of the colossal power of the ocean, which, when we arrived, lay tranquil and far away at ebb, playing the innocent.

In the foreground the thin clerkly figure of the Bailiff's secretary bent over his notes, as he established in shocked nasal tones the extent of the damage done and took due evidence of it to make his official report. I was amused by the contrast – rather like that of the king and his jester – on the one hand the supreme majesty and might of nature, on the other the desk-bound civil servant, trying conscientiously to keep his records straight.

St Ouen's Bay itself presented an unusual and extraordinary sight, parts of it like patches of dark swampy moorland, with the stumps of ancient trees showing here and there. The second member of our expedition, a pleasant and well-informed local man, explained that this was a sight seldom seen – the last time 15 years ago – brought about by as yet unexplained vagaries of wind and weather, but chiefly by the erosion of sand. What we were looking at was the old seabed, with the remains of a primeval forest which had existed perhaps before the islands became separated from the mainland. I took a couple of samples of this prehistoric forest, dark brown, charred and brittle and light as a feather in my hand. A unique souvenir, some 5,000 years old.

In the opinion of local residents, the quantity of sand which was shipped over to Granville on the coast of France opposite, a few years ago when the whole area was being fortified, should never have been removed. It was needed here to secure the foundations of the seawalls; now, as the sea washes the sand around the island, there is always the danger of some portion of the seawall being laid bare and breached at high tide, particularly on the west coast.

8.3.45. Elaine Fielding has 'fallen in love' in the fullest and finest sense of the word. Her mother, and she still more, have become quite devoted to me and show their affection in such touchingly selfless and undemanding fashion that I can only accept this undeserved tribute as a happy gift of fate.

In the evening, as soon as it is dark, I creep over the 'noisy garden stones', the gravel approach to their door. Elaine is alert to the slightest sound and comes to meet me joyfully. This is her first great love, the awakening of her youthful mind and senses, long ripening to just such an occasion. Not that she has lost her head. On the contrary, some innate sense of reserve and a wisdom beyond her years makes her master of herself and the situation, so that she tends to deal with it lightly, with lots of jokes and laughter. Still, I find it difficult to prevent her from lavishing the entire contents of her Red Cross parcel on me, or for that matter of preventing them both from sharing their meagre rations with me.

For these two women, so long living alone with each other, and since the siege even more cut off from local friends by the lack of public transport, my sudden incursion into their lives must obviously have been of greater significance for them than it could be for me: up to my eyes in work and responsibilities from morning to night. I have realised this from the way they seem to live for my arrival and listen avidly to any scrap of news or account of the day's activities I am able to impart.

Their good breeding imparts a special charm to all they say and do. Elaine is full of youthful high spirits, but also tender and serious in turn, and never lacking in some imaginative flight of fancy to transform the ordinary occasion into a special one.

It is through her that I have learned to appreciate the English language. Everything she has to say, spoken with so much sincerity in her low voice, sounds like a poem. I had never known that English-women had so much heart and feeling. Yesterday evening Elaine sat down at the piano and in a pleasant contralto voice sang songs which were entirely unknown to me. We Germans too have been 'insular' in failing to have learned the rare quality of English songs.

9.3.45. The *Vega* has arrived for the third time, this time with snow-white flour for the civilian population. I drove down to the harbour to meet the ship. Apart from this, I am thankful to say, owing to the industry of our new Platzkommandant, von Cleve, who has busied himself in settling all the details of programme, protocol, unloading of the ship, what is and more important what is not allowed, I have been relieved of much of the responsibility which fell to my lot under Heider. Then I felt bound to take the lead, now I need only follow.

On board the ship, Cleve made a gallant effort to keep up conversationally with the Swiss Colonel Iselin. Perhaps a little jealous of my fluent French, he felt called on to explain that, as a young man, he had applied himself to and mastered the Swedish language in a matter of two weeks, thus confirming my original impression of him as a bit of a play-actor.

The pleasant young French-Swiss Callias had, unfortunately, to drop out at the last moment and was replaced by an Italian-Swiss, Mariotti. Owing to the last-minute switch, Mariotti failed to be documented as an international representative of the Red Cross and is thus not authorised to meet or take part in any deliberations with members of the States.

He has the narrow well-sculpted head of the typical Italian, also the rather sunken cheeks and pouched eyes, conveying that air of worldliness if not sensuality also common to Mediterranean peoples. For the rest, he is suave, well-mannered, rather boringly of a piece, with the affability of the well-travelled businessman, whose interests are commercial rather than cerebral.

After the tumult of the past few weeks, it is a relief to be able to retire to comparative anonymity and some sort of private life. Cleve has taken over full command, so that, apart from advising him to the best of my ability, I am no longer so burdened with personal responsibility.

Heider's departure to Guernsey was preceded by a vast amount of packing and preparation; obviously his chief interest as Feldkommandant was his cognac, his cigars and his food. Now reduced to size as a mere traveller, his main concern is still with his stomach and personal well-being. For all that he bears his fate with admirable stoicism and cheerfulness. As well for him that he is not the type to brood over his fall from power or to worry too much about what the future may bring.

10.3.45. For the first time this year got into swimming trunks for a sunbathe on the beach and a run along the sands. I was in good shape for this, as I had kept in training by early morning exercises.

The commando raid on Granville has been successfully concluded from a military point of view, but has not led to any material gain apart from 70 tons of coal. A number of Americans were taken prisoners and 60 German prisoners of war freed and brought back here. Our own losses have not been announced, although they are said to be high.

11.3.45. On my return from Guernsey I was greeted by the Fielding ladies like a long-awaited traveller from some distant shore. I spent the evening with them, in an animated exchange of news and views, which extended until dawn was breaking.

Yesterday they entertained me with a reading from Shakespeare, each taking a different role. Their rendering was masterly in understanding and expressiveness. No performance could have moved me more: their melodious voices opened up to me the whole might and majesty of Shakespeare's poetic works.

12.3.45. In the morning paid a visit to Samarès Manor with Mariotti and the captain of the Swedish ship. The weather was delightfully warm and sunny. The camellias were in full bloom, the magnolias bore finger-long buds and under the old trees in the park was an Easter proliferation of crocuses, narcissi and snowdrops. (There is a red camellia which is particularly decorative; its flowers are of almost architectural design, giving an artificial effect and with its waxy dark-green leaves, it has the boring perfection of the too beautiful woman.) Our guests were much impressed by the beauty of the place and returned to their ship with their arms full of flowers.

At midday there was the usual opulent meal on board the *Vega*. Mariotti is the personification of southern courtesy and charm. He does not merely offer his hand but extends both with a warmth of greeting which we more temperate northerners permit ourselves only rarely.

The day passed in so peaceful a pursuance of social duties, excursions and receptions, that it made the horrors of the war and the suffering in Germany still more frightful to contemplate. Yet Germany is only a few hours distant by air. It is on this brief but highly perilous flight that the General will be leaving today.

The Fieldings asked me in what costume I would like them to receive me on Fasching Monday, the culmination of the pre-Lent carnival celebrations in south Germany. I suggested that Elaine might appear as Nike of Samothrace and Mrs. Fielding as Athena the goddess of wisdom.

When I arrived, the 18-year-old daughter and 38-year-old mother greeted me in the guise of two bearded Greek fisher lads, so alike as to be indistinguishable.[1] They were ready, they announced, to row the stranger stranded on their island of Phaeacia back to his home, wife and children in Ithaca-Aufsess. There they would apply for work as wood-cutters on the Oberaufsess estate, a job for which, as the owner knew, they were well-qualified. All this, clearly pleased with their great joke, they delivered in well-turned Homeric hexameters, which they had composed and learned by heart.

I am abashed, even a little conscience-stricken, by their devotion to me, for which I can make so little return. But their good breeding is such that they maintain a certain distance and reserve. The Fieldings belong to the highest academic circles. They have a wonderful library, with the complete works of leading authors. Browsing along the shelves, one comes across many signed editions of the works of famous poets and philosophers. Mrs. Fielding's father is a Nobel prize winner, her husband a scientist of international repute. Mother and daughter had remained in their house in Jersey only because the new house under construction in Mexico was not yet habitable. Mr. Fielding holds the chair of natural science and physics at the university there.

13.3.45. The fortress commander, Colonel Heine, left the island early this morning, before daylight. He is to take over the command of the troops in Guernsey. Rather a come-down and probably painful for him, but he is shortly to be compensated by promotion to General. His decency and justice are beyond doubt and have won him universal regard.

There are some people with whom I am unable to establish any satisfactory relationship; they are totally antipathetic. Schade is one of them. I do my best to hide my aversion, but this leads to a false heartiness and makes the position worse, putting me at odds with myself. Schade is at present trying, in his crafty and devious way, to have the administrative section for agriculture and forestry, with himself, Ambacher and Schmidt, removed to offices in a separate location.

Visited a farm with Mariotti[2] and Wienberg,[3] also the gardens of Rozel Manor. Car rides, sightseeing, gifts of flowers, exchanges of invitations, all just as in times of peace.

14.3.45. A letter has just arrived for me in Guernsey. It is from Aussee,[4] dated 20 January 1945. All my cultivated calm and equanimity is shattered on the instant. I find myself shaking with anxiety, in alternating hope and despair, about the fate of my wife and children, whose health and happiness lie nearest of all things in the world to my heart.

Every week on a Tuesday I call at the Soldiers' Home for a chat with Sister Marie von Wedel. The very regularity of the call seems to work wonders with her, perhaps as the one still stable event in a world of impending chaos and change. She seems at least a little less fraught, distrait and abrupt in manner. I feel greatly for her, as our families have so much in common.

In the morning a long session with Mariotti and the States' representatives. The proceedings were purely routine but unduly prolonged by Cleve's enthusiasm for the duties of his new office.

One of the items on the agenda was the handing over by the Red Cross of wax impressions for making artificial legs. These were for a young girl who had lost both her legs in an accident on the island railway line some years ago and had since grown up. The arrival of the parcel was the result of a lengthy correspondence between us and Geneva, Lisbon and London. This was surely for a worthy cause and showed that we were not indifferent to the needs of the poor and handicapped. But as we unwrapped the parcel to check the contents, a security measure imposed by the conditions of war, the Bailiff could not resist sarcastically quipping that it might contain explosives. There are times when his abrasive manner and lack of good taste are positively obnoxious.

For all his vanity and enormous self-confidence, Cleve has the happy knack of not taking, or at least putting up a good show of not taking, his own opinions for granted; in either case this has a conciliatory effect. He has fine, large blue eyes and knows how to use them; certainly a bit of an actor, if a likeable one.

Duret Aubin, the Attorney-General, wears mittens, from which his ugly, uncared-for gardener's fingers protrude comically, as from torn gloves. His nose and cheeks are perpetually ruddy. He is very much a child of nature. When the Bailiff speaks, he spontaneously and unconsciously supports him with muttered exclamations of approbation and emphasis, providing a small parliament in himself for the interested observer sitting next to him, as I was today.

In the evening took a stroll round the garden at Linden Court. It is beautifully kept and now in the full burgeoning of spring. If one never lived less comfortably than here, or ate less well than on the Red Cross ship today, one would indeed be among the favoured of mankind.

15.3.45. The letter from Altaussee has arrived. But it was only a routine report from Herr von Hindenburg,[5] from which I can only deduce that my wife must still be in prison in Linz. I am completely nonplussed and cast down. I had always hoped that she might by now have been freed. Obviously, what news there is is being deliberately withheld from me, as I have had no direct communication with the family, either from Altaussee or from Aufsess. Well-meant as it may be, this suppression of news is maddening. On the other hand, I suppose, I can only be thankful that the warrant for my arrest, which must certainly have followed my wife's incarceration, has still not arrived in the islands.

Spent the evening with the Fieldings. The relationship between mother and daughter is delightful; they tease and chaff and bring out the best in each other. Yesterday evening Mrs. Fielding was invited out and left me alone with Elaine, with an observation I felt worthy of the Marschallin in *Die Rosenkavalier*, that she was leaving behind 'a lucky girl and a well-balanced man'. Our friendship *à trois* is relaxed, easy and gay. It could only have sprung up in the extraordinary conditions of a dreadful war nearing its end, with dire necessity and want all around us. The most welcome gift I can bring them is a few logs of wood, while they reciprocate most generously with ingeniously contrived variations of sandwiches from the contents of their Red Cross parcels, no Lucullan feast this. But the meagreness of our supper table beside the fire is compensated to some extent by the one thing we still enjoy in abundance, spring flowers and flowering twigs. Our table is covered by them, as are the islands themselves. If a war could be won with flowers, these poor beleaguered islands could conquer the whole continent.

16.3.45. Important conferences, which may lead to big organisational changes. Schade has been promoted to chief agricultural expert for the island, and will be moving into the Platzkommandantur building. This at least meets my endeavours to get all the members of Military Administration under one roof. Difficult and delicate negotiations with the Bailiff, which proceeded for hours. We urgently need more potatoes for the hungry garrison on Alderney. To obtain them, however, meant breaking the agreement which had been made by Helldorf (and against which I had warned everybody at the time). The Bailiff threatened to resign. But Cleve handled the situation with great good sense and skill. The Bailiff himself acknowledges Cleve to be the cleverest man to hold the office of Feldkommandant or Platzkommandant to date, although in view of his two predecessors this is not perhaps such a great compliment.

I was interrogated by the Military Court as a witness in the case against Helldorf. He is accused of having failed to carry out orders, but I do not believe this charge can be proven. I did my best to help him.

18.3.45. After further lengthy talks, the dispute over the potatoes has been brought to a satisfactory conclusion. We shook hands warmly with the Bailiff and Attorney-General. It is true they are letting us have only 100 tons instead of the 200 tons we asked for, but this with the important proviso that they do not consider this quantity in breach of our agreement. On the grounds of successful collaboration with the States, this must be accounted a victory, although I should have been apprehensive of reporting an effective loss of 50% of our needs if I had been reporting to the Admiral as the officer solely responsible. Cleve is so firmly in the saddle that he can afford a compromise which in the case of his predecessors might have been considered a weakness. No doubt he worked hard in presenting his case to gain the undoubted approbation of the German authorities, and has also not failed to impress this on the States.

Cleve grows in stature with his mounting popularity and his response to it, particularly as expressed in his confidence in his staff. He has come to rely so much on my advice that Pokorny has jokingly accused me of being the *eminence grise* of a whole succession of Commandants.

After long shilly-shallying, Cleve has at last decided to move in with me at Linden Court. We had long since agreed that our private lives would remain private and neither would intrude on the other. This despite the Admiral having practically impressed an oath of chastity on his officers! All that this has achieved is to stress the importance of not being found out. Such affairs should in any case be conducted with discretion and with a proper regard for decorum and good taste.

The rearrangement of the Platzkommandantur to accommodate the agriculture and forestry section has now been completed along the lines I suggested. If the daily sight of Schade is not particularly agreeable, at least all the business conducted by him comes under my scrutiny.

This morning we had a visit from our new fortress and divisional commander, General Wulf, who has replaced Heine. He is the archetype of the professional soldier, a second Ludendorff, with no whit of personal warmth or affability and no interest in anything but purely military affairs. His features are fleshy but well-formed; nose, mouth and chin set in a firm line. In his own professional field we may expect his decisions to be clear, concise and final. For the more diplomatic aspects of his appointment he has no propensity at all, as he made clear from the start by declining to meet the Bailiff, on the grounds of lack of interest. His attitude towards the civilian sector and his responsibilities as supreme commander of this small foreign land and its inhabitants seems one of rejection, even of aversion. As his physiognomy indicates he is the bluff soldier, interested only in hard facts and military action.

19.3.45. Mrs. Fielding plays the piano beautifully. She has introduced me to and taught me to appreciate Ravel. The two of them think up some new entertainment for every evening. I am often hard put to it to decide of which I am more fond, mother or daughter. They are, for their part, above all jealousy.

21.3.45. Since Cleve has moved into the house, I have withdrawn to my own room, which I have fitted up with more comfortable furniture. Here I enjoy my solitude.

Invited Counsellor Hauschild to tea. He comes from Gmunden; has recently been posted to us from Germany to advise on agricultural matters and arrived here recently by air. An affable little Austrian, he has a clever pointed face and small watchful eyes. He is very full of himself and his mission, with the bustling self-importance of the hard-working, conscientious, but rather narrow-minded civil servant, all in keeping with his physical appearance, his short but paunchy figure. His qualifications are undoubted, and his dedication to his job. He is also quite the diplomat, weighing his words carefully, if primarily with the object of making a good impression and gaining proper recognition for himself. The first task he has undertaken is the complete reorganisation of milk supplies. These are to be increased (!) and the surplus devoted to producing nourishing by-products, such as yoghurt and cottage cheese, etc. Thus the supply of calories will be increased in the long term, without killing, as it were, the golden goose, or, in this case, the Jersey cow which supplies them, for the more short-term benefits of meat.

Cleve moved into Linden Court with reluctance. He really wanted to live alone. So he cannot complain if I have made myself scarce, which was what he had led me to understand he required of me. I am only too happy to escape from his unending declamatory monologue. He is very much the actor, not only in dominating the stage and not allowing anyone else a word, but in his habit of switching, as at the fall of a curtain, from a grave face to one illuminated by a broad smile revealing dazzling – but, as I so unfortunately discovered this morning – false teeth. His signature, starting off in large letters, but dwindling to a

squiggle at the end, seems to match his propensity to start off playing a
big role, without carrying it through to the end.

25.3.45. The progress of the war – with the Allies now over the Rhine
and the Russians advancing on all sectors of the eastern front – is such
that it leaves one with little inclination to record daily events in our
little backwater. I retire into a world of books, but find little consolation
there.

A greater solace is my friendship with the Fieldings, which becomes
ever more firmly established. Their magnanimity is boundless and they
are gifted in their expression of it, always finding the right things to say
and do. Our relationship is unique in its happy blend of tactful reserve
and lighthearted companionship.

26.3.45. The Admiral is here again. He called a meeting of officers and
addressed us with great eloquence, confiding to us the full facts of the
situation here and his assessment of it. He is a master of rhetoric and
always knows how to grip his audience.

Two things strike me about him, his round shoulders, typical of the
bookman rather than the man of action, and his high forehead, typical
of the thinker. The army officers must find him a puzzlingly alien being.
He belongs to that category of Nazi who are so carried away and
bemused by their own oratory that they can never be reckoned to be
dealing honestly either with themselves or with others. The Admiral
would not be out of place as an evangelical pastor speaking from the
pulpit. Certainly he could not proclaim his political, as against his
religious, beliefs with more fervour or conviction.

In the afternoon there was a meeting between the Admiral and the
Bailiff. From this I was excluded. No doubt the Admiral's adjutant
Reich, who might better be described as his confidential clerk, has
taken exception to my tendency to candid comment, and has chalked
up another black mark against me. This lack of trust is most
disheartening. My name, my friendship with General von Schmettow,
my reputation for moderation, all count against me with the new
regime, so that I am barely tolerated. It has even, it has come to my
knowledge, been suggested that I should be exiled to Alderney, as
Intendant there, to detach me from my alleged anglophile contacts and
preoccupations.

All this at a time when the Americans are advancing on my home.
Würzburg has already fallen. All our homes have been overrun or are
about to be overrun by the foe, yet this senseless discord rules among
us here. To raise any sensible and reasoned objection to any course of
action proposed here is merely to risk being labelled a defeatist.

I can already foresee that Hauschild's grandiose scheme for revolutionising the milk industry is doomed to failure. But to point this out, on the grounds of my greater experience in local affairs, would only further incense Reich and Hauschild against me, without in any way helping the local population. So I hold my tongue. We have reached a complete breakdown, not only materially but in morale. The Admiral was by no means unjustified in making an appeal for trust between us the central theme of his address, although of course one never knows with him how much he is inspired by rhetoric and how much by honest intent.

In the evening the Admiral came to visit us at Linden Court. After his departure, Cleve lit up another big cigar to talk over the occasion with me for another couple of hours; that is, to indulge in his customary monologue. He is, one feels – another aspect of his play-acting nature – not seeking approbation so much as a sounding-board for his opinions. He is also, surprisingly and rather disarmingly, himself aware of this, as he showed by asking if I did not think he was becoming too talkative. An honest reply would have been too discourteous.

2.4.45. A whole week has passed since I last made an entry in this diary. The news of the war in Germany, now rapidly approaching the final defeat, inhibits the urge to set down our small local happenings. The spring is so lovely here this year, the countryside burgeoning under the late warm rains, that one can forget the situation for hours on end. Easter, too, passed pleasantly, with good company and good food, thanks largely to the unfailing affection and hospitality of the Fieldings. In continuing to see them I am breaking the Admiral's latest order, which came into force on 1 April and which forbids any social contact with the local population.

On Easter Sunday Cleve and I were invited to tea with Mrs. Riley at Rozel Manor. The cakes were of pre-war quality. In our conversation, conducted in the light half-ironic style customary on the English social occasion, we touched on our present situation. Cleve hinted that the end of war would not necessarily mean an unconditional surrender of the islands. He quoted a speech allegedly once made by Churchill, describing the islands as 'millstones around the neck of England'. It should therefore not be difficult to strike a little bargain to rid England of this weight of responsibility. It was merely a matter of skilled negotiation and not overstepping the bounds of moderation in putting our conditions. I chimed in jokingly to say that after the War I would write a comedy entitled 'Who besieged Whom?'; it was in fact a comic situation with the British besieging not only us but their fellow-countrymen and with both sides beleaguered by the sea. Mrs. Riley offered to put the manor at our disposal for peace negotiations and also jokingly considered whether she would still have enough supplies in her cellar to provide us with refreshments.

On Easter Monday there was a grand set-to with the Bailiff on the question of milk supplies. Hauschild's plan for a big reorganisation is already proving impracticable. Hauschild lost his temper, which in turn moved the Bailiff to wrath. It was clearly not an atmosphere in which to continue discussion and the meeting was adjourned until the Tuesday after Easter.

4.4.45. In this state of siege one must view with concern the poor physical condition of the troops and the measures taken to offset it, i.e., the reduction of military exercises to a minimum. I am doubtful about the success of this policy and feel it has been carried to excess in imposing an almost complete idleness which has led to a general apathy and sickliness more harmful than an occasional overtaxing of physical strength. Physical well-being depends on a modicum of bodily exercise, no matter how ill nourished the body.

5.4.45. Meanwhile the big argument on milk supplies has been settled, after a fashion. What has been achieved, after three weeks of negotiations, is meagre enough. I could have achieved as much with far less expenditure of time and energy. In short, the situation remains much the same as before. The only concession we have gained is that in future all supplies of skimmed milk will come to us, for the production of cottage cheese for the troops. This should, supposedly, reduce the troops' requirements for meat. Hauschild's demands for increased milk supplies will I fear founder on the simple facts of supply and demand. We have been through all this before.

At least I am glad that I no longer bear sole responsibility. This must now devolve in a large measure on Hauschild, our new agricultural adviser, and Reich, the Admiral's adjutant, both of whom played a leading part in the negotiations. I should have felt myself falling short of my duty to have come away from such prolonged discussions with so little to show for it. I should also have felt particularly concerned about other pertinent matters which were shelved or deferred by our new negotiators. As, for example, an Easter egg for the troops, which, paradoxically, they had never lacked until our new rulers introduced their 'tougher line' policy. There is no denying that Helldorf, with his flair for the practical and common sense, if less conventional, methods, did very much better. All that has happened under the new regime is a doubling or tripling of staffs and organisational plans, with the result of still less in the way of practical achievement. Our Commander-in-Chief in France experienced this. It seems that this tendency to over-organisation is an inbuilt flaw in the German character.

6.4.45. Since the change in command, the malaise of mistrust among us has steadily increased. Every word one utters must be carefully weighed. To argue about anything, even with obvious good sense, invites the charge of a 'traitorous' lack of belief in our final victory. (As if anyone could believe in this with half of Germany now under enemy occupation.)

Ambacher, for instance, is at present on trial before the military court, merely for having countered the silly and extravagant talk of a young lieutenant in his regiment with the observation that the enemy could not be driven out of Germany with broomsticks!

The Navy here, like the Party in Germany, occupies the key posts and enjoys special rights. In future, nobody will be allowed on board the Red Cross ship except naval personnel. That the Red Cross delegates may find it odd that Schneeberger in Guernsey and myself in Jersey are so suddenly excluded and that this may reflect adversely on our authority in dealing with them, counts for nothing. And the passes authorising access to the ship are to be issued by, of all people, the very naval officer previously subjected to disciplinary action for drunk and disorderly conduct aboard her!

The naval captain, Reich, falls short of his responsibilities in every respect. We no longer receive any clear directives from Staff Headquarters and the change in command has not gained a single advantage for the German side; on the contrary, the flood of new orders has merely stiffened local resistance. The new system of milk deliveries is working so badly that I have felt obliged to intervene in the worst cases of defalcation, although I am in no way responsible. Hauschild, too, while starting off with dazzling plans and all the enthusiasm of the beginner, and not perhaps without an eye to his own advancement, has proved to be lacking in the resilience and determination necessary to carry his own plans through on a practical basis.

The old and tried members of my staff rally round me and assure me that everything worked much more smoothly and with less expenditure of manpower and effort in the days when I was in sole command of civilian affairs. As I have genuinely done my best to fall in with the new policy of employing a host of new experts, have even been impressed by some of their ideas and hoped for good results, I write without personal bias. Perhaps I have erred in the other direction and should have insisted more strongly on my own superior knowledge of local affairs. Not that the validity of the claim would be allowed by Captain Reich.

It is a great mistake to entrust persons of modest background, such as Reich, with his former experience as a bank clerk, with the responsibilities of high office. They are naturally on the defensive, suspecting that their authority could be challenged, and this can only have a detrimental overall effect.

These wonderful spring days and my preoccupation with botany and biology help to keep the petty vexations of life at bay. Rain and sunshine alternate in happy sequence and nature responds a hundred-fold in proliferating growth. The hedges around Linden Court thicken into impenetrable green walls. The daffodils wither and the cherry trees approach their zenith in a delicate profusion of blossom crowning every twig. I choose the best blooms to give to friends and deck my office desk with flowers.

In the evening our neighbours, Mrs. Fielding and her daughter, visited us in Linden Court for the first time, making a discreet entrance through the back door. They were in high spirits over the invitation and clearly enjoyed the social occasion, finding it hard to break up even long after midnight. Their laughter and animated conversation were rather dangerously loud in respect of passing patrols, who might have gained the impression that a much larger party was in progress. Cleve and I agreed that Elaine was especially talented and quick-witted. We both greatly enjoyed the ladies' company. Rising to the occasion, Cleve excelled himself in recounting droll anecdotes which kept us all laughing; he was most entertaining.

7.4.45. Stinging-nettles, sorrel, lettuce and cauliflower now introduce a welcome variety to our recent diet of root vegetables. With a small supply of beet syrup and some extra vegetables, I have been fortunate enough to get through the last few weeks, when supplies were at their lowest, rather better than most people. The meals aboard the Red Cross ships, the Saturday evening suppers with the Fieldings and the little extras in fruit and vegetables from my good friend the Jesuit father, have also provided their share of additional sustenance.

So I find myself still in good physical and mental health, and hope to maintain this state by keeping to the strict regimen I have long since set myself: regular physical exercise and mental exercise in the shape of a regular language study. To succumb to circumstance, to lapse into apathy is, as I have daily cause to note, a mistaken policy in the struggle for survival in these days of emergency.

The faint reverberation of gunfire from distant St Nazaire is all that disturbs this peaceful Saturday afternoon. At home the enemy front draws ever more menacingly near.

8.4.45. The implementation of Hauschild's grand project for stepping up milk supplies has shown that the target cannot be reached without the help of the civilian population. And the islanders are not only ever less inclined to co-operate as our own situation worsens; the revelation of our increased demands has led to an increase in their resistance. Even Hauschild has himself come to admit the actuality of the opposition to his scheme. He may imagine the situation could be retrieved by some drastic intervention on our part, such as making a change in the island leadership. In this he would be greatly mistaken. Such drastic exercise of power would merely stiffen a resistance which does not stem from any particular individuals but is rooted in the whole community.

The only alternative would be for the forces to take over an increasing share in the farming. Experience shows however that, apart from the technical difficulties, this would hardly be likely to lead to any greater success. It will now be for the Admiral to decide whether we are to continue to manoeuvre with the States Committee, as the elected representatives of the people, retaining their marginal co-operation, or resort to force and declare open war on them.

Hauschild's plan was feasible only on paper; brought up against the realities of the situation it proves impracticable. My own opinion is that our best course would be to continue our juggling and negotiating with the States. This does not preclude slipping in tougher measures here and there as expedient. To change over to a complete assumption of power at this stage would cost us too much and guarantee us too little. I have set down these thoughts in a memorandum addressed to Cleve, for use at his discretion. I could not bring myself to address it to Reich, a touchy little man, apt to take any expression of opinion as a personal challenge to his authority, while unable to control his vastly inflated staff. I have no confidence in him.

In the afternoon we sat round on the sun terrace at Newland House, drinking tea and chatting. Gloomy speculation on the future led us to praise the present and to admit that, up to now, our lot had been so much more fortunate than most Germans. Hauschild prophesied guerrilla warfare in Germany. None of us can have the slightest conception of what may lie before us. We also spoke very freely about the mistakes of the past, although denunciation is the order of the day, even in small circles. Still, we have not quite reached the extremes of the Spanish Inquisition, when even a rebellious look in the eye could be taken for heresy and suitably punished.

Gathered two magnificent bouquets for the *Vega* at Samarès Manor and 'enjoyed myself', as the English say, in the process.

Back in the office was confronted by the Commander-in-Chief's new standing orders, all of 30 pages long. So typically German: organisation and classification. At the same time the whole unwieldy apparatus works to ever less effect. An entire page is given over to hieroglyphs such as G I, G II, a II, Qu II, etc., close on a hundred designations for the various detachments and details. Any attempt to get to grips with practical affairs must be defeated by this military algebra. We are lacking in clever heads at the top who could relate action to reality and meet the exigencies of the situation by a wise deployment of manpower rather than by a duplication of office.

In comparison, the opposition's system is enviably simple, smooth-running and effective, and the members of the States Superior Council, set up to deal with occupation conditions, are united in mutual trust, knowledge of affairs and the common aim of putting up a good stand against the Germans.

One can only laugh, if rather wryly, at this stupendous compilation, not least at the futility of its issue at all at this late date.

9.4.45. Have been reading an amusing book by the French writer Delteil, on St Francis of Assisi's conversations with the birds. The good saint wanders through the world, at peace with himself and all nature, communing with the animals, feeding the birds, but noting how the inhabitants of the world subsist by preying on and devouring each other. This disturbs the good man not at all, but leads him to the sensible conclusion that the world would be a cold and barren planet without these natural processes of life and death. In short, our role is to eat or be eaten, *'La veritable concorde réside dans l'estomac mes frères, la suprême fraternité, c'est la fraternité des ventres'*.

In the evening we entertained the two Swiss doctors from the Red Cross Commission at Linden Court. The conversation turned princi-pally on foreign travel; Cleve making a leading contribution with a graphic and convincing account of Greece and its people. The elder of the doctors, a good-looking man, told us about his trips to Kilimanjaro, North Africa and latterly Greenland, but it seemed with more enthusiasm for the extent of his travels than for conveying an impression of the places visited. This urge to claim acquaintance with far horizons is a noticeable component in the Swiss character, perhaps owing to the claustrophobic smallness of their own country. They react to this either centripetally, by settling on their own small plot in peace, or centrifugally by ranging restlessly about the world. In neither case can they shake off the confines of their place of birth.

A pretty Irishwoman called on me in the office today. She is desperately anxious to get away on the Red Cross ship in order to reach England and from there take passage to India, where her fiancé has been awaiting her for the past six years. I have been doing my best to help her. Today she ingenuously offered any help which she, as a neutral, could extend me in return; I must for instance have a wife and family in Germany. A depressing reminder of how soon we shall be, if we are not already, reliant on the compassion and charity of others.

10.4.45. Even now the Americans are advancing on my home-town and the Russians on the town of Linz. The Americans are reported as 24 kms. east of Bamberg, coming down from Coburg. The Russians, to all effect already the masters of Vienna, are advancing on Linz. My mind is in a turmoil of anxiety for my family and hope that they may survive these dreadful days. It now really seems that my wife may be freed by the Russians. What an absurdity of fate! And what terrors may she be suffering in these final hours.

Here, meanwhile, we are engaged in a series of conferences with the Red Cross Commission on the evacuation of the sick. The number to be transported is small and the inhabitants' general lack of response to the scheme a mute testimonial of good treatment and a supportable life. Conference after conference, too, among ourselves on all the sticky issues of the day. On reactivating the fishing industry, where the chief difficulty is getting the local fishermen to work for us. On keeping account of the milk supply and its by-products, a problem bedevilled by a hundred obstacles in connection with the dairies, transport, deliveries, controls, etc., and hardly likely to be solved by discussion. On the water supply, the allocation of coal, the allocation of petrol, etc. Fewer conferences would be needed with men of initiative and clearer vision at the helm. Instead we have fanatics and utopians, intolerant of any commonsense objections to their plans. In voicing my own doubts I immediately became suspect as a nonconformist and learned to hold my tongue.

There is as much a fashion in attitudes of mind as in modes of dress. To have scruples on any subject is as outdated as wearing high collars or long hair. In the present climate of political and military thought nobody can afford such eccentricities.

I am amused to think how often, in the five peaceful years of German occupation of the island, fashion has changed with regard to the island's most vulnerable points of attack. At first there was no doubt at all that this would be in the west. Bunkers, strongpoints and heavy artillery were concentrated there. With the fall of Normandy military opinion veered to the east as the area liable to enemy attack, with a resultant feverish activity in shifting defences, requisitioning more buildings, land, materials etc. Suddenly the area of interest shifted to the centre of the island, where it was now clear to the military commanders that the spearhead of the attack would be made by paratroopers, and suitable boobytrap defences were set up. Our new General has decided on the north coast as his scene of an imaginary enemy attack and is busily engaged in deploying our forces and setting up our defences there.

Meanwhile, in Germany, our foes are closing in all sides and there will soon be nothing left to defend.

11.4.45. The day began with a full-throated dawn chorus of birds. The morning sun glistened on the rain-drenched foliage of the multi-coloured shrubs now coming into leaf in the garden of Linden Court. In this background of green and gold, the cherry trees, all of varieties cultivated for their wealth of blossom, appeared at their best in a cloud of colour ranging from palest pink to deepest red. After three days of drought and an icy east wind, a sudden heavy shower has restored and revivified thirsting nature.

All units are now busily engaged in setting up nets along the shore to trap fish. This was preceded by a stampede to local tennis courts to acquire the necessary nets, conducted with the customary lack of military co-ordination and consequent waste of material. One bright O.T. man has distinguished himself by tackling the problem in positively scientific style and coming up with the best solution. It was, he decided, not enough to stretch wide-mouthed V shaped nets on the seabed facing the incoming tide. In addition he set up, further out to sea, a vertical net barrier. Thus the fish swept in by the sea were caught in his artful trap in greater numbers. Figures showed that this method had substantially increased his catch.

12.4.45. Discussion follows discussion, without any noticeable improvement in the situation. At the last big meeting of the vastly inflated H.Q. staff to consider the problem of providing sustenance for the troops, I amused myself by observing the varying expressions of those taking part. Some looked completely vacant, others were frowningly intent on following the proceedings. The least impressive person present was undoubtedly the presiding officer of this, at least numerically, imposing assembly, Captain Reich. On the previous evening we had been fellow-guests at a reception given for the Red Cross commissioners, when my previous impression of him as a small-time official had been confirmed and I had felt positively embarrassed *vis-a-vis* our Swiss visitors for his lack of *savoir faire* and the shameless way in which he made up to them.

Reich, like Hauschild, leans to extremism, with all the adjuncts of the police state. Hauschild is fond of declaring in resigned tones that it only needs somebody to be shot, then all would go better. Precisely the opposite would of course obtain. He is merely looking for an excuse for his own shortcomings. With his grandiose scheme for transforming the milk production, drawn up on paper for no less than a year ahead, he has not reckoned with local opposition and has failed to counter this by all the little tricks of diplomacy and patient negotiations which would have been necessary to implement even the initial stages. Instead he complains from one conference to another at the lack of progress.

Extremism is taking over, not only in our relations with the island governments but among ourselves. We are playing out on a smaller stage the same tragedy which is now leading to the annihilation of Germany. In Guernsey a medical officer was recruited to report on 'morale'. He has just betrayed some of his own comrades and thus been instrumental in their posting to 'exile' in Alderney. On his return to Guernsey, Reich immediately sent us an urgent request for a list of 100 Germans who might similarly qualify for political quarantine. I refused to have anything to do with the business; Cleve has with difficulty mustered up barely half the required number of names.

14.4.45. I am terribly shaken by the latest news of Bayreuth. The town refused to surrender. It was then bombed and bombarded until, after three hours, the white flags appeared. By then of course it was too late, the whole town was in flames. So this beautiful and ancient town of my youth will exist no more, and all for the sake of a set of fools remaining just three more hours in command. This urge to self-destruction is criminal and pathological and has nothing to do with true heroism or loyalty to one's country.

The Swedish captain of the *Vega* told us that our government, that is the government of Bavaria, is now in Constance. The battlefront will by now have passed over Oberaufsess.

Von Cleve is highly flattering about my acquaintance with the Fieldings, whose visit gave him such an excellent opportunity to shine as a raconteur. In his opinion they are the two best-looking women in the island. He had, he declares, never before encountered such charming and lady-like representatives of the English nation. When I consider the female company he entertained here the other evening, I can well believe him. He is very anxious to invite the Fieldings again and repeat our happy evening.

19.4.45. The last four days have been so hectic, so packed with anxious thoughts and action, that there has not been a free minute to write about all that was happening. Now I am starting on the third exercise book and consigning the others to the past and a safe hiding place. Each volume has, curiously enough, started with some particularly ominous event, the ushering in, as it were, of a new era. The first began with the news of my wife's arrest by the Gestapo, the second with the news of the General's fall from power. This, the third, commences with a record of my transfer to Guernsey.

At first I was in doubt as to whether this sudden and surprising posting was a posting in the proper sense at all, but rather the result of a signal from Germany for my arrest.

I had long been prepared for this contingency and had my flight to France planned to the last detail. I had identity documents as a French labourer, bearing my photograph and duly stamped by my own office, in fact by my own hand. My fellow-conspirators were three young local people, two men and a girl. Their little sailing yawl lay in Gorey harbour. With my help they had gradually fitted it up with two outboard motors, a supply of petrol and a week's rations. Wetzstein, who is in command of the Gorey coastal area, would, if need be, have covered our escape, although I had not yet told him how advanced our plans were. One avoids burdening friends with possibly dangerous knowledge.

Now the time had come to decide whether to put this plan into effect. Did the summons from Guernsey in fact mean that I had now, like my wife, been proclaimed an enemy of the State? Was the posting to Guernsey merely a ruse to have me arrested there, rather than in Jersey, where it might have been embarrassing in view of my known good relations with the States? With the fanatics now in power and calling for heads to roll, mine would provide a sufficiently alarming example. I appealed to my good friend X, whom I have already mentioned in these pages as a reliable source at the Naval Communications Centre and who had never failed to keep me posted on radio signals from Germany. But if I was to leave for France it would have had to be almost immediately. To avoid taking the ship to Guernsey by going into hiding with my friends would have ruined our plan which depended on my having a car and wearing a uniform to bluff my way past the sentries.

So I decided to make the attempt on the night of 16/17 April. This was with a heavy heart. I had hoped to be able to hold out here until the end and bring things to a decent and honourable conclusion. Much as I detest the regime and its followers, I still felt responsible for the duties to which I had been appointed. I hurriedly wrote a few farewell letters and placed them in safe keeping.

Then, only a few hours before we were due to leave Gorey on 16 April, I heard from X that my transfer to Guernsey was merely one of a new wave of postings and that nothing against me had been reported from Germany, nor had any further complaints against me come to light. I knew I could trust X absolutely and at the eleventh hour called off the escape.

My young friends were deeply disappointed. They had been waiting for weeks for the word go and were cheerfully unconcerned about the risks. But I could not commit myself to this desperate venture merely for their sakes. I did my best to dissuade them from making the attempt alone, pointing out that the war was nearly over and if they did get to England it would be too late to join up and take part in it. They were unconvinced and I feared they would make the attempt as soon as the opportunity offered. On subsequent nights, as it happened, nature took a hand with such strong westerly winds that the tide failed to reach the mooring-place and the little boat could not have been launched.

The posting was a complete surprise not only to me but also to the Platzkommandant, von Cleve, who as my commanding officer would normally have expected to be consulted. No reasons have been given. I am being replaced in Jersey by Counsellor Schneeberger, previously in charge of the civil affairs sector of our branch administration in Guernsey. The best that can be said for the switch is that we are both well-versed in the intricacies of the local governments and experienced in dealing with their representatives, amicably and to our best advantage, despite the unwelcome wartime measures we have been called on to negotiate. Further postings had meanwhile followed. Pokorny was suspended from office pending orders for secondment.

Having abandoned my plan to flee to France, it remained to take leave of the island where I had spent the last three and a half years. This spring has been the loveliest of all, the sudden heat bringing out leaves, flowers and blossom in simultaneous rich profusion. Taking leave of my many friends meant a strict division of the remaining hours. With the obligation, on a posting, to take the next ship for Guernsey, which was to depart on the 18th, I was left with barely a day and a half.

I invited the Attorney-General to meet me in the garden at Langford House. There we had a very frank and friendly talk. Sitting on the smooth lawn, with the wisteria, tulips and fruit trees in blossom all around, it was difficult to imagine that the threat of war, in its final and most dreadful stages, still hung over this peaceful isle.

At Samarès Manor Miss White was, for the first of the many times I had called on her, not at home. Only her little Scottie terrier, Roy, greeted me as an old friend. Besides some cigarettes and a bottle of red wine, I also left her a letter. I had latterly not visited her so often. Over the years her views had narrowed and her fund of stories grown stale by repetition. As the caretaker of the finest manor, with the most beautiful and lavishly laid out grounds, she had always enjoyed a privileged position with us Germans, a position which, to do her justice, she utilised to the best advantage of the absent owner. It is characteristic of her and of our attitude towards her, that she had continued to press, through Colonel Lindner, for a receipt for a horse, for which she had long received payment, and for a paper testifying that we had removed a chaise-longue. These were the only two items the Germans had taken from Samarès Manor, the richest estate in the island. But Miss White had become out of touch with world events, especially with what was happening in Germany.

I spent the evening with the Fieldings. They were both very cast down. Even before parting, we were already exchanging those

recollections of past experiences which will in future be the only link
between us. I could not prevent them from lavishing on me all sorts of
delicacies from the Red Cross parcels which had just been issued. Just
as they had offered me a hiding-place here on the island if I needed one,
at risk of their lives, so they now offered me and my family a place of
refuge if we should need one in the future. When I arrived in Guernsey
and opened the envelope they had pressed on me at parting, I found ten
English pound notes, a good luck charm and a charming letter from
each. And when I left the house next day on my way to the harbour,
they were standing at their garden gate to see me go.

The day of departure commenced with an early breakfast at Rozel
Manor, to which Mrs. Riley had invited me at 8 a.m. The table was laid
in the large room with the open fireplace, and in this and in the
adjoining room stood at least twenty colourful arrangements of
glorious tulips in as many differing hues.

We conversed very frankly and cordially. In these few years so many
people, known to us both, have come and gone, the scene has changed
drastically for the worse, and now the final day of reckoning is near.
Our friendship was a genuine one, based on a strong community of
interests. I confided to her the negatives of my numerous photographs
of the island. These she will keep for me in some safe hiding-place.

We took a last walk through the garden, now reaching an apex of
spring. Never had there been such a profusion of blossom. The lilies
had this spring spread still further over the manorial fishpond. The
wisteria covering the walls of the little gothic chapel was just coming
into flower, a delicate bluish tracery strung over the tangled network of
creeper, through which the granite glowed roseate.

Our path led finally to the Philosopher's Wall, with a view over a sea
of azaleas to those heroic old trees I had come to know and love so well.
The gnarled beeches in their fresh spring green made a brave show of
youth. It was indeed here at Rozel Manor that I rediscovered that
idyllic world of my childhood's dreams, with palm trees, exotic
vegetation, docile wildlife – all as depicted in the framed oleograph
which had hung above my nursery bed.

On the way back to town, I made a brief call on Wetzstein, who
seemed more concerned about my posting and my future fate than I am
myself. The leave-taking of my colleagues at the office which followed
was almost too much for my overwrought nerves. The officers
presented me with an engraved silver napkin-ring; the men with a book
omitting the customary, indeed almost obligatory 'Heil Hitler' in the
inscription, which merely stated in simple terms that in these difficult
times they could not have wished for a better or more considerate chief.

The last call of the morning, on the way to the harbour, was at the
Royal Court, where Cleve accompanied me for a final leave-taking of

the Bailiff and the Attorney-General. Both expressed their regret at my departure, the latter at least genuinely. At the entrance to the court buildings, Jurat Bree, with others of the Superiors Council and the manager of the electricity works, Mr. Burrell, were waiting to give me a final handshake and expression of their good wishes. As the car left, Ralph Mollet, the Bailiff's secretary, gave a final wave and called 'We shall remember you, you were a gentleman'.

I could scarcely have wished for a better send-off, nor perhaps, although not of my own choosing, a better time to leave, at the height of the loveliest spring I had known in the island and at a turning-point from which the situation could only deteriorate until the now inevitable end of the occupation.

At the harbour there was quite a crowd of officers, some waiting to board the ship, others seeing me off. My posting was by no means an individual case. There had been a widespread last minute general post. What good this can lead to remains to be seen. Colonel Lindner had been called up in the middle of the previous night and ordered to catch the ship the next day. No reason for these postings have been divulged and all enquiries have been fobbed off from one office to another. Such a trading in persons and positions was something we had never previously experienced.

Cleve obviously found it hard to part with me. He not only valued my professional advice but had taken a great personal liking to me since we had been sharing billets. He also regarded my posting as something of a personal affront, as, against all the rules, his opinion had not been asked. He had written a personal letter to Admiral Hüffmeier, which he asked me to deliver.

On the morning of the 19th I called on the Admiral in his modest residence. He was sitting in a small glass-covered veranda, bent over a stack of files. I first handed him the Platzkommandant's letter. In this Cleve succinctly summed up the folly of this latest series of postings, pointing out the stiffness of local resistance and the dangers of provoking it to open rebellion by these latest measures. He also wrote frankly and courageously in warning against the adoption of hastily conceived and harsh measures against the local population, in this merely repeating what he had so often recently said on the telephone to Guernsey. But I could see that the Admiral was not impressed or likely to change his policy. (In fact, as I learned later, only an hour after my ship cast off from Jersey, he had sent an urgent telex to that island, threatening the Bailiff and all island officials with the most extreme penalties, if the present milk delivery of 10 thousand litres a day was not increased to 20 thousand litres, the target set by Hauschild, by 25 April.)

The Admiral then explained the reasons for my posting. Our Guernsey administrator, Schneeberger, had never been able to get on with the island representative for agriculture. Moreover, he had gone aboard the Red Cross ship against Hüffmeier's express orders; behaviour not to be tolerated. As far as I was concerned, the posting had been a political decision, although not directed entirely against me. As an 'exponent of compromise', it was time I was removed from my post in Jersey on account of the Bailiff there, who would certainly notice the change. The policy of moderation which I represented was now at an end. One could not wage war without standing up a few recalcitrants against the wall.

In this connection, the milk supply again cropped up. It looks as if it is this vexed question which has triggered off the hard-line policy and is likely to lead to a drastic change in our relations with the States. I handed the Admiral a copy of my memorandum on this subject. (Although presumably it would have passed on to Reich, I did not know whether it had actually reached the Admiral.)

At the same time as exerting pressure on the States with regard to milk deliveries, it was Hüffmeier's intention, he informed me, to tighten up discipline and make a general show of power. This especially in view of reliable news he had received that, on Hitler's birthday (20 April, tomorrow!) the enemy intended to declare the war at an end so that any further resistance would be regarded as guerrilla action and the customary rights and obligations of international war no longer applied. At this farrago of nonsense I tried, as politely as I could, to express my doubts about the enemy having any such intention. I said I knew the source of this story, the Captain of the *Vega*. I further pointed out the dangers of resorting to force at this stage of our dealings with the islanders. This would only stiffen their resistance. We were really obliged to co-operate with them, when our survival depended on their willingness to co-operate with us.

At this the Admiral looked very sour and saw fit to inform me how he had heard through his intelligence service of the Bailiff of Jersey's hatred of him, and his open avowal of this; that the Bailiff had falsely accused him, the Admiral, of wishing only to wipe out the population. From the expression on the Admiral's face, I could see he felt quite bitterly about the Bailiff. At their last meeting, he told me, the Bailiff had threatened him, if in veiled language, with legal proceedings after the war. But he was not to be deterred by this. If our Staff Headquarters ordered reprisals against the islanders, he would carry out these orders to the letter.

Still, I felt, it was chiefly the failure of Hauschild's scheme to double the milk supply and his efforts to cover up for this by reporting local resistance, which had first led Hüffmeier to adopt his new tough policy.

Meanwhile our own agricultural experts on administration staff have undertaken checks which show that Hauschild's estimates were completely unrealistic and could never have been achieved. But the damage is done. And I may consider myself, with this senseless posting to Guernsey, as the chief victim of Hauschild's ambitions and miscalculations.

As the Admiral was about to terminate the interview, I enquired whether I was still to function here, in Guernsey, as the head of the civil affairs branch of Military Administration for the Channel Islands. On his assuring me that I was, I pointed out that I must then regard my task here as one of even higher responsibility than in Jersey. The Admiral asked in what way and I explained that I felt my chief duty here must be that of adviser to the Commander-in-Chief on questions of international law. In this respect the naval captain, Zimmermann, lately called in to advise on questions of war at sea, was lacking in experience of local conditions which could only be acquired by living and working among the people. In all such important questions, I had hitherto stood by the Feldkommandant and later the Platzkommandant, in Jersey. This would scarcely be possible to the same extent by telephone. Here in Guernsey, I could report on matters of especial interest only to the Admiral himself. Only he would have the authority to deal with them and going through a third person could lead to misunderstandings. The Admiral agreed to a channel being set up for direct access to him on matters outside the competence of Headquarters Supply Staff (Captain Reich!) and advised me on whom to get in touch with to facilitate this.

With this I had made the first move towards consolidating my position and authority. I would gladly waive any further claim to authority and retire into peaceful anonymity, which was perhaps what was expected of me at this stage. But as fate has landed me here and I felt I might still be able to prevent the worst excesses of Nazi policy, I shall continue to try to play some part in affairs. With what success is doubtful, in view of the Admiral's increasing tendency to extremism. Yet he seems to me open to argument and willing to give a hearing to opposing viewpoints. Reich is a very different proposition; a narrow-minded and rabid demagogue. Unfortunately as the Admiral's chief adviser and sycophant henchman, he dominates him by playing up to the worst side of his character.

So I left the Admiral, feeling that, even after making a tentative first move, I should probably still be out-manoeuvred by the arch-Nazi Reich. However, if I have gained the reputation for being the 'leading exponent of compromise', this is certainly the time and place to put my reputation to the test in trying to exert every influence I can bring to bear on the leading characters in our islands drama, even those most antipathetic to me.

In the afternoon I had a meeting with Reich. With him, too, I put myself out to try to see some good in him, as without this no good could come of trying to work with him. He is eminently approachable and apparently eager to meet one halfway with a typical Rhineland warmth and sociability. But this is an initial impression and belied by the crafty little eyes behind their spectacles. It is certainly his influence on the Admiral which has led to this inconsiderate trading in posts and persons. His very short-sightedness perhaps makes him better at dealing with statistics and the abstract problem rather than the human element. He is, however, by no means unskilled in argument; can present his case with a quiet confidence and seeming impartiality which, I can see, would carry great weight with the Admiral. Hüffmeier seems, with his excitable nature, over-impressionable and unfortunately apt to over-react and attach undue importance to every trifling matter brought to his attention. And the island network of snoopers and informants continues its unholy work.

Reich explained to me in his complacent manner, as of a lecturer addressing his students, that he did not regard this present phase of the war as altogether unfavourable. (With the Russians close to Berlin and the Americans to Dresden?) With the islands in our hands, we were still in a position to strike a bargain with the enemy to the advantage of Germany. Well and good. I am all for making the most of any assets we still possess and not selling out cheaply. But to imagine that we could still achieve a quasi-victory by trading the islands against total surrender in Germany seems to me so ludicrous, that I can only attribute the idea to that dangerous Nazi capacity for self-delusion, which decked with similar specious argument, has led us to our present plight.

I went back to my billets with the uneasy feeling that nothing here made sense, that everyone was engaged in a perilous game of self-deception. The Admiral, irascible as he may be, given to exaggeration and too easily swayed by trifles, is basically honourable, means well and believes in what he says. It would be difficult to influence Reich. Pigheaded and lacking in any breadth of vision, he is motivated not so much by honourable intentions as by a determination to serve the *Zeitgeist* as at present represented in the person of the Admiral.

20.4.45. Hitler's birthday was celebrated by a rousing speech given by the Admiral. He is certainly a worthy pupil of Goebbels. The Realkino, where the big gathering of troops was held, was decked out in the best Nazi tradition, huge flags, floodlights, attendant orchestra, etc. The

Admiral and his adjutant, so sadly lacking in inches, appeared on the platform as 'the long and short of it'. Hüffmeier snapped smartly to attention and greeted the assembly with a loud 'Heil Hitler', which was vociferously returned.

Taking his stand on the rostrum, he allowed half a minute to elapse in solemn silence. Then this scion of a family of Protestant pastors began his National Socialist sermon, speaking with evangelical fervour but on behalf of Adolf instead of God. He spoke, too, with consummate skill, first engaging the common sentiments of his listeners, then speaking frankly, glossing nothing over, the more compellingly to carry them away in a final surge of emotion. What German could resist this heady mixture? I was not myself altogether immune to its appeal. But the critical faculty intervened and after half an hour I could feel only mounting fury at this meretricious and deceptive show. Yet, so effective was it, that if I had dared to make some protest, I should certainly have been in danger of being lynched by the bemused audience.

Reich had issued an order permitting the troops to buy vegetables in the market and at all the greengrocers. This followed a report to him that not all vegetables had been sold by the end of the day. Certainly the troops are undernourished. Certainly, too, the ample supply of vegetables delivered directly to them is still insufficient to satisfy the demands of their empty bellies. But this permission to buy on the open market resulted in some ugly scenes and the new purchasers' insatiable hunger led to every shop being sold out almost immediately. There were inevitably clashes and scuffles in which of course soldiers came off victors against the local housewives. The farmers threatened to go on strike and cut off all supplies to the troops and the whole island was in an uproar.

We had to call a conference with States officials to try to settle the problem. The question was, how to secure for the troops any surplus on the civilian market. All sorts of complicated schemes were mooted. Finally I suggested that the local people should be allowed to buy in the morning and the troops in the afternoon; thus the civilians would be given the chance to cover their requirements and the troops to profit from any surplus. This was agreed and the conference was concluded to the satisfaction of both sides. The next day I was mentioned in the Guernsey press as having cut the Gordian knot. I record the matter only as a rare instance of being able to live up to my reputation as an 'exponent of compromise' in my new post, which as a purely nominal one, carrying little authority, otherwise affords me little satisfaction.

I had first intended to take over Schneeberger's quarters in the house he shared with Hauschild. But the thought of living under the same roof with the man who concocted the two-year plan for increased deliveries of milk and called for blood when they failed to materialise was too much for me. So I decided to forego the advantages of the vegetable garden, comfortable accommodation and my rights as the head of the organisation, and instead moved in with my good and trusty Heider who has landed up here as Ortskommandant. My modest attic room, with its views over Elizabeth College, Jethou, Herm and Sark, where I live like some romantic 18th-century poet, more than suffices me. An old-fashioned windmill, designed to power greenhouses, provides electricity to read by and hear the essential enemy news reports on the radio. The general atmosphere among us is insupportable, with every man suspicious of the next and denunciations the order of the day. I avoid all social life and my only contacts are the Blücher ladies, on whose discretion I know I can rely absolutely.

23.4.45. Since my arrival, Helldorf has also called to see me. He is under surveillance pending his court martial. The Admiral fears him, not without good reason, and would doubtless be glad to find some means of eliminating him from the scene. Helldorf, for his part, more than reciprocates the Admiral's animosity and is bitterly resentful of having been thrown out of office and called up for trial. With every justification. He spoke with utter and terrifying frankness. The possibility we had only touched on at this meeting a few days ago was finally agreed between us when I visited him in his quarters today. This is that we are close on the time when the Admiral will have to be put out of action and that one of us will have to do it. This is on two grounds, the Admiral's declared intentions, one, not to accept unconditional surrender and two, in the event of surrender, to blow up all the arms and ammunition in the islands, which would be half destroyed in the process. Helldorf said he would do the deed himself and would only need my support and assistance in certain matters.

We conspired until deep in the night, speaking in low voices and going to the door from time to time to make sure no one was eavesdropping. I would never have imagined that such weighty deliberations between determined men could take place in such an atmosphere of cops and robbers. We grew quite merry on port and assassination plans. What had happened to our moral scruples in thus planning to kill in cold blood? They had been disposed of in the long sleepless nights which inexorably led us to decide on this act of deliverance. In the past few months I have felt a hardening of a resolve which will permit no further compromise with or concession to these enemies of humanity.

Every day I hide this diary behind the loose wallpaper in the adjoining room.

24.4.45. I have no further interest at all in my work. Fortunately, the multiplicity of new and overlapping posts, created to improve administration, makes it easy to avoid being much involved. (And with all this over-organisation, less gets done than ever.) In this state of idleness and comparative ease, I find myself sharing the material philosophy of my house-mate, Heider, who has never lived in any other way. He takes care of his stomach, looks after the running of the house and improves the commissariat by profitable exchanges, and knows all the local rumours. It is the philosophy of the old soldier who lives for the day and makes the most of it. And I am duly grateful for this comparatively protected existence. At the moment he is planning to invite along a couple of local girls, of questionable repute, for a jolly evening, which will be helped along no doubt by his apparently inexhaustible supplies of cognac and he greatly looks forward to it.

I was recently introduced to the Austrian General Dini, a totally insignificant air force officer who has reached his rank only through the war and seems to have lost most of his Viennese charm in the process. We had neither of us the slightest interest in the other; for me he is the typical non-intellectual serviceman and he no doubt regards me as a mere administrative big-wig, the civilian in uniform. Our conversation was stilted. In an effort to make some contribution to it, I inadvertently remarked that I was on tenterhooks to know exactly where the advancing Russians and Americans would meet up in Germany and Austria. A bad mistake of course. Although the advancing Allies are now only 70 kilometres apart, to mention this fact is taboo, indeed dangerous, as an offence against the 'will to victory'. Reason seems to have no more validity, at least as applied to contemporary events.

In the evening I had a 'phone call from Cleve. He has been much put out by my posting and desperately worried about the Admiral's ultimatum to the States' Superior Council. A full sitting of the States was called to deal with this. It says much for Cleve's skill and single-mindedness that this ended up by the States agreeing to do their best to step up the milk supply. The farmers voluntarily gave up their meat ration and the heavy workers' representatives agreed to their meat rations being cut by half. All this could only have been achieved by Cleve exerting all his influence and exploiting the goodwill he has won with the States, particularly in winning them over to believe, against their natural mistrust, that the Admiral would *not* defend the islands to the bitter end. That, of course, is a matter which is still to be resolved.

25.4.45. Today took a trip by motor-boat to Jethou. The ostensible reason was to salvage valuable books from the owner's library there. In fact an excuse to get away and enjoy a carefree day at sea among the little islands and out of reach of any sudden surprise or confrontation.

In the once cultivated garden on the little island, now so sadly run to seed, dark red roses were still blooming. In the similarly neglected and already plundered library, there was still a wealth of books, chiefly on gardening and of a scope and variety which would astonish the gardening enthusiast in Germany.

The young naval lieutenant and I scrambled around the island looking for seagulls' eggs and found a couple of cormorants' eggs on a dangerous overhang. We chatted about all sorts of things. The poor young fellow, whom I found most likeable, has a disabled right arm, the result of one of Hüffmeier's senseless forays against the mainland. Yet he idolises the Admiral, whose martial ambition has partially crippled him, and his one thought in searching the plundered house was to find something which might please the Admiral. If only he knew the plan I am involved in! It made me feel quite base and conscience-stricken. Is it our part in life as men to make war, whether or not in a good cause and become so enamoured of it that loyalty outweighs wisdom in following a phantom? And can I myself find no peace or ease of mind even on such a lovely day and peaceful expedition as this?

26.4.45. If wars could be won with flowers, we could from these islands conquer the whole continent. Never has there been a spring with such a riot of blossom.

I had a meeting with the naval Captain Zimmermann, of the Admiral's Staff, to whom I had occasion to refer in the early pages of this diary as the stylish young lieutenant, who, with his arm upflung in the Nazi salute, presented the very picture of the sentimental, patriotic postcard. We spoke about setting up a channel to give me immediate access to the Admiral on particularly delicate legal matters, of international import. The last thing I want to do is to create still another office with some mysterious symbol in standing orders; only to ensure that I have the means of advising the Admiral directly, as possibly the only person in the islands with such long experience of fencing with the Bailiffs on these delicate matters.

Called on Colonel Heine who gave me a warm and friendly reception. In Jersey, under the old regime, we had always worked well together. He is now nominally head of the army here, but is bypassed on every side and has no real power. He admitted ruefully that his position here was very different to what it had been in Jersey.

Not long ago, it seems, Hauschild gave a lecture to troops taking part in the N.S.F.O. [National Socialist Leadership Organisation] course. His theme was the absolute sovereignty we had achieved in the islands, which we would continue to occupy for at least another two years. The British would not attack them and we would hold them as a valuable bargaining point in negotiating the peace treaty. It was incumbent on

all loyal Nazis openly to proclaim their faith in this policy and thus to
silence any expression of doubt in the cowardly ranks of the sceptics.

26.4.45. In this eleventh hour of the war, the Admiral has suddenly
become interested in Carey Castle, a fine old Adam- style house, which
had hitherto remained untouched by us, and ordered that it be made
into an officers' club. This impressive building, of truly feudal
appearance and furnished in appropriate style, is ideally situated, high
above the town. The view over the well-kept gardens, with their rare
and ancient trees, falls sheer down to the harbour and Castle Cornet,
with the sea as a blue backdrop.

As the administration of service clubs falls within the competence of
the Platzkommandantur, I also became involved in the project, and
found myself making quite a hobby of rearranging pictures and
furniture and introducing additional items to achieve the best artistic
effect. Certainly a ludicrous occupation for the last days of this long
and bloody world-wide war. But there is another reason for this
apparently senseless activity. The club is also the Admiral's current
hobby and preoccupation, and thus provides an innocuous ground on
which to establish closer relations with him for a far from innocuous
purpose. I have learned that, at 9 a.m. precisely, he walks over there
every morning for a glass of curdled milk provided by Sister Hanna and
to inspect and express satisfaction with my latest innovations. So I have
been able to report to Helldorf the exact time and route of his morning
walk through the park.

Often, when we are talking about the fitting up of the club, one
subject at least on which the Admiral and I are on common ground, I
can scarcely credit my own duplicity. Should I not rather be warning
him? But I realise that things have gone too far for that. Politically we
are farther than ever apart. Since my first conversation with him, he has
become even more radical in attitude and more under the influence of
Reich. There is nothing I could do now to win him over to a more
moderate course. Especially as I have myself recently again been under
attack by the extremist elements, so that I scarcely any longer feel
secure, even in my attic room. It only needs a radio message from
Germany and I am finished.

27.4.45. Heider's two girl friends have paid us their promised visit. A
pair of saucy, common young things, all set to entertain with a fund of
silly stories. But they brought with them an ample supply of white
bread, an undreamed of luxury. We ate that evening until appetite was
really satisfied and for once without turnip tops. It was such a feast
that, with the aid of alcohol, everyone was soon in rollicking good
humour, which soon took a macabre turn in jokes about the last days of

Pompeii, the last party, the end which could come tomorrow. Germany, freedom, life, money, titles, rank, all at an end. The two girls became ever more cheeky and forward. Heider, I could see, as Rhinelander, bachelor and commercial traveller, felt much at home in this carnival atmosphere and was enjoying himself enormously. But suddenly for me, something snapped. I could endure it no longer and slipped unobtrusively away to my attic room and to bed.

Not much later, I was disturbed there by one of the girls, presumably directed to my room by Heider, who, with her grasping hand, made such an overture to sexual intercourse as I had never before experienced. This ended with my unceremoniously chucking her out. Heider of course chaffed me about this the next morning, indicating by expressive gestures how he had taken advantage of the situation. He is such a confirmed and unrepentant hedonist that one cannot take offence, only recognise him for what he is and join in his laughter.

28.4.45. Suddenly and totally unexpectedly, Helldorf has been banished to the island of Herm, where there is not a single inhabitant and the only house is the decayed and plundered one-time luxury villa of the former English tenant. The ostensible reason for his 'posting' to this desolate and isolated island is to make a study of its possible utilisation for agricultural purposes. This news was a great shock to me. Had Helldorf, out of his unbridled hatred for the Admiral, let slip some compromising information? Had one of his undercover connections been brought to light? I await further developments from hour to hour with increasing trepidation.

29.4.45. To get away from it all, even if only for a few hours, I made some excuse for a trip to Brecqhou, the only one of the lesser islands I had not yet visited. We set out by motor-boat on a warm, still day. In Sark we took a small boat in tow, and approached Brecqhou through the bizarre world of craggy rocks flanking its little bay. At the landing-stage was a wooden stairway, much eroded by salt water and slippery with moss and seaweed. This gave way to stone steps leading in serpentine turns up the steep cliff.

The lines for a cable-car strung across the bay were rather puzzling. But apparently it was used to transport cargo brought in by ship to the top of the island. The vistas disclosed on the ascent showed how enchantingly this island is situated compared with all the others. The view from here was still more beautiful than from Herm and Jethou. On the other hand this island is almost entirely lacking in vegetation. There are not even any ferns. Only the bluebells seem at home, covering the bare island in a blue light reflecting the sea.

The former owner, a Captain Clark, with that disregard for cost only possible for the very wealthy, had built himself a fine modern house, in a sheltered position facing west. He had also obviously tried to lay out a garden, in the shelter of a thick stone encircling wall. But the evidence for any success he may have had has long since been destroyed by time and marauding rabbits.

I was interested to note the remains of his attempt at afforestation, in the shape of up-ended tar-barrels, which as one approaches the island give the curious effect of an outbreak of warts on the landscape. In their shelter he had tried to cultivate pine saplings. But these, like all other imported plants, had also succumbed to the depredations of time and the rabbits.

Besides the cliff path we had climbed, there is also a steep road leading from the otherwise almost inaccessible harbour to the house. This road is only about 500 metres long, but was sufficient excuse for the owner to keep a fleet of three powerful, expensive cars on the island.

The house unfortunately proved to have been broken into and as shamelessly plundered as those on Herm and Jethou. Only the books are the last things to disappear, as items of little interest to the looter. We took a few pieces of furniture for the use of the Standort Kommandantur in fitting-up quarters.

In the library I found some photographs of the former owner. These showed him as rather morose-looking but well set up and immaculately dressed; no doubt a man who had always indulged his every whim. There was an album full of press-cuttings, with photographs of him leading in his winners at the races and taking prizes as a breeder of pedigree cattle and sheep. Other pictures showed him arriving on his luxury yacht in Egypt, India, etc., and others attending formal functions in morning coat and grey top hat. This 'private view' of the life and times of one of the richest men in England was an odd sensation, the more so as one felt these times would never return. Whether, after the war, he would be able to afford such merely additional luxuries as a private cable-car and private electricity and waterworks on a remote island seemed doubtful. Not only for him but for all his like in England and in Europe. It was a glimpse of a lost world and a lost lifestyle.

Our little ship left the island with an oddly assorted cargo: chairs, curtains, vases and crockery, and among all this the buckets which our practical sailors had commandeered and spent the time busily filling with limpets. All credit to their hard work. I seated myself comfortably in one of the salvaged armchairs and observed the wildlife around us on the run back to Guernsey over the still mirror-calm sea.

The cormorants swam with bodies submerged, only their necks emerging from the water. The puffins rocked peacefully on the gentle swell, undisturbed by our proximity. Lieutenant M. took a couple of shots at them with a carbine but missed. The little creatures flapped their wings in fright but evidently did not connect the noise with our ship and soon settled down again quite near us. Suddenly there was a deafening explosion. It was the Strassburg battery in Guernsey, firing over our heads. The blast reverberated round all the little bays and the gulls rose in screaming protest. Then utter silence descended again on an utterly calm sea, where only some streaks and eddies warned of the craggy conformation of the seabed below. The islands lay bathed in peaceful evening light, each wrapped in its own dreamy reverie and connected with the others only by the long lines of seabirds in continual passage between them. It was hard to imagine the real world with the war now in its last horrifying throes in Germany, even more incongruous to consider assassination and possible arrest.

30.4.45. The Red Cross ship has arrived again, with all the activities customary to the occasion. This time my French-speaking friend Callias was on board again, and he brought me a welcome gift of good Swiss chocolate. The usual invitations between us have also followed and I have again had to blush for Reich's small-mindedness and lack of social graces. The Admiral has refused to set foot on the ship again, as, on its last visit, the Captain had failed to fly his flag at half-mast for Hitler's birthday and only did so in the end under dire threats from the Admiral.

Accompanied the Red Cross delegates on a tour of Victor Hugo's house. This has been preserved as he left it and is one of the island's tourist attractions. It is crammed with furniture in the heavy and over-ornate style of the period and hung with imitation Gobelins. The extravagance of a basically uncertain age, combined with the poet's own leanings to the fantastic, resulted in a truly formidable collection of period pieces. Victor Hugo also shared the contemporary taste for large and gloomy pictures and grisly statuary. Even the pretty little garden, set on a steep incline, has its Chinese dragons and other crumbling horrors. His vanity is displayed in the all too frequent introduction of the initials 'V.H.' as a decorative motif in the furnishings, a weakness the stout republican shared with the Emperor Napoleon. Today one senses his poetic spirit only in his obvious love for wide and untrammelled views, as evidenced by the round balconies, large windows and rooftop *atelier* of a house built, in this respect, far in advance of its time. Here in a house so ideally situated, with a free outlook over all the islands and surrounded by family and friends, it would be possible to live happily enough, even in exile.

One of our party, Medical Officer Rupp, a thoroughly unpleasant type, indulged his salacious fancies about Hugo's second wife in every room. He had heard or read somewhere that she had been the cause of the poet's expulsion from Jersey by the puritanical islanders. (The actual reason was political and connected with the publication in a newspaper run by local French exiles of an 'open letter' published by exiles in London attacking Queen Victoria for her visit to Napoleon III in Paris.) In the bedroom, Rupp bounced about on the bed and pronounced it very comfortable, with winks and grins. The guide, who had no inkling of what all these antics were about, came off best with a lavish tip in money and even more precious cigarettes.

In the afternoon Pokorny arrived from Jersey. He has at this eleventh hour and most unjustly been posted to Alderney, all a part of this reign of terror. I spent an hour talking to him at the harbour. Fortunately he accepts his fate in a philosophical spirit, the more so as the end is now so very near. He brought me gifts and letters from the Fieldings and the silver napkin-ring from my colleagues in the Jersey administration, now engraved with their chosen inscription.

Reich invited me along for the evening, together with the people from the *Vega*. I was able to enjoy a really free and uninhibited talk with Callias, as nobody can understand our French. He has become a good friend and is also anxious to do all he can for me in the future. I have the impression that his offer to stay on here for the short time remaining, as International Red Cross representative in matters affecting prisoners-of-war, was largely inspired by his attachment to me.

Chapter Six

May 1945

1.5.45. Lacking the vital information I had counted on receiving from Helldorf, I am out of touch with the situation and at a loss how to proceed. It seems increasingly doubtful whether I shall be able, alone, to decide on the right moment for the fateful act. Nor do I know on whom Helldorf was otherwise relying for support. He must have had other backers for his projected coup, but failed or perhaps had no time to brief me before his departure to Herm and I have heard nothing from him since. I have made some exploratory calls on leading service commanders, including Colonel Heine, but could elicit nothing more than complaints about their own particular problems and difficulties. The leaders of the States of Guernsey – unlike their counterparts in Jersey, on whom I might have counted for some support – are elderly and rather feeble figures. This opinion was confirmed when, in an effort to establish closer contact with them, I personally delivered their Red Cross parcels to their homes; they are definitely not the stuff of which revolutionaries are made.

Our first conference with the Red Cross delegates and members of the Guernsey States took place in Carey Castle, the large and newly equipped officers' club. The Bailiff, rosy-cheeked and grandfatherly Victor Carey, whispered to me that the conference chamber had once been his grandmother's bedroom.

The President of the Controlling Committee, John Leale, white-haired and ascetic in feature, inspires me with a growing liking and respect. He seems to have an inner strength, based I am sure on a deep religious belief, which enables him to take a detached view of all that passes, without irony or bitterness. With his young secretary, too, Louis Guillemette – formerly the secretary of the Bailiff – I have long since made my peace and established good relations. Guillemette is a bright and industrious fellow, assuming a great deal of responsibility in a comparatively junior post, and obviously eager to extend his horizons beyond the narrow confines of Guernsey. He is most appreciative of good treatment and recognition of his merits, and, I think, of my lack of formality.

When, in the course of the conference, Reich grossly insulted the meticulously correct Leale by trying to insinuate that he was a party to peculation, I jumped to the defence of this good and upright man, whom I find so congenial. I was glad to do so. I have latterly noticed how quickly I have fallen into the habit of showing, outwardly at least, as much cordiality to those who are uncongenial to me as to those for whom such feeling comes from the heart. Even if adopted as deliberate policy in an effort to exert a moderating influence, it is an art in which I would not wish to become too proficient.

2.5.45. It is illuminating to know that the Admiral comes from a long line of North German pastors. His brothers are pastors, too. Certainly his address to the assembled troops yesterday had all the attributes of a sermon; in delivery, as he first stood with his head turned up to heaven as if invoking the blessing of the Almighty, then flung his arms wide, then placed a hand on heart, and not less so in content, which would have been described by country parishioners attending a stern sermon on hellfire and damnation as 'telling them good and proper'.

Just at this moment news has come through by radio-telephone from Germany that Hitler has fallen and that his successor is Dönitz. Now everything is happening so swiftly that one can only wait in suspense for the next news. The Admiral here must clearly acknowledge the authority of the Führer's successor as his own commander-in-chief and head of the navy as well now of the nation. Any other choice might well have stiffened his determination to disregard authority and carry on fighting of his own accord.

In the evening I visited Countess Blücher and Princess Radzivill in their tastefully and lavishly appointed home. They have some large and wonderful paintings by David of Napoleon and his campaigns, the booty brought back by their grandfather Field Marshal Blücher of Prussia, an ally of England in the Napoleonic wars, which would more properly belong in a French museum.

The ladies are of liberal education and outlook and fluent in many languages. They are above all very sympathetic listeners, and the opportunity to unburden myself generally, leads I am afraid, to my talking far too much.

We have ranged over a wide variety of topics, including the League of Nations, which prompted the Princess to show me a book of photographs of the League Palace in Geneva, which had been presented to her in recognition of her services as an interpreter there.

Both ladies are greatly attached to the islands and well versed in their history and lore. We spoke about the curious atmospheric effects of local weather. These have been particularly noticeable in the last few days, as the clouds, which had brought with them icy rain, roll away from the islands. Where they still break into distant showers, it is as if, in the dazzling sunshine, sea and sky merge in an interchange of light and become indistinguishable from each other. This aspect of nature was best captured by Turner, whose paintings are bathed in a pervading light which unites heaven and earth and dispenses with all dividing lines between them. When I mentioned this, my hostesses of course immediately brought out a really beautiful book on Turner to show me, with excellent colour reproductions of his works. And after they had also provided me with a large glass of cognac, to which one is now totally unaccustomed, what more could be needed to loosen the tongue?

3.5.45. Captain von Cleve still rings me up to ask my advice on all important matters. Just from his tone of voice I can tell how utterly weary and worn-out he has become in struggling to cope with the problems of administration alone. He is not the man to come to decisions in solitary cogitation. What I have sometimes referred to as his tendency to play to the gallery is in fact a real need to think aloud, to formulate his ideas by trying them out on an understanding partner. In this respect we complemented each other very well, although of course he misses me more than I miss him.

What is plaguing him at the moment is the growing insolence and importunity of the Bailiff of Jersey. Coutanche is now demanding that, as a gesture of goodwill, we should abdicate at least a part of our control over island affairs, as he cannot otherwise guarantee the maintenance of peace and good order. He also suggests that it would be expedient to lift the ban on listening to the B.B.C. This is all subterfuge on his part and designed to increase his own prestige and standing with the population. With the end of the occupation practically in sight, he is clearly determined to emerge from it as the strong and popular leader.

I strongly advised Cleve against taking any such steps. He should rather, I urged him, issue a warning notice to the people of the island, calling on them to keep calm. This I dictated to him over the 'phone and set down here for the record.

> *Proclamation.* During the past years of occupation, there has been no riotous behaviour on the part of the population or clashes between them and the troops. The German authorities are determined to maintain, and have the power to enforce the maintenance of such law and order until the end of the occupation. There must therefore be no public marches, assemblies or demonstrations. Those who transgress this order will be most severely dealt with, in the belief that in the present situation, any relaxation of discipline or disturbance of the public peace by hotheads, can only be to the detriment of a defenceless populace.

Our chief concern and the subject of endless debate continues to be the horrifying and increasing extent of theft by the hungry soldiers. The only people who gain are those farmers who will exchange food for stolen goods, and unless this situation can be brought under control, all

estimates of supplies becomes meaningless. Up to now we have found
no means of checking it. Orders to fire on sight at night; posting guards
overnight in the greenhouses; dividing the whole island into strictly
patrolled areas; reduction of rations by the value of the goods stolen; all
have proved ineffective. We have come to a strange pass in which
organisation, backed by military authority, fails to work against the
more pressing realities of hunger and want.

In talking to the ordinary soldiers, mostly the older men, I for the
first time encountered a mutinous attitude: 'When you're hungry,
nowhere's any good'. 'Don't care whether I'm here or in Canada or
where I am as long as I can eat my fill again'. 'Now you have taken away
our last pleasure, the three cigarettes a day', etc. The majority of the
men are certainly in no mood to fight. Even if still physically able, they
have lost all heart for it. The very idea of carrying on here for months
after the war has ended in Germany – and only the incurable optimist
could contemplate it – must founder on this most important consideration, the human factor. The long period of inaction has weakened the
troops and undermined their morale.

5.5.45. Inspected the camp of the French colonial troops, the
Moroccans, with the two Red Cross delegates and the usual over-
swollen train of German officers, some present by right of office, others
not. Apart from the need to assert their own importance, one cannot
avoid the impression that this assiduous attendance on the Commission is chiefly prompted by a hankering after the odd cigarette or the
possibility of making some small profitable deal.

This inspection of a prisoner-of-war camp at a time when our armies
are capitulating one after another in a Germany near collapse has for us
a grim topicality on which for the moment it is best not to dwell. Just
now, as regards rations, the Moroccans are the best nourished people in
the island. Apart from a lack of adequate clothing, they have no
complaints.

We walked through the clean and tidy rooms. In one of the rooms a
soldier was deep in prayer to Allah. Kneeling on a piece of sacking,
murmuring the ritual prayers and throwing himself face down in an
ecstasy of devotion, he did not even notice our passing.

The Moroccans are essentially a childlike people, accepting what fate
brings without much concern and living wholly for the day. Several of
them made a positively dashing appearance and they seemed blessed
with a natural insouciant cheerfulness.

Reich seemed rather taken aback by my chatting with the prisoners
in French, after I had conducted the foregoing conference in English. A
fluency in foreign tongues always impresses those not similarly gifted.
Yesterday, for once, Reich found me quite useful, although he

customarily regards my manner of conducting business, with a light touch, patience and good humour – as opposed to his heavily doctrinaire approach – with the utmost suspicion.

That evening President Leale and Guillemette sought me out for a little talk on the immediate future. I was quite open with them, concealing nothing and conceding nothing. I think I was able to make clear to them the German point of view at this moment of defeat. President Leale's eyes were moist as I spoke about Germany's tragic destiny in being forced to submit to Russian domination, to a yoke we could never abide, while losing the war to Britain and America we could face without the same bitterness. I could see he felt for me. We parted in mutual understanding and respect.

Later in the evening, I at last heard the news for which I had so long been waiting. Linz has been occupied after capitulating without resistance. Now I at least know for certain that my wife must by now have been released from her odious confinement. This induces such a mood of euphoria that I even allow myself to hope that I may soon be reunited with her. Callias has told me that the Americans are in urgent need of administrative staff. In this he sees great possibilities for me. Who could be better suited to assist in the general work of reconstruction under an Anglo-American occupation than an administrative official with a knowledge of foreign languages and long experience on British territory?

7.5.45. The early morning news on the wireless announced, if still unofficially, total capitulation by Germany. The local population is in a fever of anticipation as to coming events. We discussed with States' representatives the best means of maintaining peace and public order until the end. President Leale made handsome acknowledgement of the exemplary behaviour of the occupying troops throughout the occupation, and promised to bring this to the attention of the British forces as soon as they landed. How much this attitude differs from that of the Bailiff of Jersey, who is so much more concerned with his own public image. From him, I fear, we can expect no such fair treatment.

Cleve has put in a request, signed by the Fortress Commander, General Wulf, for my return to Jersey, where it is claimed that I am urgently needed to deal with civilian affairs. I would personally not be averse to going back, but feel I might be more useful here. Although my duties here are less onerous, I have at least a chance to bring some influence to bear on the Admiral. Surrounded as he is by a crowd of would-be imitators and sycophants which his strong and fanatical personality inevitably attracts, I would appear an unlikely choice as adviser. But I have latterly noticed that he seems increasingly inclined to lend an ear to my counsels. The news of Hitler's death and Dönitz's appointment as his successor seems also to have had a salutory effect on the Admiral. I often have the impression that he is torn by some inner conflict of conscience amounting to a frenzy. He could indeed do with a friend to whom he could turn for disinterested advice. The *camarilla* merely parrot his own extremist views. But the turn in the historical page seems to have had some effect even on the Admiral's fanatical convictions.

All is now approaching an end. There can be no further doubt about the general capitulation. All sorts of people call on us at the office to express their sympathy and wish us well. The workers in our canteens and kitchens carry on with their job. It is amazing how much goodwill we encounter and how little opposition or bitterness.

At midday I was invited to the last of the well-remembered opulent meals aboard the Red Cross ship. The captain was particularly cordial. He has fallen out with the Admiral, because the latter requested him to fly the flag at half-mast for Hitler's death. By way of retaliation, he did not include the Admiral in the invitation, on the grounds that he would be in mourning. By now I have become acquainted and one might also say friends with everybody aboard the *Vega* from the Captain to the steward.

In the evening Callias and I drove out to pay some last farewell calls. We visited General Heine and members of the States. This last historic day thus passed in an atmosphere of goodwill and amity.

8.5.45. The actual surrender of the islands came as something of an anti-climax, although not, unfortunately, without its dramatic moments. The Admiral, in a fit of silly pique and pride, at first threatened to fire on the English ships when they arrived a few hours before the agreed time. The ships withdrew, but he thus lost his one and only chance of negotiation and merely angered the victorious enemy. To exacerbate them further, his envoy, the theatrical Lieutenant-Commander Zimmermann, sent to make the first contact aboard the leading British ship, greeted its commander with upflung arm and the Hitler salute. One can only guess at the feelings of the astounded British officer, but must assume that for once the English response to the comical failed, and he was both offended and outraged. We felt the effects of this in the inimical manner in which we were subsequently treated. With one foolish gesture of defiance, all the goodwill earned by the troops in years of exemplary behaviour had been destroyed.

That the Admiral surrendered without, as he had threatened, blowing up all the arms and ammunition, was due to the orders he received directly from his supreme commander, Dönitz. But his intention came perilously near to being put into effect.

On this last day it fell to my lot, together with Reich, to perform one more official duty in making the formal return of the island to the States of Guernsey. This was effected briefly if worthily enough in the single sentence I spoke in English: 'The war is over; we herewith hand back the islands to you'. All the members of the States were assembled. We faced each other with polite but wordless bows like so many Chinese mummers. We concluded by pointing out to the States that it now lay within their own discretion to authorise the flagging of public buildings.

At that we took our departure without another word. The policemen on duty at the door saluted us politely. There has never been any enmity between the islands and the Germans. This may, admittedly, at least in part be due to the remoteness of the islands from the centre of hostilities and their being spared the worst excesses of war.

When the first reporters arrived and asked the Bailiff of Guernsey and President Leale to tell them something about the behaviour of the German troops during the Occupation, both replied that it had been exemplary. The reporters protested that the time was hardly ripe for the publication of such news and it was not what their readers expected. Both these honourable men remained adamant in defending their view and the reporters were forced to retire, diappointed and in disarray.

My diary must close with this final tribute to British fair play.

Envoi

I had in fact still to spend two years in England as a P.o.W., all this time still in ignorance of my wife's fate, before I was finally reunited with her. But even this difficult period had in retrospect its humorous moments and compensating memories, such as my encounter with the local postman, a tough character. I recorded this years later in a little book of reminiscences, and append it here as giving something of the flavour of my enforced stay in England.

When, as a P.o.W., I worked voluntarily on the land, I encountered the local postman three times a day; once in the early morning and twice later when he passed my place of work on his rounds. In the 16 months I worked there, this amounted, with the deduction of holidays, to 1,200 times. This was not in a busy centre, but in a remote village in Northumbria, where even the Romans had dared press on no further, but had built the nearby Hadrian's Wall as a defence against the Scots. The garden where I worked had once belonged to the villa of a captain of Roman legionaries, and German prisoners may well have worked there some 1,500 years ago. The postman and I never exchanged a word, yet I came to regard him quite affectionately as part and parcel of the local scene.

In the village of Bardon Mill on the Tyne, it was not the farmers who were the early risers, but the landworkers, arriving by bus from the town. The town woke the country and the landworkers the farmers. Post office and railway were alike geared to deliver letters and newspapers to the breakfast tables of the country dwellers, just as at home the baker delivers the breakfast rolls.

I first met the postman when I was on my way from the bus to my kindly hosts at the *Fox and Hounds* and he was on his way to the bus station to pick up the mail. He was always accompanied by the local postmaster, a nicety of procedure I would have liked to ask him about. But, having learned that he was an ex-regular of the British Raj in India, after a lifetime of soldiering still serving in an official capacity, I felt he might consider such an enquiry impertinent. It had to remain one of the puzzles of life in England which was never resolved.

With the opening of the post office, the village came to life. Cats and dogs in astonishing numbers were let out of doors. Ducks waddled, quacking loudly, to the brook for their morning swim. Milk was

191

delivered discreetly at back doors. The elderly spinster from next door collected her morning paper, which was carried before her by her ancient dog.

I too started on my daily routine and appointed task. This was to dig up and restore to order the garden previously mentioned, now sadly run to seed, which was situated above the village bridge, a task which occupied many months. At first I flung myself into physical labour as an antidote to thought, but the village worthies who came along to observe and pronounce knowledgeably on my progress seemed shocked by such unseemly haste. So I soon reduced my tempo to the more leisurely pace of local life. This seemed to meet with general approval, as expressed in not only passing the time of day but speaking about the weather.

Only the postman never addressed a word to me, although he passed me often enough; as I have already mentioned, 1,200 times in all. Not that he was dumb by any means, as every time he passed me he sang loudly in a raucous voice what appeared to be a soldier's marching song. I was never able to make out the words, although the tune became familiar enough. Was it some old battle song of the Hindu Kush? Why did he sing only when he passed me? To express disapproval of a mere European P.o.W., or solidarity with a fellow old campaigner?

I had meanwhile become an acknowledged figure in village life. Everybody passed the time of day with me, except the postman. Once when I was sweating to wrest out a tree stump, one villager even progressed beyond speaking about the weather to enquire 'Happy at your work?'. At first I was furious, but glancing at his friendly face, happily realised in time that no sarcasm was intended, it was a mere figure of speech. So, despite the truly foul weather, I managed to reply 'Oh yes, it's not so bad today'. Which I think earned me another good mark.

I cannot say that I ever regarded the postman as an unsympathetic figure; his stiff-backed aloofness conveyed no sense of personal animosity. Soon, I missed him when he failed to put in an appearance as much as I would have missed the cheeky thrush which snatched worms from under my spade or the friendly Scottish sheepdog which licked my hands and fraternised with me daily. All prisoners-of-war must feel a special affinity with these dumb creatures, who seem in comparison so free but are in fact the prisoners of their own instincts and limitations. For the postman, this sturdy veteran of the Indian army, who still in his old age tramped the countryside in all winds and weathers, faithfully delivering his mail, I came to have a special respect, even affection. I ceased to speculate about his attitude to me and accepted him as part of the background of life.

At last my date of repatriation was announced and I caught the early bus to the village for the last time. My good hosts at the *Fox and Hounds* loaded me with gifts. There was also a packet of cigarettes left there for me by the postman! This time, I was resolved, I would certainly speak to him. But the postman was too clever for me. Why spoil a friendship with unnecessary talk? Instead he made a long and laborious detour. I saw him pass in the distance but heard no song. What the words had been I shall never know, but perhaps after all they were meant to cheer me with some consolatory allusion to the hard lot of the soldier in a foreign land.

Footnotes

Chapter One

1. Presumably, as conscientious objectors, buyers for the German forces – not to be confused with the Jerseymen and Guernseymen who, nominated by States and with the permission of the German authorities, purchased on behalf of the islands' civilian populations in France.
2. For legal, legislative and administrative purposes, the Channel Islands are still divided into two bailiwicks (Guernsey and Jersey), each presided over by a Bailiff assisted by 12 jurats, on the old constitutional pattern which once prevailed in Normandy.
3. The German editor and censor in the local newspaper office.
4. 'The Little Treasure Trove' – a pot-pourri of verses, songs, etc.
5. General Graf Rudolf von Schmettow.
6. The representative of the British Crown and the most senior government official in the bailiwick after the Bailiff.

Chapter Two

1. Schloss Greifenstein was the seat of the Stauffenburg family (see next note).
2. Colonel Count Claus von Stauffenburg placed the bomb in the abortive attempt on Hitler's life which took place on 20 July 1944.
3. Dr. Hans Auerbach was the author of the book *Die Kanalinslen, Jersey, Guernsey, Sark*, giving an historical account of the islands, which was commissioned by the German Commander-in-Chief on Jersey and published in the spring of 1942.

Chapter Three

1. H.U.V.: Heeresunterkunftsverwaltung, the quartermaster's office.
2. This talk was with a Catholic priest attached to the troops, who was confessor to the naval forces. He had long been on intimate terms with the author, and was the only person to whom the Baron confided that his wife was to be arraigned before the People's Court and that in all probability he would be himself. The priest was on good terms with all the naval wireless operators, who transcribed all the messages from Germany and it was arranged that any concerning the Baron should be conveyed to him first, and that any ordering his arrest or having a similar threatening import should if possible be suppressed altogether.
3. In fact, towards the end of the war Baroness von Aufsess was released from prison not by her film-star brother but by her second brother Dieter von Klippstein, who was an officer in the Luftwaffe.

Chapter Four

1. Militärverwaltungsrat: military administrative councillor.

2. Although the *Vega* had only just arrived in Guernsey on her second trip and was still awaited in Jersey, a second distribution of parcels was made on 7 February from the stocks which she had brought on her first trip.

Chapter Five
1. Mrs. and Miss Fielding were leading figures in local amateur dramatics.
2. Mariotti had been accredited by this time.
3. Weinberg was the Captain of the *Vega*.
4. Baroness von Aufsess was living in Ausee (Austria) when she was arrested and put in gaol in Linz.
5. Herr von Hindenburg was a friend of the Aufsess family.

Index